MW01201572

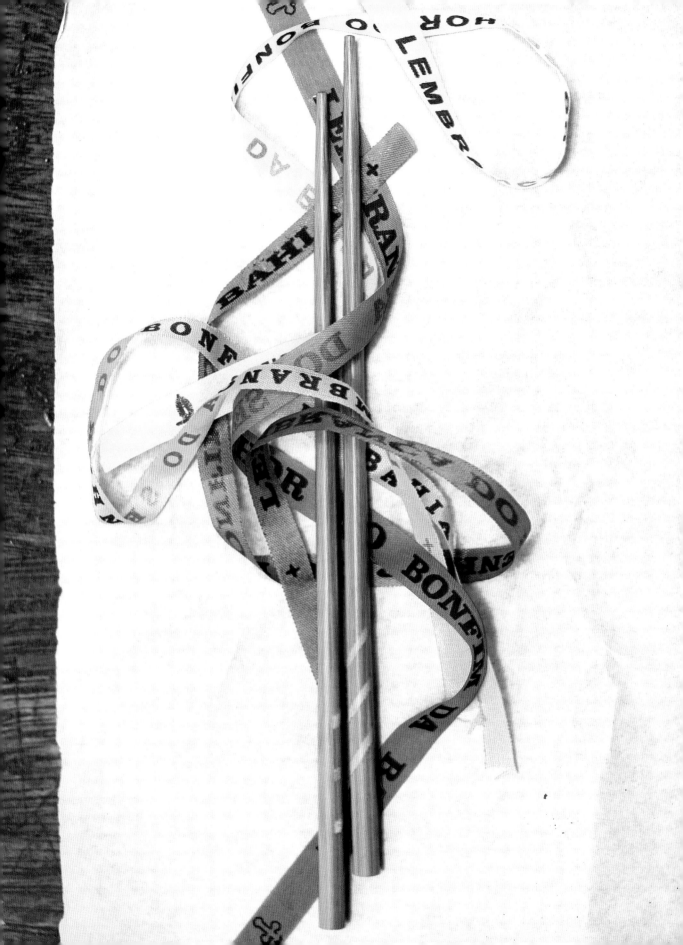

NIKKEI
CUISINE
Japanese Food the South American Way

LUIZ HARA

jacqui
small

Photography by Lisa Linder

First published in 2015 by Jacqui Small LLP
An imprint of Aurum Press
74–77 White Lion Street, London N1 9PF

Text copyright © Luiz Hara 2015 except the following:
pages 28–29 © Toshiro Konishi 2015
pages 42–43 © Jorge Muñoz & Kioki Ii 2015
pages 46–47 © Hajime Kasuga 2015
pages 58–59 © Adriano Kanashiro 2015
pages 70–71 © Tsuyoshi Murakami 2015
pages 86–87 © Mitsuharu Tsumura 2015
pages 152–153 © Diego Oka 2015
pages 174–175 © Pedro Duarte 2015
pages 186–187 © Jordan Sclare 2015
pages 212–213 © Shin Koike 2015

Design and layout copyright © Jacqui Small 2015
Photographic copyright (pages 12–13) © Ricardo Hara 2015
(www.ricardohara.com.br)

Publisher: Jacqui Small
Senior Commissioning Editor: Fritha Saunders
Managing Editor: Emma Heyworth-Dunn
Project Manager and Editor: Nikki Sims
Design and Art Direction: Manisha Patel
Photographer: Lisa Linder
Food Stylist: Luiz Hara
Prop Stylist: Cynthia Inions
Production: Maeve Healy

ISBN: 978 1 910254 20 2

A catalogue record for this book is available from the British Library.

2017 2016 2015
10 9 8 7 6 5 4 3 2 1

Printed in China

When following the recipes, stick to one set of measurements
(metric, imperial or cups). Measurements used in the recipes are
based on the following conversions:
25g = 1oz
1 tsp = 5ml
1 tbsp = 15ml
30ml = 1fl oz
240ml = 8fl oz = 1 cup (for both liquid and dry volume ingredients).
Note that the weight of dry ingredients varies according to the
volume so 1 cup of flour weighs less than 1 cup of sugar.

CONTENTS

WHAT IS NIKKEI CUISINE?

Nikkei is derived from the Japanese word 'nikkeijin', which refers to Japanese people who migrated overseas and their descendants, including me and my family. Nikkei cuisine, therefore, is the cooking of the Japanese diaspora. Japanese migrants have found themselves in a variety of cultures and contexts but have often maintained a loyalty to their native cuisine. This has required local adaptation: the so-called Nikkei community has embraced a new country's ingredients and assimilated these into their own cooking using Japanese techniques. So, Nikkei cooking is found wherever in the world Japanese immigrants and their descendants are. But, for historical reasons, two countries have had substantially more Japanese immigrants than most of the rest of the world – Brazil and Peru. And it is these South American countries that are particularly noted for their Nikkei cooking.

Brazil has the largest Japanese population of any country outside Japan and it was there that my grandparents migrated and where I was born. Since their arrival, the Nikkei have made a tremendous contribution to agriculture, introducing a number of Japanese fruit and vegetable stocks to Brazil, as well as greatly improving the cultivation of native varietals; work that still continues. On arrival, the Nikkei had to adapt to a predominantly meat-worshipping nation but, because of the large numbers of migrants, they were quick to set up artisan production of tofu, soy sauce, miso (fermented soya beans) and even udon noodles to satisfy the needs of the newly arrived community. Peru has a smaller Nikkei population than Brazil, but since both it and Japan have a Pacific coastline (on opposite sides of the ocean) they share many fish species. With a stronger native agriculture and food heritage, Peru has been the crucible for creating a vibrant Nikkei cooking culture. Peruvian Nikkei dishes often use the maritime abundance brought to the coastline by the Humboldt Current, as well as the unique *aji* peppers, lime, corn and yucca, not to mention the more than 3,000 varieties of potatoes.

So, it is fair to say that in Brazil the Nikkei greatly improved agricultural methods and introduced the wider population to authentic Japanese and Nikkei cuisines in restaurants, which now outnumber both the Brazilian barbecue eateries known as *churrascarias* and even the pizzerias. Japanese street-food is also hugely popular in Brazil thanks to the Nikkei community who serve their own versions of deep-fried gyoza (*pastéis*), yakisoba and takoyaki (fried octopus balls) to name just a few. In contrast, in Peru the Nikkei massively expanded the repertoire of Pacific fish used and improved the methods of preparation of popular national dishes, for example *ceviche*. They also introduced novel ways of preparing fish such as the *tiradito* – sashimi-style raw fish served with a citrus *leche de tigre* sauce.

Japanese migration to South America – a potted history
After 300 years of almost total isolation from the outside world, the Meiji Restoration in 1868 saw an opening up of Japan to migration both in and out of the country. This major modernisation of Japanese society not only ended the feudal system, which had been in place for hundreds of years, but also had some adverse effects on the economy particularly in

— 6 —

SIGNALEMENT

Domicile: *Tochigi-ken.*

Statut familial: *2ᵉ fille de M. Kiyomatsu, chef de famille.*

Profession: *Agriculture*

Taille: *1.40 m.*

Particularités physiques:

Taille et particularités physiques des personnes accompagnant le porteur:

Signature du porteur:

— 7 —

PHOTOGRAPH
PHOTOGRAPHIE

rural areas. In addition, after the Sino-Japanese (1894–95) and Russo-Japanese (1904–05) wars, Japan had difficulty reabsorbing its returning soldiers and large numbers of Japanese citizens decided to search for a new life overseas. The government of Japan, in fact, entered into agreements with other nations, including Brazil and Peru, to encourage and support the emigration of its own nationals.

Japanese emigration began in the 1870s, and over the next 50 years around one million citizens emigrated. Major destinations were Brazil, Hawaii and Manchuria (taking around 25% each), with the rest heading all over the world – 4% ending up in Peru. Most Japanese in Hawaii migrated there before it was annexed by the USA and from there many moved on to California. The emigrants were, on average, better educated than those who remained and many left home with dreams of riches in the Americas. In South America, the opportunities available were in farming – for sugar in Peru, and coffee in Brazil. The first vessel, the *Sakura Maru*, arrived in Callao, Peru in 1899. Nine years later in Brazil, the first 781 Japanese men, women and children arrived in Santos aboard the *Kasato Maru*. This later influx was intended to solve the coffee farming manpower crisis caused by the abolition of slavery in Brazil in 1888. In Japan, campaigns advertising opportunities in Brazil promised great gains for all willing to work on coffee farms. The long trip from Japan to Brazil – it took 52 days from Kobe to São Paolo – was subsidised by the Brazilian government. These were powerfully attractive to Japanese workers seeking a better life outside of their home country. However, the newly arrived workers would soon discover harsher conditions than they had anticipated, akin to those endured by the newly liberated slaves. Even though Japanese immigrants had lived in frugal conditions in Japan, these could not compare to what awaited them in Brazil.

According to Tomoo Handa's book *The Japanese Immigrant – a History of their Life in Brazil*, by 1912 over 60% of Nikkei had left the farms to move to the cities in search of better living conditions and work in professions more similar to their own. Many settled in the São Paulo neighbourhood of Liberdade and set up what were later to become the many restaurants in this area. Most of the Japanese migrants to Peru and Brazil imagined their stay as temporary – a way to achieve prosperity before returning home. However, the advent of the Second World War and the demise of Japan resulted in most of them considering South America as their permanent home.

My family – a story of migration

My grandfather, Takeshi Hara, was officially an American, born to Japanese parents in Hawaii in 1907. He arrived in Brazil with his parents as a young child and embraced his adopted country as his own. He fell in love with the South American lifestyle, so much so that he ran off with a voluptuous Uruguayan woman, before his scandalised family sent him packing to a close-knit Japanese farming community in the interior of São Paulo state to mend his ways, and it was here that he met my Japanese grandmother Seki Suzuki. Born in 1912 in Fukuoka on the Japanese island of Kyushu, she was brought to Brazil in 1927 when she was 15 by an aunt who was migrating with her whole family and needed to make up numbers for the departure of their ship. She was promised that she would soon be returned to her family in Japan, but my grandfather and love got the better of her and so Brazil became her new home.

After losing their coffee farm to severe frost, my grandparents migrated to the city of São Paulo and set up a fruit and vegetable shop with their family including my father, Yasuo Hara. One of seven children, my dad was a natural entrepreneur – he soon realised that fruit and veg would not earn him the money he dreamed of. So, he bought a VW Beetle, learned how to drive it and started off on his first career as a travelling salesman, buying and selling watches across southern Brazil. It was during this phase of his life that he met my mother Ana-Maria Saladini in the state of Paraná. They returned to the city of São Paulo where they settled down, opening a watch and jewellery shop, and starting a family – my sisters Jacqueline and Patricia, myself and then my brother Ricardo.

When their marriage ended, we stayed with our father and were raised by my Japanese grandmother and aunt Yoshiko Hara, luckily both excellent cooks. It was from this period that my appreciation of Nikkei cooking started, both through the cooking of my grandmother at home and through visiting many of Liberdade's Japanese restaurants with my father. Little did I know it at the time, but these formative food experiences would later shape my life. Aged 19 I came to London as part of my Brazilian university degree in hotel management. I was meant to return to Brazil the following year to continue my studies, but met my British partner and, rather like my grandmother many years before me, I never left. After taking a business degree at a London university, I spent over 10 years working in finance and investment banking. It was during this time that I started writing The London Foodie blog as a creative platform for my foodie cravings. The blog led me to quit my job, to retrain at Le Cordon Bleu and to launch the Japanese and Nikkei supper club at my London home in 2012.

Modern Nikkei life

Today, the Japanese community in Brazil is the largest outside Japan, with most Nikkei living in the southern states of São Paulo and Paraná. The Nikkei in Brazil are fully integrated in society and inter-racial marriage, like that of my parents, is commonplace. Japanese immigration continues today, although in smaller numbers. The second largest Nikkei community in South America is in Peru, centred in Lima, with significant numbers still in the northern areas of Peru to which migration first occurred, including Trujillo, Huancayo and Chiclayo. The Nikkei have made a substantial impact in Peru, including in the political sphere. For example, in 1990 Alberto Fujimori was the first Asian to be elected president in any country outside of Asia. He was re-elected in 1995. Of all the communities that make up the cultural melting pots of modern Brazil and Peru, the Nikkei are among the better educated and most prosperous. They are prominent in the professions, agriculture, commerce and finance.

Nikkei cuisine – how did it all begin?

The Japanese were in for a big surprise when they arrived in South America when it came to food. Coming from a nation that banned the killing of cattle until 1872, their diet was primarily pescatarian and could not be more different from that they encountered in Brazil. Brazilian food at the time was rich in pork fat, cassava and corn. The only culinary similarity was the Brazilian fondness for rice, although the Japanese were astonished to see it fried in pork fat and combined with beans, the latter used only to make desserts back home. There was no fresh fish in the countryside and the main meat available on the plantations was jerk beef, which the new arrivals found repugnant. They also had to change from drinking their beloved green tea to the potent brew of coffee.

A great deal of adaptation was required of the Nikkei to adjust to this way of life. They made use of native varieties of fruit and vegetables and began to take a liking to fresh meat and poultry. Within their homes, they would use these newly discovered ingredients to create their own versions of dishes they once enjoyed in their home country. Nikkei cuisine therefore was born out of necessity around the start of the 20th century in the homes of Japanese immigrants. Conversely, these immigrants also had an impact on the food and agriculture of their new host nations. In Brazil, the Nikkei introduced a number of their native fruit and vegetables, including their beloved kabocha pumpkin, the persimmon (called *kaki* in both Japan and Brazil) and the ponca citrus fruit (it's a varietal of the Japanese tangerine). They also made the cultivation of numerous Brazilian vegetables more efficient, many of which had never before been commercially planted.

With the advent of Japanese multinationals, such as Toyota, Mitsubishi and Panasonic, opening factories in South America in the 1970s and 1980s, a new wave of white-collar Japanese immigrants arrived to run these operations. Many chefs, including most famously Nobu Matsuhisa, were recruited from Japan to cater for these new arrivals and to teach Nikkei chefs Japanese cooking skills. Other notable Japanese chefs were Toshiro Konishi in Lima and Takatomo Hachinohe in São Paulo. Although these were all fully trained professional chefs working in Japan, on arrival in South America they also discovered that importing many ingredients from Japan was difficult, if not impossible in some cases, and so once again adaptation to local ingredients was required. Nikkei cooking then went from the domestic setting to the restaurant, this time cooked by professional chefs. These top chefs added a layer of sophistication to Nikkei cuisine, passed this on to the current generation of Nikkei chefs and over the last decade have brought it to international attention.

Nikkei cuisine today

Today in Brazil and Peru, Nikkei cuisine is gaining popularity and is enjoyed both at home and in restaurants by Nikkei and non-Nikkei populations alike. In São Paulo, the Michelin-starred Nikkei chef Tsuyoshi Murakami heads one of the most coveted tables in the city, as does Adriano Kanashiro at Momotaro, whose foie gras and tuna sushi has become legendary. Shin Koike of Aizome, a Japanese national who immigrated as recently as 1994, has been a great inspiration for me and is pioneering the use of native Amazonian fruits and plants in his Nikkei cooking. In Lima, Mitsuharu Tsumura of Maido (ranked 7th in the 50 Best Restaurants of Latin America in San Pellegrino's list) offers perhaps the most sophisticated expression of Nikkei cuisine in Peru. Toshiro Konishi, considered by many to be the father of Peruvian Nikkei cuisine, is one of the most celebrated chefs in the land. Hajime Kasuga is a lecturer in Nikkei and Japanese cooking at the prestigious Le Cordon Bleu Cookery School in Lima and is a true ambassador for both cuisines.

Now, Nikkei food is gaining momentum beyond South America. Nikkei restaurants are opening across Europe and the US, perhaps reflecting an increasing appreciation of Peruvian and Brazilian cuisines in which Nikkei cooking has had a major influence. Several Nikkei restaurants have opened in London, including Chotto Matte and Sushi Samba. In Barcelona, Albert and Ferran Adrià from the late El Bulli opened their own Nikkei restaurant Pakta, earning rave reviews. In Miami, at The Mandarin Oriental, La Mar Restaurant is headed by the Nikkei chef Diego Oka to great acclaim.

The 'f' word

It is impossible to write about Nikkei cooking, combining as it does Japanese and South American elements, without considering the dreaded 'f' word – fusion. For many food purists, fusion is anathema; and particularly in relation to Japanese cuisine (washoku), which has been added to UNESCO's cultural heritage list. For me, Japanese cooking is among my favourites, and it would be upsetting to me if people suggested it was being manipulated without much thought. Nikkei cuisine is a byproduct of migration and adaptation, created over 100 years ago in South America. It was a cuisine created out of necessity; it is part of my family history and that of millions like me and so, unlike food fads, it is here to stay.

For those flying the authenticity flag, it might come as a surprise to learn that Japanese cooking itself has been influenced by many different countries, including Portugal, China and the US. Take tempura as an example – the love of battered, deep-fried foods was introduced to Japan by the Portuguese in the 16th century. The word for bread in Japanese, pan, derives from the Portuguese word *pão*. From China, perhaps the most popular imports were ramen, gyoza and mabo dofu – all now considered quintessentially Japanese. Even today, washoku is an ever-changing cuisine. The Japanese's love for fatty beef, tuna and salmon is a relatively recent phenomenon, as is their fancy for dairy produce, including cheese and double (heavy) cream; over time their lactose intolerance has reduced. These days, it is not uncommon to see California rolls on menus throughout Japan, not to mention their increasing love for spicy foods, curries and European wines.

Unthinking combinations of different cuisines are seldom successful. As Toshiro Konishi put it: 'to create Nikkei dishes, it is important to understand both Japanese and South American food cultures; simply mixing soy sauce and miso into

a Latin dish and calling it Nikkei is a violation'. While for Mitsuharu Tsumura, 'without this understanding, fusion becomes confusion'. In Tsuyoshi Murakami's opinion, 'Japanese food cannot be entirely recreated outside of Japan, and some adaptation is always necessary'. And I totally agree.

Cooking Nikkei food at home – how to use this book

In most Nikkei households, Japanese, Nikkei and the national cuisine go hand-in-hand and it would be difficult to consider one without reference to the others. At our Nikkei home in Brazil and now in the UK, we adopted the Japanese washoku philosophy of providing a balanced meal, not only in terms of nutritional value but also considering other aspects such as flavour, cooking methods, colour and presentation. One outcome of this method is that the sheer variety helps achieve satiety without excess, and my approach in this book is similar.

I have aimed to provide a varied selection of recipes that will allow you to design a menu to incorporate a range of different colours, flavours and cooking methods. A balanced Nikkei meal would start with two or three different small eats, including a soup and a raw fish *tiradito* or sashimi, followed by a more substantial fish or meat dish, accompanied by rice and vegetables and ending with a sweet and refreshing dessert. This approach differs from a more traditional Japanese menu where the rice and soup are usually served at the end of the meal.

But, there are no hard and fast rules here; in my supper club, for instance, I like serving up to ten small eats in one meal, sometimes with no main course! With friends at home, I love getting together around a hotpot, accompanied by a range of small eats. Alternatively, many of the dishes in this book could be used as an interesting starter (appetizer) or main course within a Western meal. Whatever your approach, the aim of this book is to give you the confidence and understanding to cook Nikkei dishes in your own home and to experiment with a different and exciting cuisine.

Happy cooking!

SMALL
EATS

Everyone loves a burger, and in this recipe I combine some of my favourite flavours to create a Nikkei version – meltingly tender beef, unctuous foie gras and spicy kimchi. Buttery brioche is the perfect accompaniment to foie gras, and I love lightly toasting the buns in the pan used for searing the liver, mopping up the delicious melted foie gras before assembling for added va-va-voom. And if you love a '2 for 1', the great thing about this dish is that you use some of the beef from another recipe – Braised beef short ribs cooked in soy sauce, sake and brown sugar (see page 158) – so if you attempt that recipe you could get to enjoy this one too!

BONELESS SHORT-RIB SLIDERS
WITH FOIE GRAS & KIMCHI MAYO

SERVES 4

4 pieces of Braised beef short ribs (see page 158), roughly the size of the brioche buns
100g (3½oz) lobe of foie gras liver
50g (1¾oz) kimchi pickle, plus 4 whole 2.5cm (1in) pieces for assembly
25g (1oz/2 tbsp) Japanese-style mayoneizu (see page 232) or ready-made Japanese mayonnaise
freshly ground salt and black pepper
¼ tsp shichimi pepper
1 tbsp sunflower oil
4 canapé-sized brioche buns
2 iceberg lettuce leaves, cut into 4 cups roughly the size of the brioche buns
2 tbsp spring onions (scallions), finely sliced
4 Japanese bamboo sticks, for presentation

Prepare the short ribs following the instructions on page 158. When ready, take the pieces of beef short ribs and cut them into four slices 1.5cm (½in) thick and as wide as the brioche buns. Preheat the oven to 60–70°C (140–158°F/gas mark ¼).

Cut the foie gras into four pieces about 2cm (¾in) thick and roughly as wide as the canapé-sized brioche buns. Keep refrigerated until needed.

To prepare the kimchi mayonnaise, start by chopping the kimchi pickle discarding any excess liquid from the kimchi and mixing it with the Japanese mayonnaise. Add a couple of pinches of salt and the shichimi pepper. Check the seasoning and adjust if necessary.

Heat the oil in a non-stick frying pan (or skillet) and fry the slices of short-rib beef on a medium heat for a couple of minutes on each side. Transfer to a plate and keep warm in the preheated oven.

Wipe the same pan dry with kitchen paper, (paper towels) return it to the heat and when smoking hot, add the pieces of foie gras and brown on both sides (it should take only about 30 seconds on each side), season well with freshly ground salt and pepper. Transfer to a plate and keep warm. Alternatively, if you prefer, you can use a blow-torch to sear the foie gras slices on each side in a frying pan (or skillet); this way less of the liver will melt than in the frying pan (skillet) method.

Halve the brioche buns and quickly fry them in the fat left from cooking the foie gras liver.

Place the bottom halves on a plate, top each with an iceberg lettuce cup followed by a piece of kimchi pickle, then place 1 teaspoon of kimchi mayo in the centre, followed by a piece of beef short rib and another of foie gras, and finally a few slices of spring onion (scallion) over the top. Carefully place the top halves of the brioche buns over the tower of ingredients and gently pierce the slider through with a Japanese bamboo stick to hold the various layers together. Serve immediately.

Made with pastry that is paper-thin, filled with a variety of savoury or sweet fillings and then deep-fried, *pastéis* are lighter and crispier than *empanadas*. They are believed to have been created when Japanese immigrants started deep-frying gyoza (Japanese dumplings) to sell as snacks at weekly fruit and vegetable street markets, known in Brazil as *feiras*. *Pastéis* stalls are usually run by Nikkei families at such markets and their delicious *pastéis* are everyone's reward after a morning's shopping. Popular flavours are ham and cheese, shredded chicken with cream cheese, and minced (ground) beef or pork with hard-boiled egg, but below are two of my favourites. I find that gyoza wrappers work perfectly well and save time. *Pastéis* are delicious served as appetisers or simply on their own with a glass of chilled beer.

PASTÉIS OF CHICKEN, CREAM CHEESE & GREEN OLIVES

MAKES 30–40 SMALL *PASTÉIS*

450g (1lb) boneless, skinless chicken breasts
1 tbsp chicken bouillon powder
2 tbsp sunflower oil, plus extra for deep-frying
1 medium onion, very finely chopped
3 spring onions (scallions), chopped
2 garlic cloves, crushed
1 tsp dried oregano
1 tbsp cornflour (cornstarch)
2 tbsp tomato purée (paste)
juice of ½ lime
4 tbsp flat-leaf parsley, roughly chopped
freshly ground salt and black pepper
250g (9oz) good-quality gyoza wrappers
100g (3½oz/½ cup) cream cheese
20–30 pitted green olives, halved lengthways
lime wedges, to serve
Tabasco (or other hot pepper) sauce, to serve (optional)

First, make the filling. Place the chicken breasts in a pan with the bouillon powder and cover with water. Bring to the boil and simmer for 5 minutes. Turn off the heat and let it stand, covered, for a further 10 minutes. Remove the poached chicken and set aside, reserving the broth. When the chicken has cooled down enough to handle, shred it finely and then refrigerate until needed.

Heat the sunflower oil in a pan and fry the onion and spring onions (scallions) until soft. Add the garlic, dried oregano and cornflour (cornstarch) and mix well. Next, add the tomato purée (paste) along with 250ml (8½fl oz/1 cup) of the reserved chicken broth and simmer until the mixture starts to thicken slightly. Then, add the shredded chicken and mix well, adding a little more chicken broth if the mixture seems a little dry.

Remove from the heat and stir in the lime juice and chopped parsley, and mix well. Season with salt and pepper to taste.

Now, you're ready to prepare the *pastéis*. Place a gyoza wrapper on your work surface (counter). Then, place 1 tablespoon of the chicken mixture, ½ a teaspoon of cream cheese and half a green olive in the middle of the wrapper. Dip your finger in water and use it to moisten the edges of the wrapper. Fold it over the filling, pressing the edges together and then pinching them with a fork all the way around. Repeat with the remaining wrappers (if the wrappers are small, use two wrappers to make one *pastél*).

Fill a pan with 5cm (2in) of sunflower oil or heat a deep-fryer to 180°C (350°F). Fry the *pastéis* in batches until golden brown. Drain on kitchen paper (paper towels) and serve warm with a dash of hot pepper sauce (if using).

Variation – **Ham, cheese & tomato *pastéis***
Place a small cube of mozzarella cheese, a little chopped ham, ½ a slice of tomato, a sprinkle of dried oregano and salt and pepper over a gyoza wrapper, fold it over, and deep-fry, as above. Enjoy!

I have loved popcorn since I was a kid, and at university it saw me through endless nights of revision; today it remains one of my guilty pleasures. Popcorn is a versatile snack that can be flavoured in many different ways – with shichimi pepper or wasabi for a little spice, with black sesame caramel for those sweet cravings, with red miso powder for a Marmite-like (umami-like) savouriness or with matcha salt for something a tad different. It's a doddle to make and goes really well with any aperitif.

POPCORN FIVE WAYS

SERVES 2

For the shichimi pepper flavour:
2 tbsp sunflower oil
100g (3½oz/½ cup) popcorn
  kernels
3 tbsp unsalted butter
1 tsp salt
1 tbsp shichimi pepper

SHICHIMI PEPPER

In a pan with a lid, heat the sunflower oil on a high heat until hot and smoking. Add the popcorn kernels and cover with the lid. The popcorn should start popping very soon after this, and after a couple of minutes when there is a time gap of 1–2 seconds between pops, turn the heat off, leaving the pan covered until the corn stops popping.

Transfer the popcorn from the pan into a large bowl. Add the butter to the pan and, over a low heat, melt the butter until foaming but not browned. Pour the foaming butter over the popcorn and give it a good shake.

Season with salt and the shichimi pepper, and mix well until well combined. Check for seasoning and add more salt or shichimi pepper, if desired. Serve.

For the hot wasabi butter flavour:
2 tbsp sunflower oil
100g (3½oz/½ cup) popcorn
  kernels
3 tbsp unsalted butter
½ tsp salt
1 tsp wasabi salt

HOT WASABI

Prepare the popcorn as per instructions for shichimi pepper flavour but without seasoning.

Season with the salt and wasabi salt, and mix until well combined. Check for seasoning and add more salt or wasabi salt, if desired. Serve.

For the black sesame caramel flavour:
2 tbsp sunflower oil
100g (3½oz/½ cup popcorn
  kernels
300g (10½oz/1½ cups)
  caster (superfine) sugar
50g (1¾oz/3½ tbsp) unsalted
  butter
50g (1¾oz/⅓ cup) toasted
  black sesame seeds

BLACK SESAME CARAMEL

Prepare the popcorn as for shichimi pepper flavour but don't add the butter or seasoning.

In a pan large enough to accommodate the caramel and all the popped corn, add the caster (superfine) sugar and over a medium heat, cook the sugar to a light, amber-coloured caramel. Add the butter and, using a wooden spoon, mix it well into the caramel, then add the toasted black sesame seeds, mixing it well again until combined. Tip in the cooked popcorn and fold into the caramel, so that all the popcorn is coated in the sesame caramel.

Transfer it from the pan to a bowl, don't be tempted to try it at this stage as it will be super-hot – let it cool down. The caramel will solidify as it cools down, so you'll need to break it up using a rolling pin. Serve.

For the red miso flavour:
2 tbsp sunflower oil
100g (3½oz/½ cup) popcorn
3 tbsp unsalted butter
½ tsp salt
1½ tbsp Red miso powder
  (see page 241)

RED MISO

Prepare the popcorn as per instructions for shichimi pepper flavour but without seasoning.

Season with the salt and red miso powder, and mix until well combined. Check for seasoning and add more salt or red miso powder, if desired. Serve.

For the matcha flavour:
2 tbsp sunflower oil
100g (3½oz/½ cup) popcorn
3 tbsp unsalted butter
½ tsp salt
1 tsp matcha salt

MATCHA SALT

Prepare the popcorn as per instructions for shichimi pepper flavour but without seasoning.

Season with the salt and matcha salt, and mix until well combined. Check for seasoning and add more salt or matcha salt, if desired. Serve.

Few can resist a lip-smacking and crispy deep-fried chicken, whether it's as *frango à passarinho* in Brazil or kara-age in Japan. Here I use shio kouji (fermented rice culture and salt) to marinate the chicken for extra umaminess. Lately, shio kouji has had a comeback as an ingredient in Japan – it adds a rich flavour to dishes, tenderises fish and meat, and is thought to have health benefits. Lotus root, known in Japan as renkon, is not an everyday veggie in the West, but if you haven't tried it yet, you will find that it makes for deliciously crunchy chips (fries) that are dead easy to make!

KOUJI FRIED CHICKEN & RENKON CHIPS

WITH A NANBAN DIPPING SAUCE

SERVES 2

For the kouji fried chicken:
500g (1lb 2oz) skin-on, boneless chicken thighs, cut into 2.5cm (1in) pieces
4 tbsp shio kouji
2 tsp grated ginger
2 garlic cloves, crushed
2 tsp soy sauce
juice of 1 lime
sunflower oil, for deep-frying
50g (1¾oz/½ cup) cornflour (cornstarch)
50g (1¾oz/⅓ cup) plain (all-purpose) flour
½ tsp salt
½ tsp ground white pepper

For the renkon chips:
400g (14oz) renkon lotus root, washed
1 tsp rice vinegar
400ml (13½fl oz/1¾ cups) water
Maldon sea salt flakes, to taste
1 tsp dried seaweed flakes (known as aonori)

For the nanban dipping sauce:
50ml (2fl oz/¼ cup) soy sauce
50ml (2fl oz/¼ cup) rice vinegar
½ tsp sugar
1 garlic clove, crushed
1 red chilli, deseeded and finely chopped

Combine the chicken pieces with the shio kouji, ginger, garlic, soy sauce and lime in a bowl, cover with clingfilm (plastic wrap) and marinate for at least 4 hours and up to 24 hours in the fridge.

When you are getting ready to cook the chicken, make the dipping sauce. Mix all the ingredients together in a bowl, stirring well to dissolve the sugar. Set aside.

Then, heat a pan with sunflower oil to 160°C (310°F) for deep-frying. While the oil is heating, prepare the renkon chips (fries). The lotus root can be peeled if you wish to remove the outer skin, I like keeping it for extra colour. Using a mandolin or a sharp knife, cut the root into 5mm (¼in) round slices; any thinner than this and the chips (fries) will become crisps (potato chips)! Mix the rice vinegar and water in a bowl and soak the renkon slices for about 5 minutes.

Next, in a separate bowl, mix the flours with the salt and ground white pepper. Add a few pieces of chicken to the bowl, coating them well with the seasoned flour; do this just before adding the chicken to the hot oil each time. Gently drop each piece of chicken into the pan and deep-fry until golden brown; this should take about 5 minutes. Fry only a few pieces of chicken at a time – overcrowding the pan will bring the temperature of the oil down too much and the chicken will be stewed in the oil rather than crisply fried. While the chicken is frying, drain the renkon and pat dry using a tea-towel (dish towel).

When the chicken is ready, transfer it to a plate lined with kitchen paper (paper towels) and keep them warm while you fry the renkon chips (fries) in the same oil.

Check the temperature of the oil is still about 160°C (310°F). I use a thermometer for this, but if you don't have one, pop a slice of renkon into the hot oil: it should take a couple of seconds to come up to the surface; if it comes up quicker than that then the oil is too hot and, conversely, if it sits at the bottom of the pan for longer than 2 seconds, the oil is not hot enough. Add a few slices of renkon to the oil at a time and deep-fry for about 4 minutes or until the slices are golden brown. Transfer them to a plate lined with kitchen paper (paper towels) and season with Maldon sea salt flakes.

Serve the kouji fried chicken and renkon chips (fries) immediately with the nanban dipping sauce and a sprinkle of dried seaweed flakes.

Regarded by many as the father of Peruvian Nikkei cuisine, Toshiro Konishi is one of the most revered chefs in Peru today. Arriving in Lima in the 1970s, Konishi-san fell in love with the Peruvian people and the wonderful native ingredients of the Andean land and sea, never returning to live in Japan.

I was lucky enough to meet him in Peru and try this delicious daikon dish. Konishi-san is a larger-than-life character, with a contagious laugh and a generosity of spirit that made me like him instantly.

When he is not at one of his two busy restaurant kitchens – Toshiro's at San Isidro, Peru, or Toshiro Robatayaki in Bogota, Colombia – he is travelling the world championing Peruvian Nikkei cuisine or lecturing at the San Ignacio de Loyola University in Lima, where he is a visiting professor of culinary arts.

TOSHIRO'S DAIKON NIMONO NIKU – MISO FLAVOUR

SERVES 4

1 large Japanese daikon
2 litres (3½ pints/8 cups) water
100g (3½oz/½ cup) short-grain white rice
1 litre (1¾ pints/4 cups) dashi (from 1 litre (1¾ pints/4 cups) water and 1 tsp instant dashi powder)
100ml (3½fl oz/7 tbsp) soy sauce
100ml (3½fl oz/7 tbsp) mirin
10cm x 10cm (4in x 4in) dashi konbu

For the sauce:
100g (3½oz/½ cup) inaka miso (red miso)
100g (3½oz/½ cup) sugar
100ml (3½fl oz/½ cup) sake
2 egg yolks
2 tsp sunflower oil
2 jalapeño chillies, finely chopped
150g (5½oz) minced (ground) beef
100g (3½oz) spring onions (scallions), chopped, plus extra shredded to garnish
1 tsp toasted sesame oil
a little yuzu kosho, to taste
a little yuzu peel, to garnish

Peel the daikon and cut it across into 4cm (1½in)-thick slices. Ensure these are free of sharp edges (cut these off). Cut a slit in each slice from one side 1cm (½in) towards the centre. Put the water and rice in a pan and bring to the boil. Once boiled, place the daikon slices in the pan for about 5 minutes then remove, discarding the rice from cooking the daikon. This softening of the daikon is known as shitayude and removes any bitterness and smell.

Next, put the dashi, soy sauce, mirin, dashi konbu followed by the daikon slices into a separate medium pan and boil over a medium heat. Instead of using a lid, cover the top of the pan with foil. Once it's boiled, turn the heat to low and simmer for about an hour. After this, turn off the heat and leave it as it is.

Meanwhile, make the sauce. Add the miso, sugar, sake and egg yolks to a separate pan (let's call this pan B) over a medium heat and mix together, without burning them. Keep mixing gently with a spatula until it bubbles up then turn off the heat.

In another pan, heat the oil and add the jalapeños, minced (ground) beef and spring onions (scallions) and stir-fry until cooked through. Add this mixture to pan B.

Allow pan B to simmer over a low heat, add the sesame oil and the yuzu kosho, to taste. Meanwhile, shred the yuzu peel.

Once the daikon is very soft (insert a toothpick gently through one of the pieces to see), place the daikon slices into individual soup bowls and add about one-quarter of the remaining broth. Place the sauce on top of the daikon pieces, to taste, and then garnish with the yuzu peel and shredded spring onion (scallion).

Known in the UK as salt and pepper squid, in Peru as *chicharrón de calamar* and as *lula frita* in Brazil, my version of this popular dish uses sansho pepper – one of my favourite Japanese ingredients. If you've not heard of sansho pepper before, it is the pulverised peppercorns of the Japanese prickly ash tree. This Nikkei take on this universally popular squid dish should be crispy, with a feather-like texture and when paired with this intensely aromatic Japanese condiment I think it's a winner of a dish. I love serving this with an exceptionally well-chilled beer.

SALT & SANSHO PEPPER SQUID

SERVES 2

1 long red chilli, thinly sliced
2 spring onions (scallions), thinly sliced
sunflower oil, for shallow-frying and deep-frying
200g (7oz) fresh squid tubes, cleaned
75ml (2¾fl oz/5 tbsp) water
30g (1¼oz/¼ cup) plain (all-purpose) flour
a pinch of baking powder
40g (1½oz/¼ cup) potato flour
30g (1¼oz/¼ cup) cornflour (cornstarch)
½ tsp toasted black sesame seeds, to garnish
2 lime wedges, to serve

For the pepper & salt mix:
½ tsp sansho pepper
½ tsp freshly ground black pepper
½ tbsp Maldon sea salt flakes

In a bowl, first make the pepper and salt mix and combine the ingredients well.

Heat 2 tablespoons of sunflower oil in a non-stick frying pan (or skillet). When the pan has heated through and the oil is hot, shallow-fry the chilli and spring onion (scallion) slices for a few seconds until lightly wilted, then transfer them to a plate lined with kitchen paper (paper towels) and set aside until garnishing the dish.

Cut the squid tubes so that they open flat and lightly score one surface in a criss-cross pattern; this will help cooking and prevent the squid from curling up too much. Cut the squid into 1.5cm (½in) slices (not rings).

In a deep pan, heat the oil for deep-frying the squid to about 180°C (350°F).

Make a batter by mixing the water, flour and baking powder in a bowl. Coat the squid pieces in the batter, then let them drain over a wire rack for a minute.

In a separate bowl, mix the potato flour and cornflour (cornstarch) together and then coat the battered squid, shaking off any excess flour as you go.

Deep-fry the squid pieces for about 1 minute in a couple of batches, do not overcrowd the pan or the temperature of the oil will drop too fast and the squid will not crisp up. Transfer the cooked squid to a plate lined with kitchen paper (paper towels).

Coat the fried squid with the pepper and salt mix, top with the fried chilli and spring onion (scallion) and sprinkle over the toasted black sesame seeds. Serve immediately with wedges of lime.

One of the most popular dishes in Japan, tamagoyaki is a multi-layered omelette and a bento box favourite. It can be eaten on top of sushi, on its own as a snack or as a side dish as part of a Japanese or Nikkei meal. Don't be put off by the techniques required to make this dish – as with crêpes, practice makes perfect, and once you get the hang of it, you'll be hooked. Here I give a recipe for a basic mixture, and use it to make three versions – plain, with foie gras and with crab.

JAPANESE ROLLED OMELETTE, THREE WAYS
PLAIN TAMAGOYAKI & WITH CRAB & WITH FOIE GRAS

SERVES 6 – MAKES 3 ROLLED OMELETTES

For the plain tamagoyaki mixture:
18 large eggs
2 tsp instant dashi powder
3 tbsp mirin
3 tbsp caster (superfine) sugar
2 tbsp light soy sauce
a couple of pinches of salt
50ml (2fl oz/¼ cup) sunflower oil

For the garnish (optional):
300g (10½oz) daikon piece, finely grated and excess water squeezed out
a few drops of light soy sauce

For the crab tamagoyaki:
⅓ portion of the plain tamagoyaki mixture (above)
3 tbsp finely chopped chives
100g (3½oz) white crab meat

For the foie gras tamagoyaki:
⅓ portion of the plain tamagoyaki mixture (above)
100g (3½oz) lobe of foie gras liver, cut into 2cm (¾in) thick, 15cm (6in) long batons (thin sticks) (the length should be roughly the same width as the tamagoyaki pan)

For this recipe, you'll need a non-stick, square tamagoyaki pan and a sushi rolling mat.

Break the eggs into a large measuring jug (cup) and gently mix just so that the yolks and whites are roughly mixed (if the eggs are overbeaten, the omelette will not be light).

In a bowl, add the instant dashi powder, mirin, caster (superfine) sugar, soy sauce and salt and mix until the sugar and salt have dissolved (no powder or grains remain). Pour the dashi mixture into the beaten eggs and fold gently. Read off the volume of the tamagoyaki mixture and divide it into three equal parts – one for plain, one for crab and one for the foie gras tamagoyaki. Transfer one-third of the mixture into a smaller jug (pitcher) for the first omelette, which makes it easier to pour the mixture into the tamagoyaki pan.

Heat the tamagoyaki pan over a medium heat until hot. Keep the temperature of the pan constant so that the eggs cook quickly but do not burn, colour too quickly or become rubbery. Measure out the oil into a cup and dip a small cloth or some folded kitchen paper (paper towel) into the oil. Use chopsticks to hold the cloth or paper and wipe the pan so that it is only lightly greased. Keep this handy as you'll use it throughout the cooking process. Next, drop a tiny amount of egg mixture in the middle of the pan; if it sizzles, the pan is hot enough. Adjust the heat to keep the pan at this temperature throughout.

A good tamagoyaki has many fine layers and is super-light; the omelette should not be golden or lightly browned as it will be overcooked. **1** Pour about 10% of the egg mixture into the pan or just enough to coat the pan with a really fine layer across the bottom. Tilt the pan so that the egg mixture spreads in an even thin layer over the bottom. **2–4** When the egg starts bubbling up around the edges and is starting to set, roll it up away from you using chopsticks and/or a spatula as you would a Swiss (jelly) roll. The egg mixture should be lightly wet when being rolled or the layers of cooked egg will not stick together.

5 Keep the rolled omelette in the pan but slide it to the other end, grease the pan again with the oiled cloth or kitchen paper (paper towel), pour another thin layer of egg mixture, roughly 10%, into the empty side of the pan. **6** Lift up the first roll with chopsticks and let the egg mix run underneath while tilting the pan to coat it evenly. **7** When this new layer is half-set, roll the first omelette away from you so that a new layer rolls around it. **8** Then, pull the two-layered omelette towards you again, oil the pan and add another lot of egg mix to the pan.

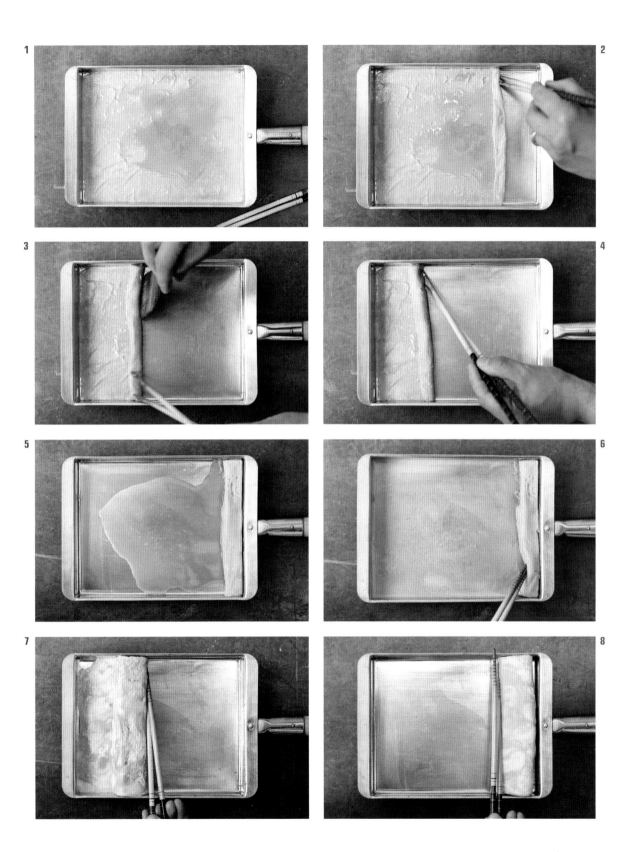

9

10

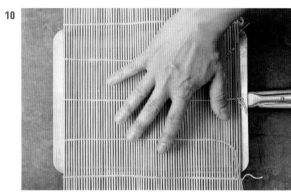

11

12

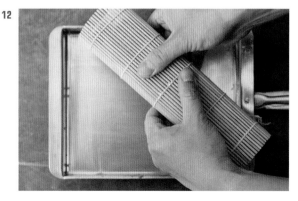

9 Repeat this process of rolling and adding a little of the egg mixture until all of the egg mix is used up – you should now have one complete multi-layered tamagoyaki.

10 Carefully flip the tamagoyaki onto a bamboo sushi mat, it should be about a 4cm (1½in)-thick block. **11–12** Roll up the omelette gently but firmly in the mat (I find that placing a rubber band around it helps to keep it closed) and leave it to stand, rolled up and lightly weighed down by a small non-breakable object (I often use a small tin) for 5 minutes.

13 (main picture) Unroll the mat and then cut the omelette into 1–2cm (½–¾in)-thick slices and serve with the grated daikon flavoured with a few drops of soy sauce (if using). If you are not eating it straightaway, wrap it in clingfilm (plastic wrap) and keep in the fridge for up to 24 hours.

FOR THE FILLED TAMAGOYAKI:

For the **crab tamagoyaki**, add the chopped chives to one of the reserved thirds of plain egg mixture. Before adding the egg, stir the chives around so they are evenly distributed. Cook as for the plain version above, but adding a scattering of white crab meat over the thin layers of egg mixture just before rolling them in the hot pan. As before, roll the multi-layered omelette within a sushi mat, weigh it down and slice it up. Serve lightly warm or at room temperature.

With the remaining third of the plain egg mixture, make the **foie gras version**. The foie gras batons (sticks) will be placed in the first omelette layer from one side of the pan to the other. To do this, the first layer will need to be slightly thicker than subsequent ones. When the pan is hot enough, pour about one-quarter of the egg into the pan. Place the foie gras batons (sticks) from one side of the pan to the other and 3cm (1¼in) from the start of the omelette; when the omelette is starting to set, carefully flip the 3cm (1¼in) omelette border over the foie gras and gently continue to roll it, so that the foie gras is in the middle of the first omelette layer. Continue to roll the tamagoyaki, as for the plain one above, until all the mix is used. Roll the multi-layered omelette within a sushi mat, weigh it down and slice it up. It is best served warm.

Quinoa has been eaten in the Peruvian Andes for thousands of years. The black variety I use here has a toasty aniseed flavour that complements the scallops and sweet but citrusy kumquat. It's an elegant starter (appetizer) to any meal.

SCALLOPS WITH BLACK QUINOA TABBOULEH & CANDIED KUMQUATS

SERVES 6

6 large scallops, roe on
6 large scallop shells
1 tbsp extra virgin olive oil,
   for frying
a little salt-sludge (add a few
   drops of water to salt until it
   looks like sand)

For the candied kumquats:
120g (4oz/⅔ cup) sugar
1 tbsp glucose (or honey)
2 tbsp water
200g (7oz) kumquats, halved
2 tbsp pistachio kernels
2 tbsp cachaça or sake

For the black quinoa tabbouleh:
50g (1¾oz/⅓ cup) black quinoa
15g (½oz/⅓ cup) flat-leaf
   parsley
15g (½oz/1 cup) mint leaves
15g (½oz/1½ cups) dill fronds
15g (½oz) spring onions
   (scallions)
25g (1oz) banana shallot
½ small ripe avocado (about
   75g (2¾oz)), finely cubed

For the dressing:
4 tbsp yuzu (or lemon) juice
½ tsp sugar
2 tbsp extra virgin olive oil
1 red chilli (about 12g (⅓oz)),
   deseeded and finely diced
1 tsp Maldon sea salt flakes

For the garnish:
a sprinkle of shichimi pepper
Maldon sea salt flakes
micro herbs

First, make the candied kumquat. Mix the sugar, glucose (or honey) and water in a small pan, stirring until the sugar has dissolved and bring it to 120°C (248°F). Add the kumquat halves and the pistachios and cook for 3 minutes. Turn the heat off and let the sugar syrup cool. Once cool, add the cachaça or sake, whichever you prefer, and gently mix. Keep in a sterilised jar in the fridge until needed.

Next, prepare the tabbouleh. Add the quinoa to lightly salted boiling water (use twice the volume of water as quinoa) and once it returns to boiling point cover the pan and simmer very gently for 17 minutes. Turn off the heat and let it rest for a further 5 minutes, without taking the lid off. After this time, use a fork to fluff the quinoa. All the water should have been absorbed by the seeds, but if not cook the quinoa on a low heat, uncovered for a couple of minutes more until the water evaporates. Then, let the quinoa cool completely.

Make the dressing. In a bowl, combine the yuzu or lemon juice with the sugar, whisk well until the sugar has dissolved. Add the olive oil, chilli and salt, and mix until combined.

Next, finely chop the herbs, spring onions (scallions) and finely dice the shallot. Now assemble the tabbouleh. In a separate bowl, gently mix the chopped herbs, spring onions (scallions) and shallot into the cooked quinoa. Drizzle over half of the tabbouleh dressing and mix well. Finally, fold the cubed avocado gently into the black quinoa tabbouleh to avoid breaking up the avocado. Check for seasoning and adjust if necessary. Set aside briefly.

If you have a blow-torch, brown the scallops on both sides until lightly charred; if you don't have a blow-torch, heat a non-stick frying pan (or skillet) with a little olive oil until very hot and pan-fry the scallops for 30 seconds on each side.

I like using the scallop shells to serve this dish. Put a mound of the salt sludge in the middle of a small serving plate on which the scallop shell will sit; this mixture will stop the shell rattling around the plate.

To serve, place a tablespoon of black quinoa tabbouleh in the middle of each scallop shell, top this with a charred scallop. Now add half a candied kumquat with a few pistachios by the side of each scallop with half a teaspoon of the kumquat liquor. Then, using the reserved tabbouleh dressing, drizzle over the scallops, finishing with a sprinkle of shichimi pepper, Maldon sea salt flakes and a scattering of micro herbs.

Spaghetti alla Giapponese is my Nikkei take on the perennial favourite spaghetti Bolognese, or Spag Bol in many homes. The inspiration for this dish comes from the large Italian community in Southern Brazil. At home in São Paulo, whatever we cooked, we would add a splash or two of soy sauce, even if we were cooking pasta! This fun, tongue-in-cheek kind of dish uses fine strips of squid 'spaghetti', a spicy miso Bolognese sauce and chopped egg yolks for the Parmesan cheese.

SPAGHETTI ALLA GIAPPONESE
SQUID SPAGHETTI WITH SPICY MISO BOLOGNESE

SERVES 4

For the squid 'spaghetti':
500g (1lb 2oz) fresh squid
 tubes, cleaned
4 tbsp sake

For the spicy miso Bolognese:
50g (1¾oz/¼ cup) brown
 miso
2 tbsp mirin
1 tbsp soy sauce
1 tbsp sugar
1 tbsp cornflour (cornstarch)
1 tbsp sesame oil
100ml (3½fl oz/½ cup) water
100g (3½oz/¾ cup) tinned
 whole bamboo shoots,
 chopped into 5mm (¼in)
 cubes
2 tbsp vegetable oil
200g (7oz) minced (ground)
 pork
2 garlic cloves, crushed
2 tbsp Chinese soybean chilli
 paste or tobanjan paste
1 egg, to garnish

Cut the squid tubes so that they open flat. Place one sheet of squid over the other to form a block and wrap this tightly in clingfilm (plastic wrap). Partially freeze the squid for 45 minutes to 1 hour.

In the meantime, make the miso seasoning. In a bowl, add the brown miso, mirin, soy sauce, sugar, cornflour (cornstarch), sesame oil and water and mix well. Set aside.

Bring a pan of salted water to the boil, add the bamboo shoots and simmer for 5 minutes, drain and set aside.

Next, heat the vegetable oil in large wok until smoking, add the minced (ground) and garlic, then brown the meat for a couple of minutes. Stir in the chopped bamboo shoots, the Chinese soybean chilli paste and finally the miso seasoning. Adjust the seasoning by adding more tobanjan paste or soy sauce, if desired.

Remove the squid block from the freezer and slice it lengthways using an electric slicer or a super-sharp knife to make 5mm (¼in) 'spaghetti' strips. Put the squid in a bowl along with the sake and refrigerate until needed. The sake will remove any odour from the seafood and tenderise it at the same time.

Add the egg to a small pan filled with cold water. Bring the water to the boil then turn the heat down and simmer gently for 10 minutes to hard-boil the egg. Remove the hard yolk from the white (you won't need the white in this recipe) and chop the yolk very finely to resemble Parmesan cheese. Set aside.

Just before serving, bring a pan of salted water to the boil, blanch the squid for 30 seconds until it turns opaque, then drain immediately.

Using four small bowls, place a small amount of the squid 'spaghetti' in the middle of each bowl, followed by a tablespoon of the spicy miso Bolognese on top and a sprinkle of the finely chopped egg yolk. Serve immediately.

Nanban sauce is a Southern creation hailing from Kyushu island in Japan, with South American chillies introduced by the Portuguese in the 16th century. Loosely based on the Portuguese *escabeche*, nanban sauce is made with soy sauce, vinegar and chillies and is a great accompaniment for deep-fried meats and fish. This recipe is unusual in many ways – chicken is deep-fried until golden and crispy, then dunked in the cold Nanban sauce to marinate for a few hours. What began as hot, crispy chicken is served moist and at room temperature, having absorbed the marinade's flavours to become sweet and sour.

DEEP-FRIED CHICKEN NANBAN

SERVES 6

1 portion of Nanban sauce
    (see page 238)
1 carrot
1 celery stick
1 white onion
5cm (2in) piece of root ginger
chilli (dried red pepper) flakes
    or hot chilli sauce (optional)
vegetable oil, for deep-frying
750g (1lb 11¾oz) skin-on,
    boneless chicken thighs
200g (7oz/1½ cups) plain (all-
    purpose) flour, for dredging
1 tbsp salt

For the garnish:

1 tbsp toasted white sesame
    seeds
a handful of baby coriander
    (cilantro) leaves

Prepare the nanban sauce according to the instructions on page 238.

Peel, wash and cut the carrot and celery into fine julienne sticks of about 4cm (1½in) long and 2mm (⅛in) thick. Cut the onion into quarters and slice them lengthways very thinly. Peel and grate the ginger. Add all the sliced vegetables and grated ginger together in a large bowl (large enough to accommodate the sauce, vegetables and chicken).

Pour the prepared nanban sauce on to the vegetables, then leave the mixture marinating at room temperature for at least 30 minutes to 1 hour. Check the seasoning of the what will now be the marinade and adjust by adding chilli (dried red pepper) flakes or hot chilli sauce, if desired. Meanwhile, heat enough oil for deep-frying to 170°C/325°F.

Next, prepare the chicken by cutting it into bite-sized pieces. Mix the flour with the salt in a bowl. Dredge the chicken pieces in the seasoned flour, shaking off any excess. (I find that a large sieve (strainer) helps me with this task.) Coat a small batch at a time as the chicken will sweat if left too long and the flour will become wet and sticky before deep-frying.

Deep-fry the pieces until golden brown (about 5 minutes) – you will need to do this in batches. Place the deep-fried pieces of chicken on a wire rack over a tray to drain for a couple of minutes. Then, dunk the deep-fried chicken pieces into the large bowl of vegetables and nanban marinade; make sure that they are covered with the marinade but don't mix up too much otherwise the chicken pieces might break and spoil the presentation.

Continue until all the chicken has been deep-fried and mixed in with the marinade. Cover the bowl with clingfilm (plastic wrap) and let it sit at room temperature for at least 2 hours before serving; I find that between 4 and 6 hours is the ideal marinating time. If you prefer, you can keep the chicken in the fridge overnight and serve it the following day for a richer flavour (although the texture will be wetter). In this case, take it from the fridge a couple of hours before serving to allow it to come up to room temperature.

To serve, use a plate or bowl with some depth. Place some julienned vegetables to create a bed for the chicken in the middle of the plate, then top this with 4–5 pieces of chicken, followed by a few more vegetables and a couple of chilli slices (from the marinade). Pour 2 tablespoons of the marinade around the chicken, sprinkle over some white sesame seeds and finish it off with a smattering of baby coriander (cilantro) leaves and serve.

I thoroughly enjoyed this dish at the 1-Michelin-starred restaurant Pakta in Barcelona, headed by Peruvian chef Jorge Muñoz and Kioko Ii from Japan, a team brought together by Albert Adrià. Possibly the most celebrated Nikkei restaurant to date, Pakta has many outstanding reviews and judging by my visit deservedly so.

CAUSA OF BABY CUTTLEFISH

SERVES 6

For the *aji amarillo* paste:
500g (1lb 2oz) *aji amarillo*

For the yellow *causa*:
150g (5½oz) potatoes (for 100g (3½oz) potato purée)
20g (¾oz) *aji amarillo* paste
¼ tsp sunflower oil
¼ tsp salt

For the Osaka sauce:
25ml (¾fl oz/2 tbsp) lime juice
50g (1¾oz/2 tbsp) oyster sauce
40ml (1½fl oz/8 tsp) water
½ tsp instant dashi powder
2 tsp sesame oil

For the yuzu mayonnaise:
20g (¾oz) liquid egg (or beaten egg)
½ tsp instant dashi powder
1 tsp yuzu juice
¾ tsp soy sauce
90ml (3¼fl oz/⅓ cup) sunflower oil

For the potato chips:
750ml (1pint 6fl oz/3 cups) extra virgin olive oil
75g (2¾oz) potatoes

For the baby cuttlefish:
6 baby cuttlefish (each weighing about 10g (½oz))
1 tbsp sunflower oil
25g (1oz) mentaiko (chilli-marinated cod or pollock roe), to garnish

Make the *aji amarillo* paste. Add the *aji amarillo* to a medium pan, fill it with cold water, bring to the boil then strain the yellow chilli peppers in a colander. Repeat this process three times, then set aside. Blend the drained *aji amarillo* in a food processor until smooth. Strain the resulting paste to remove any bits of skin. Place it in a container in the fridge.

Next, make the yellow *causa*. Wash the potatoes and pat dry. Lay them on a plate, cover with clingfilm (plastic wrap) and cook in a microwave at 800W for 22 minutes. Peel and then pass through a fine sieve (strainer) or potato ricer. Set aside to cool. Once it's cold, mix together the ingredients for the yellow *causa*. Cover and set aside in a cool area.

Now, make the Osaka sauce by mixing all the ingredients (except the oil) in a blender, then turn it on and start adding the sesame oil little by little to make an emulsion. Transfer to a squeezy bottle and keep it in a cool place or in the fridge.

To make the yuzu mayonnaise, mix all the ingredients (except the oil) in a blender. With the blender running, start adding the sunflower oil little by little to make an emulsion. Transfer the mayonnaise to a squeezy bottle and transfer to the fridge until needed.

To prepare the chips (fries), heat the olive oil in a medium pan to 120°C (248°F). Preheat the oven to 50°C/122°F/gas mark ¼ and line a baking tray (baking sheet) with greaseproof (wax) paper. Peel the potatoes then cut them into circles using a 5cm (2in) round cutter. Using a mandolin, slice them into 5mm (¼in)-thick discs. Keep the potatoes in cold water and dry them using kitchen paper (paper towels) before frying. Once the oil has reached temperature, fry the potato slices, checking the temperature remains at 120°C (248°F). Once fried, place on a tray (sheet) lined with kitchen paper (paper towels) to remove excess oil. Pat dry and leave on the tray (sheet), then bake the chips (fries) for 2 hours for super-crunchy chips (fries). Set aside in an airtight container lined with greaseproof (wax) paper.

Prepare a bowl of iced salted water. Use small scissors to remove the eyes of the cuttlefish and use tweezers to remove its mouth. Dip the cuttlefish in the iced water and transfer to an airtight container lined with damp kitchen paper (paper towels). Cover the cuttlefish with more damp paper. Once all the cuttlefish are cleaned, cover and transfer to the fridge.

To serve, dot a little yuzu mayonnaise on the plate. Cut the yellow *causa* into six squares and place one square on each plate. Dot some yuzu mayonnaise on the *causa* to secure a potato chip (fry) on top. Heat the oil in a frying pan (skillet) until hot and sauté the cuttlefish; do not season as the Osaka sauce is highly flavoursome. Add the sauce and slowly reduce. Place the cuttlefish on top of the chip (fry) and sprinkle mentaiko on top.

Hakata, the capital of Kyushu island, was a main destination for early Chinese settlers in Japan. I first came across these buns, a Chinese import, in nearby Nagasaki where they are called kakuni manju. Here I spice things up with a cucumber and chilli pickle, ginger and coriander (cilantro) to partner the tender buta kakuni (pork belly, see page 162).

MY NIKKEI HAKATA BUNS
SLOW-BRAISED PORK BELLY IN STEAMED TAIWANESE BUNS WITH A CUCUMBER & CHILLI PICKLE

SERVES 6

½ portion of Super-slow braised pork belly (see page 162)
6 leaves of iceberg lettuce
6 small bunches of coriander (cilantro) leaves (just a handful of leaves per bunch)
1 spring onion (scallion)
2 tbsp chopped red ginger pickle (beni shoga)
6 double-slice Taiwanese buns (also known as Gua Bao buns, available from Chinese supermarkets)
2 tbsp cornflour (cornstarch)
50ml (2fl oz/3½ tbsp) cold water
2 tbsp rice vinegar
6 Japanese bamboo sticks, for presentation

For the cucumber & red chilli pickle:
120ml (4fl oz/½ cup) rice vinegar
120ml (4fl oz/½ cup) water
90g (3¼oz/½ cup) sugar
½ cucumber
½ red chilli
1 tbsp salt

Prepare ½ a portion of the Super-slow braised pork belly (aka pork kakuni) according to the instructions on page 162. You may prefer to use the faster pressure-cooker method.

Make the pickle by combining the vinegar, water and sugar in a medium pan and bringing it to the boil over a high heat. Remove from the heat and let it cool down for an hour.

Meanwhile, finely slice the cucumber and red chilli, keeping them separate. In a colander, sprinkle the salt over the cucumber and rub it against the slices until they are completely covered. Place a plate on top and a non-breakable object over the plate to weigh the cucumber slices down for an hour. After that time, rinse the cucumber thoroughly under running water to remove the salt, letting it drain for a minute or two. Now, add the cucumber and the slices of chilli to the cooled rice vinegar, water and sugar mix. Let the cucumber and chilli slices cure in this mixture for at least a couple of hours before using. Store in the fridge in an airtight, sealable container, where it will last for up to a month.

Next, prepare the accompaniments: cut, wash and dry the iceberg lettuce leaves, arrange the small bunches of coriander (cilantro) and finely slice the spring onion (scallion) on the diagonal. Then take the cucumber pickle slices out of the fridge to allow them to come up to room temperature. Roughly chop the red pickled ginger strands.

Line a steamer with greaseproof (wax) paper, steam the buns according to the packet instructions (about 10 minutes in full steam).

While the buns are steaming, prepare the sauce. To do this, pass the cooking broth used to cook the pork through a sieve (strainer) into a smaller pan and bring it the boil. Dissolve the cornflour (cornstarch) in a cup with the cold water and add this, little by little, using a whisk and mixing vigorously until a thick consistency is achieved; you may not need to use all the water and cornflour (cornstarch) mixture. Add the rice vinegar, mix well and check the seasoning – it should be sweet with a little acidity from the vinegar.

To assemble the Nikkei Hakata buns – one bun at a time – on a chopping (cutting) board, cut each piece of pork into three slices, carefully open the bun, place an iceberg lettuce leaf on it, two slices of pork followed by 2 tablespoons sauce over the pork, three slices of cucumber pickle and two slices of red chilli, ½ tablespoon of sliced spring onions (scallions), a few leaves of coriander (cilantro) and a sprinkling of chopped ginger pickle, close the bun and stick a bamboo skewer through it to secure it. Serve immediately.

Hajime Kasuga is one of the foremost Peruvian Nikkei chefs working in Peru today. When he is not promoting Peruvian Nikkei cuisine in Japan, the USA or Europe, he is working in Lima as a consultant to various Japanese and Nikkei restaurants or teaching Japanese and Nikkei cooking at the prestigious Le Cordon Bleu Peru, which is where I was lucky enough to meet him.

This stunning recipe is simple to make but is sure to impress – the ponzu jelly can be made a day or two in advance so all you need to do before serving Hajime's dish is to shuck the oysters and pop open a bottle of fizz!

FRESH OYSTERS, PONZU JELLY & ORANGE

SERVES 2

6 fresh oysters
finely grated zest of 1 orange

For the ponzu jelly:
90ml (3¼fl oz/⅓ cup) dashi
   (see page 230)
3g (⅔ tsp) gelatine powder
30ml (1fl oz/2 tbsp) soy
   sauce
30ml (1fl oz/2 tbsp) lime juice

To make the dashi follow the recipe for Primary dashi on page 230.

To make the ponzu jelly, heat the dashi to near boiling point, dissolve the gelatine in the hot dashi and then mix with the soy sauce and lime juice. Refrigerate for 40 minutes.

When set, cut the ponzu jelly into 5mm (¼in) cubes.

Just before serving, shuck the oysters removing any fragments or grit from the inside of the shell. Add 1–2 teaspoons of ponzu jelly cubes to each oyster, finishing off with the finely grated orange zest. Serve immediately.

Pork belly has always been one of my favourite foods – as a child I often used to take Brazilian *torresmo* (meaty pork scratchings) to school in my bento box accompanied by a dipping version of the sweet and slightly sour Japanese nanban sauce (see also page 238). Some say that childhood food memories are not to be revisited, but I think this recipe breaks the mould. Here, pork belly is triple-cooked to give tender but crispy morsels of joy. The first two stages of cooking can be done in advance. The last step, deep-frying the pork, is done just before serving and should take only a few minutes.

TRIPLE-COOKED PORK BELLY WITH A SPICY SAUCE

SERVES 6

1kg (2¼lb) pork belly piece, cut in half

6 garlic cloves, crushed

2.5cm (1in) piece of root ginger, unpeeled, washed and finely sliced

1 bay leaf, roughly crushed to release flavour

2 tsp salt

sunflower oil, for deep-frying

1 tbsp finely chopped coriander (cilantro), to garnish

6 lime wedges, to garnish

For the spicy nanban-style dipping sauce:

50ml (2fl oz/3½ tbsp) soy sauce

50ml (2fl oz/3½ tbsp) rice vinegar

½ tsp sugar

1 garlic clove, crushed

1 fresh red chilli, deseeded and finely chopped

Place the pork belly halves, crushed garlic, ginger slices, bay leaf and salt in a large pan and fill with water, covering the pork belly by 2cm (¾in). Bring to the boil and then reduce the heat to a simmer and cook for 90 minutes, skimming any scum off the surface as it cooks. Near the end of the cooking time, preheat the oven to 130°C/250°F/gas mark ½.

Remove the pork belly from its cooking liquor, place it on a rack over a deep tray and roast in the preheated oven for 45 minutes. Then, remove it from the oven and allow it to cool. Once cool, wrap the pork in plenty of clingfilm (plastic wrap) and refrigerate it until you are ready for the final cooking step and serving. The pork can be prepared up to this point three days ahead.

When you are ready for the final cooking stage, make the nanban-style dipping sauce by adding all the ingredients to a bowl and mixing well to dissolve the sugar.

Take the pork out of the fridge and unwrap. For a wondrously crispy crackling, blow-torch the skin. When cool enough to handle, cut the pork belly into 2.5cm (1in) cubes. Heat the sunflower oil until very hot, around 170°C (325°F). Deep-fry the pork belly cubes in batches for 3 minutes until golden brown (do not fry for much longer or the meat will dry out and become tough), placing them on a plate lined with kitchen paper (paper towels) while you cook the rest.

Serve the crispy pork belly cubes with a sprinkle of finely chopped coriander (cilantro), the lime wedges and the spicy nanban-style dipping sauce.

SUSHI, TIRADITOS & CEVICHES

The inspiration for this sushi trio came from a recent trip to Peru. Here, I pair the flavours of raw salmon with Peru's most popular yellow chilli, known locally as *aji amarillo*. This chilli has a bright yellow–orange colour and a unique fruitiness, in addition to its heat. The turf element is French foie gras, flavoured with a garlic teriyaki sauce. As the foie gras is blow-torched, some of its fat melts into the sweet sauce and vinegared rice – a heavenly combination. The final sushi in the trio is a nod to Peru's large Chinese community and their cuisine, known as chifa. In this sushi, lightly grilled (broiled) scallops are flavoured with a home-made mayonnaise spiced with chilli bean paste (which I have named chifa sauce).

NIKKEI 'SURF & TURF' SUSHI TRIO
BLOW-TORCHED FOIE GRAS WITH GARLIC TERIYAKI SAUCE, SALMON WITH *AJI AMARILLO* CREAM & GRILLED SCALLOP CHIFA-ZUSHI

SERVES 4–6

50ml (2fl oz/3½ tbsp) Garlic teriyaki sauce (see page 233)
50ml (2fl oz/3½ tbsp) *Aji amarillo* cream (see page 240)
50ml (2fl oz/3½ tbsp) Chifa sauce (see page 237)
a little salt-sludge (add a few drops of water to salt until it looks like sand)
Maldon sea salt flakes and freshly ground black pepper

For the sushi:
300g (10½oz/1⅓ cups) short-grain white rice
2–3 tbsp sushi seasoning
250g (9oz) sushi-grade salmon fillet
200g (7oz) foie gras
2 tbsp shredded nori
4–6 sushi-graded scallops, diced
2 tsp wasabi-flavoured tobiko eggs

You'll need 6 small scallop shells (preferably Manx Queenies, greased), a sushi barrel (handai in Japanese) or large wooden chopping (cutting) board, a fan and a rice paddle (shamoji) and 6 dry magnolia leaves (optional).

First, make the sauces, which will keep in airtight containers in the fridge; they last for different lengths of time so refer to each recipe for preparing ahead.

Prepare the rice following the instructions for making sushi rice on page 226. Shape the rice into 12–18 nigiri-zushi balls, place a layer of clingfilm (plastic wrap) or a moistened tea-towel (dish towel) over the balls to keep them from drying out.

Slice the salmon and foie gras – the slices should drape over the sushi rice balls on both sides, place them over the nigiri-zushi balls.

Preheat the grill (broiler) then assemble the scallop chifa-zushi. Divide the remaining rice over the greased scallop shells creating a bed of rice by filling the shells half full, sprinkle with the shredded nori and distribute the diced scallops evenly among the shells. Place under a hot grill (broiler) for 1–2 minutes. Take the shells from under the grill (broiler), top with the wasabi-flavoured tobiko eggs and carefully spoon the chifa sauce over the assembled shells.

You'll want to arrange one of each of the trio on a platter and remove the sauces made earlier from the fridge. Before serving, place a little salt-sludge on the serving plate to steady the shell and one chifa-zushi over it. Beside it spoon ½ tablespoon of the *aji amarillo* cream, place one salmon nigiri over the cream and a little more on top of the salmon. Place one foie gras nigiri the other side of the chifa-zushi and blow-torch if for a few seconds. Pour a little of the garlic teriyaki sauce over and sprinkle over black pepper and a couple of Maldon sea salt flakes and blow-torch again for a few more seconds. Lightly blow-torch the salmon nigiri and the scallop chifa-zushi. Once all sushi have been blow-torched, you can carefully transfer them to a dried magnolia leaf (as pictured) for a nice presentation, but this is optional. Serve immediately.

In this dish, I flavour sushi rice with the fragrant Japanese herb shiso and top it with salmon presented in two different ways – hand-chopped and cubed. The addition of wasabi lemon cream adds a kick of heat and freshness, while the avocado and daikon impart yet another layer of flavour and texture.

SALMON SUSHI, TWO WAYS

SALMON, AVOCADO & WASABI LEMON CREAM ON SHISO-FLAVOURED SUSHI RICE

SERVES 4

300g (10½oz/1¾ cups) cooked sushi rice (see page 226)

1 portion of Wasabi lemon cream (see page 237)

300g (10½oz) sushi-grade salmon fillet, skinned (tuna works well too)

50g (1¾oz) spring onion (scallion), finely chopped

1 tbsp soy sauce

1 ripe avocado, cut into 1cm (½in) cubes

a few shiso leaves, very finely chopped

1 tbsp toasted sesame seeds, plus a little extra for presentation

5cm (2in) piece of daikon radish, peeled

1 tbsp nori seaweed strips (known as kizami nori)

Prepare the rice following the instructions for making sushi rice on page 226; you'll need about half that recipe. Make a portion of Wasabi lemon cream as instructed on page 237.

Cut off any residual brown meat from the salmon fillet and discard. Finely hand-chop half of the cleaned salmon, place it in a bowl, cover and refrigerate. Cut the other salmon half into 1cm (½in) cubes, put in a separate bowl, cover and refrigerate until needed.

When you are ready to serve, gently mix the spring onions (scallions) with the finely chopped salmon, adding the soy sauce until combined.

Next, add the avocado to the bowl of cubed salmon and mix gently. Do not over-stir or the avocado will break up into the fish and spoil the presentation.

Fold the chopped shiso and the toasted sesame seeds into the rice, and mix well. Just before plating, grate the peeled daikon, squeeze out any excess water and mix into the rice.

Place a 7–8cm (2¾–3¼in)-wide cooking ring in the middle of a serving plate, and add the seasoned sushi rice to a height of about 2.5cm (1in), press lightly onto the plate. Now add a fine 1cm (½in) layer of the finely hand-chopped salmon and spring onion (scallion) mix to cover the rice. Next, remove the cooking ring gently by pulling it upwards and spoon some of the cubed avocado and salmon mix into the centre of the sushi tower. Press lightly so that the pieces are close together in the middle of the sushi, forming a small mound. You want to be able to see both textures of salmon, so do not cover the finely chopped salmon completely.

Top with a couple of tablespoons of wasabi lemon cream in a line and to one side of the sushi tower (rather than in the middle), so that the salmon is not totally covered under the cream. Finally, place some fine strips of nori seaweed on top of the sushi tower, finishing with a sprinkle of toasted sesame seeds and serve.

Created by Toshiro Konishi in Lima, the concept of *tiradito* is the Nikkei answer to Peru's much-loved *ceviche*. The fish in a *tiradito* is finely sliced like a traditional sashimi, rather than cubed as in *ceviche*, but, unlike its Japanese cousin, *tiraditos* are seasoned with a highly zingy tiger's milk (*leche de tigre*). *Tiradito* is a marriage of two distinct national cultures on one plate — if you are not fond of eating raw fish with plain soy sauce, but would like to try something with a little more va-va-voom, then this dish is for you.

TIRADITO OF SCALLOPS & SEA BASS
WITH SAMPHIRE, DILL & BURNT CUCUMBER & YUZU *LECHE DE TIGRE*

SERVES 4

50g (1¾oz) cucumber, deseeded
1 sea bass, skinned and filleted (about 500g (1lb 2oz))
4 scallops
20g (¾oz) samphire, washed
15g (½oz) spring onions (scallions), very finely sliced
freshly ground black pepper
a sprinkle of Maldon sea salt flakes

For the yuzu *leche de tigre*:
5mm (¼in)-thick slice of root ginger
1 garlic clove
juice of 2 limes
4 tbsp yuzu juice
finely grated zest of ½ lime
2 tbsp mirin
½ tbsp light soy sauce
5g (⅛oz/½ cup) dill (half finely chopped and half in small sprigs, to garnish)
2 tsp caster (superfine) sugar
½ tsp sesame oil
1 green chilli, deseeded and very finely chopped

Start by making the yuzu *leche de tigre*. Roughly chop the ginger and garlic, add to a bowl along with the lime juice and leave to infuse for 10 minutes.

Strain the mixture into another bowl, add the yuzu juice, lime zest, mirin, soy sauce, chopped dill, sugar, sesame oil and the chopped chilli, and mix well. Refrigerate until needed (this combination will keep in the fridge for 8 hours).

Peel the cucumber lengthways, leaving alternating strips of peeled and unpeeled flesh. Cut the cucumber in half lengthways and, using a teaspoon, scoop out the seeds and discard them. Cut the cucumber into 2mm (⅛in)-thick slices. Set aside.

Slice the sea bass and scallops into thin diagonal slices. Carefully place them on a clean plate, cover them with clingfilm (plastic wrap) and refrigerate until needed.

Before serving, scatter the slices of cucumber in a frying pan (or skillet) and blow-torch them until the edges are charred and then let the cucumber cool. If you don't have a blow-torch, then dry-fry the cucumber in a very hot non-stick wok or frying pan (or skillet) instead for a couple of minutes until it's lightly charred.

To serve, spread out the slices of charred cucumber on a shallow serving plate, scatter half of the samphire and half of the sliced spring onions (scallions) around the cucumber. Top with slices of sea bass and scallops and the remaining samphire and spring onions (scallions). Spoon a few tablespoons of the yuzu *leche de tigre* over the fish and greens until all the fish is in contact with this dressing.

Leave the fish to 'cook' for 2 minutes. Meanwhile, scatter a few sprigs of dill around the plate along with some freshly ground black pepper and Maldon sea salt flakes. It's now ready to serve.

Adriano Kanashiro was one of the most engaging Nikkei chefs I met in São Paulo. Like me, Adriano is a sansei or third-generation Nikkei; he was born in the town of Londrina in the southern state of Paraná where I also lived for three years as a child; we even attended the same school, but a year apart. Thirty-odd years later, when we finally met for dinner at his restaurant Momotaro in Vila Nova Conceição in São Paulo, we were surprised to find so many shared aspects to our lives. I have to say that it was one of our best meals of the trip.

Before opening Momotaro, Kanashiro worked for years as the Head Chef at the Japanese restaurant at The Grand Hyatt Hotel in São Paulo. He is one of the pioneers of Nikkei cuisine in professional restaurants in Brazil and is considered one of the most avant-garde exponents of the cuisine in the country.

Kanashiro's tuna tartare recipe is one of his most renowned dishes – I love the surprising combination of sweet teriyaki sauce with fresh fig, meaty tuna and seared foie gras – unexpected yet utterly delectable.

TARTARE OF TUNA WITH FRESH FIGS,
MASAGO CAVIAR & FOIE GRAS

SERVES 4

300g (10½oz) sushi-grade tuna, cut into 1cm (½in) cubes
2 tbsp extra virgin olive oil
fleur de sel (or Maldon sea salt flakes), to taste
1 tbsp finely chopped chives, plus extra to garnish (optional)
5 ripe figs (about 120g (4oz)), peeled and lightly crushed with a fork
30g (1¼oz) masago caviar
100g (3½oz) lobe of foie gras liver, cut into 4 equal pieces
4 tbsp teriyaki sauce (see recipe below)

For the teriyaki sauce:
200ml (7fl oz/¾ cup) sake
200ml (7fl oz/¾ cup) mirin
250ml (8½fl oz/1 cup) soy sauce
190g (6¾oz/1 cup) caster (superfine) sugar

First, make the teriyaki sauce. Place the sake and mirin in a pan and bring it to the boil. Strike a match and flambé the sake to burn off the alcohol but taking great care not to burn yourself. After all the alcohol has burnt off, turn the heat down and add the soy sauce and sugar. Mix well until the sugar has completely dissolved. Simmer gently until reduced by half. Let it cool and set aside until needed.

Now, for the tartare. Place the cubed tuna in a bowl, add 1 tablespoon of the oil, fleur de sel to taste, and the finely chopped chives then mix well. Set aside in the fridge.

In a separate bowl, add the lightly crushed figs, the masago caviar and the remaining extra virgin olive oil, mix well and refrigerate until needed.

Heat a non-stick frying pan (or skillet) until very hot, sear the pieces of foie gras for 1 minute on each side then transfer them to a plate lined with kitchen paper (paper towels).

To serve, using a medium cooking ring (about 7cm (2¾in)) positioned in the middle of a plate, create a layer of cubed tuna, followed by a layer of the fig and caviar mix and top with a slice of seared foie gras. Finish off by spooning the teriyaki sauce over the plate and around the tuna tartare, along with a few chopped chives if you like, and it's ready to serve.

Created in the 1960s in Los Angeles, California rolls are possibly the most iconic example of Nikkei cooking. Legend has it that Japanese chefs decided to substitute raw tuna (not a common part of the diet outside of Japan at that time) with crab and avocado, to invent the now incredibly popular rolls. There are dozens of variations on this classic theme, and here I recreate this recipe with the original flavour combination (though I favour crab meat rather than crab sticks).

CALIFORNIA INSIDE-OUT MAKI ROLL

WITH CRAB, AVOCADO, CUCUMBER & TOBIKO EGGS

MAKES 3 ROLLS/18 PIECES

300g (10½oz/1¾ cups) cooked sushi rice (see page 226)

2 sheets of nori seaweed, cut in half

6 tbsp orange tobiko eggs

1 tsp wasabi paste, plus a little extra to serve

3 tbsp pickled ginger slices, to serve

3 tbsp soy sauce, to serve

For the filling:

1 tsp wasabi paste

1 tbsp Japanese-style mayoneizu (see page 232) or ready-made Japanese mayonnaise

a pinch of salt

120g (4oz) white crab meat in chunks (preferably fresh but tinned works too)

10cm (4in) piece of cucumber

1 small ripe avocado

For the vinegared water:

3 tbsp rice vinegar

200ml (7fl oz/¾ cup) water

To make California rolls, you'll need a sushi mat. Prepare the rice following the instructions for making sushi rice on page 226.

Next, mix the wasabi paste, Japanese mayonnaise and salt until well combined, gently fold this into the crab avoiding breaking up the chunks of crab meat. Refrigerate until needed.

Cut the cucumber in half lengthways and, using a teaspoon, scrape out the watery seeds and discard those. Cut the cucumber halves into 10cm (4in) long sticks 1cm (½in) thick. Peel the avocado, cut in half lengthways, then lengthways again into slices 1cm (½in) thick and about 10cm (4in) long. Place the avocado sticks on a plate along with the avocado stone (pit) to help prevent the flesh going brown.

Once all the ingredients are prepared, lay a sushi mat on a work surface (counter) and cover it with clingfilm (plastic wrap). Mix the ingredients for the vinegared water in a bowl.

1 Place half of a nori sheet on the mat. Dip your hands in the vinegared water, shake off any excess moisture, take a good handful of rice (about 100g (3½oz/½ cup) or a third of what you have) and place in the middle of the nori sheet. Using wet fingers, quickly spread this out so you have an even layer of rice, about 5mm (¼in) thick, to the edges of the nori. Now, pick up the rice-covered nori and quickly turn it over on the mat so that the nori side faces up.

Spread one-third of the wasabi paste from one end of the nori sheet to the other in a line. **2** Lay the crab meat mixture from one end of the nori sheet to the other in a line about 2.5cm (1in) away from you or one-third into the sheet. **3** Beside it, lay a line of cucumber sticks and another of the avocado on top.

4–5 Lift up the edge of the mat closest to you and, while holding the fillings in place with your fingers, start rolling the rice-covered nori sheet to join the edges together. First, roll the rice over the fillings leaving 1cm (½in) of rice still untouched, tuck the filling in by gently pressing with the sushi mat, move the roll forwards and now squeeze the end of the nori sheet against the 1cm (½in) rice gap for the roll to seal at that point. **6–8** Gently squeeze along the length of the roll to mould it together. Use gentler but firm pressure to shape the sushi log into a round or square shape, as desired. Cover the surface of the rice with one-third of the tobiko eggs.

Wrap in clingfilm (plastic wrap) and place in a cool place until you are ready to cut and eat. Do not place the sushi in the fridge or the rice will harden and the texture will be lost. **9** Remove the clingfilm (plastic wrap) just before serving.

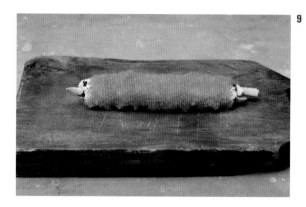

10 When you're ready to serve, dip a cloth or tea-towel (dish towel) in the vinegared water, moisten a very sharp knife and cut each roll in half. **11–12** Place the two halves next to each other, moisten the knife again and cut twice to give six equally sized pieces. Serve with a little wasabi paste, pickled slices of ginger and soy sauce on the side.

13 (main picture) At home, we leave some of the filling sticking out at the end of each roll, so that whoever takes those less-than-perfect end pieces will be compensated by the extra filling. If you prefer, you can cut the end bits off but I prefer the less-wasteful approach.

In this recipe, fine slices of sashimi salmon are seasoned with a zingy Nikkei *leche de tigre* and coriander oil. If you have not made coriander oil before I urge you to have a go — this fantastic condiment is easy to make and will add a bright green colour and a refreshing herby flavour to this and many other dishes. The jalapeño salsa, here, adds texture, making this a superbly light one-course meal — perhaps just accompanied by a glass of wine.

SALMON SASHIMI THE SOUTH AMERICAN WAY

WITH NIKKEI *LECHE DE TIGRE* & JALAPEÑO SALSA

SERVES 4

1 portion of Nikkei *leche de tigre* (see page 239)
2 tbsp Coriander oil (see page 236)
400g (14oz) sushi-grade salmon fillet, skinned
Maldon salt flakes, to garnish
shichimi pepper, to garnish

For the jalapeño salsa:
½ large cucumber
1 red jalapeño chilli
1 avocado
½ banana shallot
30 coriander (cilantro) leaves, including some to garnish
a pinch of salt
1 tbsp olive oil
1 tbsp lime juice

Get ahead by preparing the Nikkei *leche de tigre* and Coriander oil following the instructions on pages 239 and 236.

Next, prepare the salsa. Cut the cucumber in half lengthways and, using a teaspoon, scrape out the watery seeds and discard them. Dice the cucumber into 5mm (¼in) cubes. Deseed and very finely dice the jalapeño chilli. Peel, remove the stone (pit) and dice the avocado into 5mm (¼in) cubes. Peel the banana shallot and chop it very finely. Place the coriander (cilantro) leaves one on top of the other (not forgetting to reserve a few leaves for garnishing), roll them tightly as a cigar and slice very finely into hair-like strips.

In a bowl, put the diced cucumber, the chilli, two-thirds of the cubed avocado (reserving one-third for garnishing), the finely sliced coriander (cilantro) and the chopped shallots. Add the salt, olive oil and the lime juice, mixing gently as you go, then check for seasoning.

Remove any trace of brown meat from the salmon. To do this, use a sharp knife and slice off any residual brown meat from the skinned surface of the fillet.

Cut the salmon into fine slices — about 5mm (¼in) thick and 5cm (2in) long. Divide the salmon slices equally among four plates, positioning them side by side like a line of dominoes. When all the salmon has been plated, spoon 3–4 tablespoons of Nikkei *leche de tigre* over and around the salmon on each plate. Spread the salsa in a straight line in the middle of the row of salmon slices from one end to the other. Scatter a few of the remaining avocado cubes and whole coriander (cilantro) leaves around the plate and over the salmon. Drizzle a few dots of coriander oil over the fish and plate, finishing with a sprinkle of sea salt flakes and a dusting of shichimi pepper. Serve.

I love Korean food — its bold flavours and the insane use of garlic, chilli and fermented cabbage. When developing this recipe, Psy's *Gangnam Style* song was all the rage and it seemed the perfect name for this dish. I have drawn inspiration from the flavours and colours of Korea to create this sushi dish, my homage to this fascinating cuisine.

SEA BASS SUSHI GANGNAM STYLE

WITH YUZU-PON DRESSING, PICKLED DAIKON & CARROTS, SPINACH & SESAME

SERVES 4

½ portion of Sushi rice (see page 226)
1 small sushi-grade sea bass (150–200g (5½–7oz)), skinned and filleted
4 tbsp daikon and carrot pickle (see below)
4 tbsp spinach marinated in sesame oil (see below)
4 small super-fresh egg yolks (small eggs or quail's eggs)
4 small dollops wasabi paste
red ginger pickle (beni shoga), to garnish
black sesame seeds, to garnish

For the yuzu-pon dressing:
1 portion of Yuzu-pon sauce (see page 235)
2 tbsp toasted sesame oil
1 tsp caster (superfine) sugar
½ small onion, very finely chopped

For the daikon & carrot pickle:
150g (5½oz) daikon
150g (5½oz) carrot
Maldon sea salt flakes
100ml (3½fl oz/½ cup) rice vinegar
100ml (3½fl oz/½ cup) water
50g (1¾oz/¼ cup) sugar

For the spinach marinated in sesame oil:
100g (3½oz) baby spinach
½ tsp sesame oil
a pinch of Maldon sea salt flakes

You can make the yuzu-pon dressing and the daikon and carrot pickle up to a week in advance; the pickle has to be made at least the night before you want to serve this dish.

Prepare half a portion of rice following the instructions on page 226. Next, make the yuzu-pon dressing. First, make a portion of the Yuzu-pon sauce (see page 235). To this, add the toasted sesame oil, sugar and the finely chopped onion and mix well. Let it rest for at least an hour before using; it will keep for up to a week in an airtight container in the fridge.

Next, make the pickle. Peel and wash the daikon and carrot and then, using a mandolin or the coarser side of a food processor's julienne disc, julienne the vegetables. Transfer them to a colander with the sea salt, mix well and let drain for 1 hour. Next, combine the vinegar, water and sugar in a medium pan and bring it to the boil over a high heat. Remove from the heat and let it cool for an hour. Rinse the salt off the daikon and carrots, add to the cooled vinegar mixture, stir well, cover and refrigerate overnight. Drain before serving.

Wilt the spinach in boiling water for 30 seconds, then transfer to a bowl of iced water. Let the spinach cool down completely, drain and gently squeeze out the water from the spinach with your hands. Transfer to a bowl, add the sesame oil and salt and mix. Cover and refrigerate for up to 24 hours.

The sea bass will have been skinned and filleted by your fishmonger but you will need to remove any residual bits of skin, pin-bone the fish and slice it thinly.

To plate, using a 7cm (2¾in) cooking ring, place a small amount of rice in the middle of each plate, press down gently to create a disc, smear a dollop of wasabi paste evenly over the surface of the rice, spread a tablespoon of daikon and carrot pickle over the top and remove the ring; then move on to the other plates. Arrange a few slices of fish around the top in a circle, place a tablespoon of the sesame-spinach in the middle of the tower arranged in such a way as to hold the egg yolk, which should now be carefully placed over it. Next, place a couple of strips of red ginger over the yolk, drizzle 2 tablespoons of yuzu-pon dressing around the rice on the plate and finish with a sprinkle of black sesame seeds over the plate. It's now ready to serve.

MAKES 3 ROLLS/18 PIECES

⅔ portion of Sushi rice (see page 226)

1 portion of Nikkei *leche de tigre* (see page 239)

1 small, ripe avocado

sunflower oil, for deep-frying

6 ebi furai* (home-made or shop-bought)

200g (7oz) tuna, cut into 5cm (2in)-wide, 2mm (⅛in)-thick slices

3 nori sheets, cut ⅓ off each sheet

120g (4oz/½ cup) cream cheese

1 spring onion (scallion), very finely sliced

1 tsp shichimi pepper

For the vinegared water:
3 tbsp rice vinegar
200ml (7fl oz/¾ cup) water

For serving:
1 tsp wasabi paste
3 tbsp pickled ginger slices
3 tbsp soy sauce

* Ebi furai are stretched-out prawns (shrimp) about 10cm (4in) long and coated in panko breadcrumbs. You can make your own or buy them (a quicker and surprisingly cheaper option) from the freezer compartments of most Japanese food stores; they can be deep-fried from frozen.

To make these maki acevichado, you'll need a sushi mat. Get ahead by preparing the Sushi rice and Nikkei *leche de tigre* following the instructions on pages 226 and 239.

Peel the avocado, cut in half lengthways, then lengthways again into slices 1cm (½in) thick and about 10cm (4in) long. Place the avocado sticks on a plate along with the avocado stone (pit) to help prevent the flesh from going brown.

Heat the oil in a medium pan until hot, about 170°C/325°F. Deep-fry the stretched prawns (shrimp) (ebi furai) for a few minutes until golden. Remove from the pan with a slotted spoon and let them rest on a plate lined with kitchen paper (paper towels) until needed.

Cover the sliced tuna with clingfilm (plastic wrap) and refrigerate until needed. Once all the ingredients are prepared, you are ready to roll. Lay a sushi mat on a work surface (counter) and cover it with clingfilm (plastic wrap). Mix the vinegared water ingredients together.

Place ⅔ of a nori sheet on the mat. Dip your hands in the vinegared water, shake off any excess moisture, take a good handful of rice (about 130g (4½oz/¾ cup) or a third of the rice you have) and place in the middle of the nori sheet. Using wet fingers, quickly spread this out so that you have an even layer of rice, 5mm (¼in) thick, to the edges of the nori.

Pick up the rice-covered nori and quickly turn it over on the mat so that the nori side now faces up. Lay a 1cm (½in) line of cream cheese from one end of the nori sheet to the other (a piping (pastry) bag can be useful or just use a teaspoon). Beside it, make a line by laying two pieces of the deep-fried prawns (shrimp) and another line of avocado on top.

Lift up the edge of the mat closest to you, and while holding the fillings in place with your fingers, start rolling the rice-covered nori sheet to join the edges together. First, roll the rice over the fillings leaving 1cm (½in) of rice still untouched, tuck the filling in by gently pressing with the sushi mat, move the roll forwards and now squeeze the end of the nori sheet against the 1cm (½in) rice gap for the roll to seal at that point.

Lift the sushi mat from over the maki-zushi and cover the roll with the tuna slices. Now, place the sushi mat over the tuna and gently squeeze the top and sides of the sushi roll to mould them together. Use gentler but firm pressure to shape the sushi log into a round or square shape. Wrap in clingfilm (plastic wrap) and place in a cool place until ready to cut. Do not place the sushi in the fridge or the rice will harden. Remove the clingfilm (plastic wrap) just before serving. When ready to serve, dip a cloth or tea-towel (dish towel) in the vinegared water, moisten a very sharp knife and cut each roll in half. Place the two halves next to each other, moisten the knife and cut twice to give six equally sized pieces. Finish with a drizzle of Nikkei *leche de tigre*, a sprinkle of sliced spring onions (scallions) and a dusting of shichimi pepper. Serve with wasabi paste, pickled slices of ginger and soy sauce.

Cook's note The steps on how to roll an inside-out sushi, such as California roll or Peruvian maki acevichado can be followed on pages 61–62.

One of the most interesting sushi I ate when I first visited Peru was maki acevichado – a classic of Nikkei cooking there. The Nikkei *leche de tigre* is a delicious addition to the sushi rice, and the cream cheese (a contentious ingredient for many sushi purists) works very well in this eclectic combination. There is a different version of maki acevichado in nearly every restaurant in Peru – Japanese, Nikkei or otherwise.

PERUVIAN MAKI ACEVICHADO

TUNA, PRAWNS & AVOCADO WITH NIKKEI *LECHE DE TIGRE*

TSUYOSHI MURAKAMI

Tsuyoshi Murakami, known as Mura for short, is one of Brazil's most renowned chefs of Japanese and Nikkei cuisines. A larger than life sort of guy, Mura's stories and enthusiasm for life, people and good food entertain guests nearly as much as his outstanding food – and if the mood takes him, he may even sing you karaoke!

His restaurant Kinoshita, in the well-heeled district of Nova Conceição, has some of the most coveted tables in São Paulo and is a must for any foodie visitors to the city. I had a most memorable meal there when I tried his Lime butter salmon; a recipe Mura has kindly contributed below.

This year sees the publication of the first edition of the *Michelin Guide to Brazil*. I have to say that it was no surprise that Kinoshita was awarded its first Michelin star; with Mura's impeccable cooking, top-quality ingredients and super-efficient service, I am certain that there will be more to come.

LIME BUTTER SALMON

SERVES 2

120g (4oz) sushi-grade
  salmon fillet, skinned
5 tbsp light soy sauce
3 tsp lime juice
1 tbsp unsalted butter
daikon cress (or use baby
  white radish cress or baby
  cress), to garnish

Heat a non-stick frying pan (or skillet) until hot, add the salmon fillet to the pan and sear it for a few seconds on one side only.

Cut the seared salmon into slices of up to 3cm (1¼in) thick, transferring them straight onto a serving plate, side by side.

Next, in a separate pan, over a high heat, add the soy sauce, lime juice and butter. Shake the pan in a circular motion until the sauce thickens for about 1 minute. While the sauce is still hot, pour it over the slices of seared salmon.

Serve with a small tuft of daikon cress in the middle of the salmon sashimi slices.

SERVES 4

1 portion of Nikkei salmon
  anticucho marinade (see
  page 241)
1 portion of Wasabi lemon
  cream (see page 237)

For the sushi rice:
450g (1lb/2 cups) short-grain
  white rice
550ml (19fl oz/2½ cups)
  water
6–9 tbsp ready-made sushi
  seasoning

For the toppings:
½ portion of Plain tamagoyaki
  (see page 32)
1 lemon, cut into 1cm (½in)
  slices
sunflower oil, for deep-frying
  and for greasing
1 red chilli, deseeded and
  finely sliced on the diagonal
12 mangetout (snow peas)
400g (14oz) sushi-grade
  salmon
1 tsp mirin
1 tsp soy sauce
40g (1½oz) ikura (salmon roe)
½ small cucumber, deseeded
½ ripe avocado
10 shiso leaves
2 tbsp toasted white sesame
  seeds, plus a sprinkle
1 tbsp very finely chopped
  chives

Make the Nikkei salmon *anticucho* marinade and the Wasabi lemon cream following the instructions on pages 241 and 237; the wasabi lemon cream can be made up to three days ahead. Then, prepare the rice following the instructions for making sushi rice on page 226 but increasing the quantities to those shown here. Set aside.

Next, prepare all the toppings. Start with the Japanese rolled omelette (tamagoyaki), by following the instructions on page 32. Set aside until needed.

Scorch the lemon slices on both sides using a very hot griddle pan. Set aside on a plate.

Heat the sunflower oil until 140°C/275°F, deep-fry the chilli slices for 30 seconds; do not allow them to burn. Quickly transfer them to a plate lined with kitchen paper (paper towels).

Blanch the mangetout (snow peas) in boiling water for 30 seconds. Drain and plunge them into cold water; once cold, pat dry and slice finely on the diagonal, refrigerate until needed.

Cut half the salmon into 2cm (¾in) cubes, mix into the *anticucho* marinade, cover and marinate for 20 minutes. Meanwhile, cut the remaining salmon into 1cm (½in) cubes, place them in a separate bowl and refrigerate until needed. Next, preheat the grill (broiler) to hot, line a shallow baking tray (baking sheet) with foil and grease the foil with a little oil.

Gently mix the mirin and soy sauce into the ikura. Cover and refrigerate until needed.

Dice the cucumber and avocado into 1cm (½in) cubes and refrigerate until needed.

After 20 minutes of marinating, spread the salmon cubes out on the greased baking tray (baking sheet), and place under a very hot grill (broiler) for 6–8 minutes or until browning around the edges. Remove from the grill (broiler) and allow to cool. Meanwhile, place the shiso leaves one on top of the other, roll them tightly like a cigar and then slice very thinly.

Once the sushi rice has been seasoned and is at room temperature, mix the thin slices of shiso leaves, toasted white sesame seeds and 4–6 cubes of grilled (broiled) *anticucho* salmon. Mix well until thoroughly combined, the salmon will break up into smaller pieces and flavour the rice. Transfer this rice to a large serving bowl, spreading it out to cover the base of the bowl; the layer should be roughly 2–3cm (¾–1¼in) deep. Ideally, you would use a wooden sushi barrel (a handai or hangiri), but any unvarnished wooden bowl would work.

Place all the ingredients around the bowl – the avocado, chopped chives, mangetout (snow peas), raw salmon and remaining grilled (broiled) salmon, the seasoned ikura, the scorched lemon slices, the cucumber, the tamagoyaki (in 1cm (½in) cubes) and crispy chilli slices.

Chirashi-zushi means scattered sushi, and you should use your creativity to present the ingredients, scattering them over the sushi rice. I like to start with the weightier ingredients – the grilled (broiled) and raw salmon and avocado cubes. The slices of lemon could be next, followed by the cubed omelette and cucumber. Finish with the ikura, mangetout (snow peas) and a sprinkle of chopped chives and sesame seeds. Place the deep-fried chilli slices in a mound in the middle of the bowl and it's ready to serve with the wasabi lemon cream.

In the West we seem to see little else than the ubiquitous maki rolls or nigiri in terms of sushi, but there is so much more; chirashi-zushi is only one example. Literally meaning 'scattered sushi', this is a style of sushi where colourful toppings are scattered over the sushi rice, which is served family style. In this salmon-based dish, I use my Nikkei *anticucho* dressing to impart smokiness and heat. Make this for a special occasion; it is a visually striking dish that is sure to impress!

NIKKEI CHIRASHI-ZUSHI

GRILLED SALMON *ANTICUCHO*, SALMON SASHIMI, IKURA CAVIAR, LEMON & AVOCADO

A Francophile version of the much-loved *ceviche*, this sea bream tartare recipe was inspired by my days at Le Cordon Bleu. It uses a variety of herbs together with wasabi and lemon to create an aromatic marinade for the raw fish. The apples, as well as forming a bed for the sea bream, also provide a delicious crunch and refreshing acidity.

SEA BREAM TARTARE

WITH LEMON, GREEN HERBS & WASABI DRESSING ON JULIENNED APPLES

SERVES 4

10g (¼oz/¼ cup) shiso
10g (¼oz/⅓ cup) tarragon
10g (¼oz/½ cup) mint
10g (¼oz/½ cup) basil
10g (¼oz) chives
1 spring onion (scallion)
freshly ground salt and black
 pepper
200g (7oz) sushi-grade sea
 bream fillets, skinned
2 Granny Smith apples, cored
 but with the skin on
a little extra virgin olive oil,
 to garnish

For the wasabi dressing:
15g (½oz/1 tbsp) wasabi
 paste
4 tbsp sunflower oil
2 tsp toasted sesame oil
finely grated zest and juice
 of 1 lemon

Start by making the dressing. In a bowl, add the wasabi paste, the sunflower and toasted sesame oils and the lemon juice and zest. Whisk until the wasabi has completely dissolved.

Now, prepare the herbs. Wash and pat dry all the herbs, separating four small sprigs each of the mint and basil for garnishing later. Finely chop the spring onion (scallion) and the leaves of shiso, tarragon, mint and basil. Place all the chopped herbs together in a largish bowl, cover and pop in the fridge. Finely chop the chives. Refrigerate until needed.

Add the dressing to the bowl of chopped herbs, season with a little freshly ground salt and pepper and return the bowl to the fridge.

Pin-bone the sea bream fillets, remove any remaining skin, then cut into 1cm (½in) cubes. Add the cubed sea bream to the bowl of herbs and wasabi dressing and mix well. Re-cover the bowl and leave in a cool place while you julienne the apples. The sea bream should not marinate for more than 10 minutes, so you will need to work fast.

Cut the apples into quarters and then, ideally using a mandolin, slice into thin julienne strips; if you do not have a mandolin, you can cut the apple quarters into slices and then into thin julienne strips using a sharp knife. The apple will start to oxidise soon after being cut, so time is of the essence.

To plate the tartare, I like to use an 8cm (3¼in) cooking ring, which makes for a neat presentation. Place the cooking ring in the middle of a serving plate, make a bed of apple matchsticks about 2cm (¾in) tall (don't be tempted to make it much higher than this or the ratio of sea bream to apple will not be balanced), then top with the herby sea bream tartare again to about 2cm (¾in) in height, pressing gently with a spoon.

Remove the cooking ring by sliding it upwards carefully; go slowly as you don't want to topple the tower of sea bream and apple.

Place a sprig each of mint and basil over the sea bream tartare. Finish off with a drizzle of extra virgin olive oil around the fish and plate, a sprinkle of chopped chives and some freshly ground black pepper and serve straightaway.

Aji rocoto is a native Peruvian chilli with an intense heat; it's found in many guises – ground and used as a spice in sauces and soups, as a hot sauce served at the table or as a paste to flavour dishes, as in this recipe.

Palm hearts are one of the most popular foods in Brazil, and are eaten fresh in salads and pastries. In the UK and US, you can find them in jars or tins in South American shops or in larger supermarkets. I recommend using the jarred variety and avoid the tinned ones if you can. Palm hearts taste like a cross between bamboo shoot, artichoke heart and asparagus; they make a great accompaniment to heirloom tomato salad (see page 190).

Here, I use rocoto chillies and grapefruit as a basis for a *leche de tigre* in which I 'cook' cubes of sushi-grade tuna and serve it on a bed of sliced palm hearts. Quick and easy to make, it requires only a few ingredients. The *leche de tigre* can be made two days in advance. To serve, just slice a few palm hearts, dice the tuna and voilà!

TUNA, *AJI ROCOTO* & GRAPEFRUIT *LECHE DE TIGRE* ON PALM HEARTS

SERVES 4

250g (9oz) sushi-grade tuna
250g (9oz/1¾ cups) palm hearts
4 tbsp daikon cress (or a selection of micro herbs), to garnish
a sprinkle of toasted white sesame seeds, to garnish
a pinch of Maldon sea salt flakes, to garnish

For the *aji rocoto* & grapefruit *leche de tigre*:
10g (¼oz/2 tsp) ready-made *aji rocoto* paste (available from Peruvian food shops)
2 tbsp soy sauce
20g (¾oz/1½ tbsp) palm sugar (or caster (superfine) sugar)
2 tsp finely grated zest of pink grapefruit
4 tbsp pink grapefruit juice
1 tbsp lime juice
¼ tsp instant dashi powder
2 tbsp extra virgin olive oil

First, make the *aji rocoto* and grapefruit *leche de tigre* by mixing together all of the ingredients (except the olive oil) in a bowl until well combined. Check for seasoning – if more acidity is required add a tad more lime juice; or if you like it a little hotter, add a tiny bit more *aji rocoto*. Finally, add the olive oil and mix until emulsified.

Cut the tuna into 1.5cm (½in) cubes, add them to the *leche de tigre* and let it 'cook' for a maximum of 5 minutes.

Meanwhile, prepare the palm hearts. If you can't locate jarred palm hearts and have to use tinned ones then be sure to wash them under fresh water for a minute or so, taking care not to break them up. Drain and cut into 1cm (½in) round slices. Place the slices of palm heart on four plates, making up a circular base on which the cubed tuna will sit.

Share the tuna cubes equally between the serving plates, placing the cubes in the middle of the bed of palm hearts. Spoon the *leche de tigre* over the tuna cubes, carefully arrange a tuft of daikon cress (or micro herbs if using) on top of the tuna and finish with a sprinkle of toasted sesame seeds and Maldon sea salt flakes. Serve straightaway.

The Brazil nut, which technically is a seed not a nut, does actually come from Brazil, hailing from the Amazonian state of Pará in the far north of the country, where oddly enough it is known as the Pará nut.

Luckily I am not lactose intolerant, but many Asian diners at my supper club are; so, I devised this recipe with them in mind. The Brazil nut milk has a delicious flavour of the seed; it is thick and creamy and makes an ideal partner for the truffle dashi and shiitake mushrooms in this recipe's *leche de tigre*.

Marinate the sushi-grade sea bass only a few minutes before serving to avoid over-curing it. You'll need to get everything else ready first; the dressing, for instance, can be made up to a couple of days ahead.

CEVICHE OF SEA BASS
WITH BRAZIL NUT MILK, TRUFFLE DASHI & SHIITAKE MUSHROOMS

SERVES 4

½ red chilli, deseeded and
    finely chopped
1 tsp good-quality truffle oil
Maldon sea salt flakes
1 large sea bass (about 250g
    (9oz)), skinned and filleted
1 avocado, cut into 1cm (½in)
    cubes
juice of 1 lime
2 tbsp coriander (cilantro)
    cress, to garnish
2 Brazil nuts, shaved, to
    garnish
freshly ground black pepper

For the Brazil nut milk:
300g (10½oz/2 cups)
    Brazil nuts
500ml (18fl oz/2 cups) water

For the shiitake dashi:
1 tsp instant dashi powder
1 tsp caster (superfine) sugar
300ml (10fl oz/1¼ cups)
    hot water
2 large dried shiitake
    mushrooms

First, make the Brazil nut milk. Blend the nuts with the water for about 5 minutes; I do this in a food processor. Transfer the resulting mixture to a bowl, put it in the fridge and let it rest for 1 hour. Then, strain, reserving the Brazil nut milk (return this to the fridge); I like to use the crushed nuts in other recipes as a base for cakes and biscuits (cookies).

Next, make the shiitake dashi. In a bowl, dissolve the instant dashi powder and sugar in the hot water, add the mushrooms and let them rehydrate for an hour or so. Then, pour the water carefully into a separate container, avoiding any of the grit from the mushrooms that tends to sit in the bottom of the bowl. Reserve the soaking liquid; slice the mushrooms finely and set aside.

To make the dressing, add 50ml (2fl oz/¼ cup) of the mushroom soaking liquid (shiitake dashi), 100ml (3½fl oz/½ cup) of the Brazil nut milk, the chopped chilli, the truffle oil and a generous pinch of Maldon sea salt. Mix well and set aside.

Pin-bone the sea bass fillets and remove any remaining skin. Before serving cut into 1cm (½in) cubes, transfer the fish to a bowl with the cubed avocado, the lime juice and 1 teaspoon of Maldon sea salt flakes. Gently mix and let the fish 'cook' for 5 minutes.

To serve, divide the sea bass and avocado cubes between four plates, arranging them in the middle of each plate, then spoon the dressing over the fish. Place a few slices of mushrooms over each mound of fish and avocado, top with the coriander (cilantro) cress, the shaved Brazil nuts and a sprinkle of sea salt and freshly ground black pepper. Serve.

Cook's note If you are pressed for time, and for a less-expensive version, you could use ready-made unsweetened almond or hazelnut milk instead of making your own Brazil nut milk; these milks are available in all major supermarkets.

A *tostada* is a crispy tortilla with various toppings. I had some great *tostadas* in Mexico's Yucatan Peninsula a few years ago, where they were served most often with shredded chicken, refried beans, avocado, lettuce and soured cream. I loved them so much I could not wait to experiment when I got home and put my Nikkei stamp on them.

I use sashimi tuna in this version but salmon or other sushi-grade fish would also work well. This Nikkei *tostada* can be served as a colourful canapé or as an all-in-one lunch dish. It should have vibrant flavours, be full of colour and have a deliciously crunchy texture. The wasabi lemon cream is also an important touch, adding a refreshing acidity and a kick of heat. This tuna sashimi *tostada* has become a popular canapé at my Japanese and Nikkei supper clubs in London.

TUNA SASHIMI *TOSTADA*
WITH PINK GRAPEFRUIT, AVOCADO & WASABI LEMON CREAM ON CRISPY TORTILLAS

SERVES 4

2 tbsp Coriander oil (see page 236)
½ portion of Wasabi lemon cream (see page 237)
2 x 20cm (7¾in) diameter wheat flour tortillas
2 tbsp olive oil
a sprinkle of Maldon sea salt flakes, plus extra to garnish
½ pink grapefruit, peeled
150g (5½oz) sushi-grade tuna
½ small avocado, cut into 1cm (½in) cubes
2 tbsp finely diced red onions
4 tsp tobiko eggs
½ red chilli, deseeded and finely chopped, plus 2 slices to garnish
a few baby coriander (cilantro) leaves, to garnish
1 tsp toasted white sesame seeds, to garnish
a sprinkle of shichimi pepper, to garnish

Make the Coriander oil and Wasabi lemon cream following the instructions on pages 236 and 237. Keep them in the fridge until needed.

Preheat the oven to 200°C/400°F/gas mark 6, and line a baking tray (baking sheet) with non-stick baking parchment.

Prick the soft tortillas to stop them from bubbling up during baking. Brush the tortillas on both sides with olive oil, sprinkle a little sea salt over them, cut each tortilla into equal quarters, cover with a tray (to help flatten the tortillas as they cook) and bake for 2–3 minutes until lightly coloured. Turn over and bake again. Remove from the oven and transfer to a wire rack; they will crisp up further as they cool down.

Meanwhile, prepare the other ingredients. You'll need to extract the pink grapefruit flesh gently from its segments to make 1–2cm (½–¾in) triangular pieces. Set aside.

When you are just about ready to serve the tostadas, cut the tuna using a very sharp knife into thin slices 5cm (2in) wide and 2mm (⅛in) thick. If the tuna piece you have is more like a steak size and the slices you cut are not quite the measurements given, don't worry. The tuna slices will be placed alongside all of the other ingredients over the *tostada* so their size is not critical for the preparation of this dish.

Place the crispy tortilla quarters on a serving plate, close together as if the tortilla was still whole. Spoon half of the wasabi lemon cream over the tortillas. Place the thin slices of tuna over the tortilla pieces and cream. Spoon the remaining wasabi lemon cream over and around the tuna. Now scatter the pieces of grapefruit, the cubes of avocado, the finely diced red onions, the tobiko eggs and red chilli over the surface of the tortilla. Drizzle the coriander oil over the white cream, scatter a few small leaves of coriander (cilantro) and a slice of red chilli in the middle of the plate. Finish off with a sprinkle of toasted sesame seeds, a dusting of shichimi pepper and some Maldon sea salt flakes and serve.

1 portion of cooked Sushi rice
(see page 226)

½ portion of Chifa sauce (see
page 237)

8 spears baby asparagus
(about 60g (2oz))

12 medium-sized prawns
(shrimp) (about 150g
(5½oz))

4 scallops (about 120g (4oz))

150g (5½oz) baby squid with
tentacles

2 tbsp light soy sauce

1 tbsp rice vinegar

1 tbsp sesame oil

a couple of pinches of Maldon
sea salt flakes

150g (5½oz) clams

3 tbsp finely chopped chives,
plus 1 tbsp extra to garnish

1 tbsp toasted white sesame
seeds, plus extra to garnish

1 tbsp nori seaweed, ripped
into 5mm (¼in) pieces

2 tbsp tobiko eggs

a sprinkle of shichimi pepper

4 lemon wedges

Cook's note Whenever
cooking green vegetables,
I like to use 10 times
the amount of water to
vegetables, this will help
the vegetables to retain
their beautiful colour. If
you don't have a pan big
enough, I'd suggest cooking
the vegetables in a few
batches.

Prepare the rice as instructed on page 226; likewise with the Chifa sauce, see page 237.

Cut off the woody parts of the asparagus spears and discard. Cook the asparagus in plenty of salted boiling water for 2 minutes and meanwhile prepare a bowl of iced water. Remove the asparagus from the pan and plunge the spears immediately into the iced water. Once cold, drain them, cut the tips into 2.5cm (1in)-long pieces and set aside. Cut the remaining stems of the spears into 5mm (¼in)-pieces and set aside.

Prepare the seafood. Remove the shell and heads and devein all the prawns (shrimp), leaving the tails on four of the prawns (shrimp). Cut the eight remaining prawns (shrimp) in half lengthways. Chill all the prawns (shrimp). Discard the coral from the scallops, wash them and chill. Ensure the baby squid is thoroughly cleaned. Reserve four whole baby squid tubes and their tentacles for presentation and finely slice the remaining squid and tentacles. Set aside in the fridge. Place the prawns (shrimp), scallops and squid in a bowl and add the soy sauce, rice vinegar, sesame oil and the salt, mix well but gently. Let the seafood mixture marinate for 30 minutes in the fridge. Meanwhile, steam the clams for 4–5 minutes until they open completely. Discard any unopened clams.

Preheat the grill (broiler). Transfer the marinated prawns (shrimp), scallops and squid to a roasting tray lined with foil, keeping the whole prawns (shrimp), scallops and squid separate from the chopped seafood. Scatter the seafood evenly over the tray and place it under the hot grill (broiler) for 2 minutes. Remove the tray from the grill (broiler). The larger pieces, including the whole squid tubes, prawns (shrimp) with tails and scallops reserved for presentation, will possibly need another minute or so, but these will be returned to the grill (broiler) before being served.

The sushi rice should have been seasoned and cooled down to room temperature in a wooden vessel. To this vessel, add the 5mm (¼in) pieces of asparagus, the finely chopped chives, the chopped squid, the prawn (shrimp) halves, the clams (reserving eight clams for garnishing) and the toasted white sesame seeds into the rice and mix well.

I like serving this sushi in what I call a family-style way, rather than in individual portions. To do this, take a large ovenproof serving platter, preferably rectangular and lay a bed of sushi rice 2.5cm (1in) high across it. Sprinkle some crumbled pieces of nori over the rice then arrange the reserved pieces of prawns (shrimp), scallops, squid and clams on top, together with a few of the asparagus tips. Next, scatter the tobiko eggs along the rice and seafood. Drizzle a few tablespoons of chifa sauce over the top and sides, without covering the entire dish and seafood, then place it under the hot grill (broiler) for 2–3 minutes or until the sauce has browned. (If you have a blow-torch, you can use it instead of placing the entire sushi under the grill/broiler.)

Remove from the grill (broiler), garnish with finely chopped chives and sesame seeds, finishing with a sprinkle of shichimi pepper. Serve with wedges of lemon.

This is a firm favourite of mine, and a dish I like to serve family style on a large platter. A type of maze-sushi (where ingredients are mixed into the rice to flavour it), this is a colourful and visually impressive dish of sushi rice topped with a selection of delicious seafood and a spicy, creamy sauce, all finished off under a hot grill (broiler). It is a great all-in-one meal and will be like no other sushi you have ever tried. Perhaps it is to become a future favourite of yours.

GRILLED SEAFOOD SUSHI WITH A SPICY CHIFA SAUCE

Mitsuharu Tsumura – also known as Micha – is one of Peru's most celebrated Japanese Peruvian chefs. His restaurant Maido in Miraflores was ranked in the top 10 in San Pellegrino's Latin American 50 Best Restaurants list. Micha's highly sophisticated Nikkei *ceviche* – or *cebiche* – is a dish that brings to life the marriage of these two cultures.

MICHA'S NIKKEI *CEBICHE*

SERVES 1

For the dashi (makes about 1 litre (1¾ pints/4 cups):
12g (⅓oz) konbu
1 litre (1¾ pints/4 cups) water
22g (¾oz/1½ cups) katsuobushi bonito flakes

For the ponzu sauce (makes about 500ml (18fl oz/2 cups)):
100ml (3½fl oz/½ cup) rice vinegar
70ml (2¾fl oz/⅓ cup) mirin (evaporate the alcohol before using)
100ml (3½fl oz/½ cup) usukuchi (light soy sauce)
100ml (3½fl oz/½ cup) tamari (soy sauce)
80ml (3fl oz/⅓ cup) dashi
50ml (2fl oz/¼ cup) lime juice
finely grated zest of 2 lemons

For the *cebiche* sauce (makes 880ml (1½ pints/4 cups)):
30 Chulucanas limes (green with yellow hues; or use 3–4 limes)
525ml (18½fl oz/2⅓ cups) dashi
6g (⅛oz) garlic, peeled and grated
2½ tsp salt
25g (1oz) white fish trimmings
2 celery sticks, cleaned

For the Nikkei *cebiche*:
1 scallop, cleaned
2 x 2cm (¾in) cubes of fresh cabrilla or any rock fish
1 river prawn (shrimp) tail, deveined and blanched
salt, to taste
grated garlic, to taste
grated ginger, to taste
100ml (3½fl oz/½ cup) *cebiche* sauce
20ml (⅔fl oz/4 tsp) ponzu sauce
¼ Limo hot pepper (or red jalapeño chilli), diced
4 coriander (cilantro) leaves, chopped
2 sea urchins (or tobiko eggs)
20g (¾oz) red onion, julienned
1 ice cube

First, make the dashi. Soak the konbu in the water for 12 hours. Place the water and konbu in a pan over a low heat. Once the temperature reaches 80°C (176°F), add the katsuobushi bonito flakes. Then, turn off the heat and let the mixture infuse for 20 minutes, leaving the lid on. Strain the liquid through a fine sieve (strainer) using a muslin (cheesecloth) to prevent any sediments from filtering through.

To make the ponzu sauce, simply mix all the ingredients in a bowl and refrigerate.

Next, make the *cebiche* sauce. Cut the limes in half and squeeze them, making sure their juice isn't bitter. (To keep the lime juice from going bitter, be sure to squeeze only half of it using your hand.) Mix the lime juice, dashi and garlic in a bowl and add salt.

Cut the fish trimmings into small cubes and add to the mix; the purpose of this fish is only to add flavour. Crush the celery sticks with a kitchen mallet and add to the sauce and refrigerate (note: this sauce lasts only 6 hours in the fridge).

Now, to make the dish itself. Blow-torch the scallop for a few seconds only, to avoid overcooking, then dunk it in iced water for 5 seconds and set aside. Put the fish cubes in a bowl along with the prawn (shrimp) tail and scallop. Season with the salt, garlic and ginger. Next, add the *cebiche* sauce and ponzu, and mix before adding the Limo hot pepper and the coriander (cilantro). Add the sea urchin (or tobiko eggs, if using) just before serving.

Place the *cebiche* without any of its juice in a sea urchin shell or in a suitable serving bowl, as shown opposite. Sprinkle over the onion followed by the *cebiche* juice. Serve chilled. (Use the ice cube as a cooler. You could also use ice cubes made from dashi to chill the dish.)

The world is your oyster when it comes to seasoning *tiradito*. Much as I love using lime as a major component for Nikkei *leche de tigre* (Nikkei tiger's milk; see page 239), there is a whole range of different fruits to play with. So, here I use passion fruit and *aji amarillo* (a Peruvian yellow chilli) to create a zingy, punchy dressing that works really well with the fatty salmon. Finish the dish with a dusting of finely ground Espelette pepper for a gentle, fruity hint of chilli.

SALMON & PASSION FRUIT *TIRADITO*
WITH CRISPY BUTTERNUT SQUASH 'SPAGHETTI' & ESPELETTE PEPPER

SERVES 4

½ butternut squash
sunflower oil, for deep-frying
a sprinkle of Maldon sea salt
  flakes, plus extra to garnish
200g (7oz) sushi-grade
  salmon fillet, skinned
a few sprigs of chervil (or
  coriander (cilantro)), to
  garnish
a sprinkle of finely ground
  Espelette pepper (or
  shichimi pepper), to garnish

**For the passion fruit *leche
  de tigre*:**
4 small passion fruit, juice and
  seeds (around 50g (1¾oz)
  in total)
1 tsp ready-made *aji amarillo*
  paste (available from
  Peruvian food shops)
juice of 1 lemon (4 tbsp)
¼ tsp salt
1 garlic clove, cut
1cm (½in) slice of root ginger
1 tbsp mirin
1 tbsp sugar
¼ banana shallot, very finely
  chopped
2 tbsp very finely chopped
  chervil (or coriander
  (cilantro))

First, make the passion fruit *leche de tigre*. Reserve 1–2 tablespoons of passion fruit seeds and set aside. Then whizz the remaining ingredients (except the shallot and chervil) in a food processor. Next, pass the mixture through a fine sieve (strainer) and then add the finely chopped shallot and chervil. Refrigerate until needed.

Next, peel the butternut squash. Using a zester, cut fine strips of squash rather like spaghetti. Line a plate with kitchen paper (paper towels). Add the oil to a deep pan no more than one-third full (the hot oil will rise to the surface as the squash is added) and heat to 140°C (275°F). Deep-fry the butternut squash 'spaghetti' for about 2½ minutes until lightly browned, transfer to the lined plate. The squash strands will not be crispy at this stage but don't worry – they will crisp up as they cool. Season with sea salt.

Remove any residual brown flesh from the salmon fillet. Cut the salmon into thin slices and arrange them in a single row over each of four serving plates. For each plate, spoon 2–3 tablespoons of the passion fruit *leche de tigre* over the salmon, dot the reserved passion fruit seeds around the plate, arrange a line of crispy butternut squash 'spaghetti' in the middle of the salmon row and scatter a few sprigs of chervil over the squash and on the plate. Sprinkle over some sea salt flakes and Espelette pepper and serve immediately.

RICE & NOODLES

Mentaiko is chilli cod roe and, like yuzu kosho, is one of the main food products of the island of Kyushu in Japan. It can be eaten in many ways – as a topping on white rice, dried and grated on savoury dishes or as a flavouring for spaghetti sauce, the latter being probably the most popular usage in Japan. Not strictly a Nikkei dish, I have included it here as an example of a strong European influence on Japanese cooking, popular throughout the country. I love mentaiko spaghetti, and in this version I add fresh clams and a touch of Parmesan – think *spaghetti alle vongole* meets Japanese carbonara!

MENTAIKO SPAGHETTI WITH CLAMS & PARMESAN

SERVES 4

300g (10½oz) clams
35g (1¼oz/2¼ tbsp) butter
2 tbsp extra virgin olive oil
340g (11¾oz) dried spaghetti
125g (4¼oz) mentaiko
   (chilli-marinated cod or
   pollock roe)
50g (1¾oz/¼ cup) Japanese-
   style mayoneizu (see
   page 232) or ready-made
   Japanese mayonnaise
1 egg yolk
2 tbsp soy sauce
2 tbsp mirin
1 tsp shichimi pepper, plus
   extra to garnish
2 tbsp grated Parmesan
4 tbsp finely chopped chives
a little kizami nori, to garnish
1 tbsp toasted white sesame
   seeds, to garnish

Using a colander, wash the clams under plenty of cold running water, discarding any clams that are broken or permanently open. To cook the clams, choose a medium pan with a tightly fitting lid. Heat the butter and olive oil in the pan, add the clams and cover with the lid. Cook on a medium heat for 3–4 minutes, covered all the time. If a few clams have still not opened, cook for a further minute then remove from the heat and let it rest for 1 minute more. Set aside. If any clams remained unopened after resting, discard them.

Cook the spaghetti until al dente in plenty of boiling salted water, this should take about 10 minutes. Drain the pasta.

While the pasta is cooking, prepare the pasta sauce. In a bowl large enough to fit all the sauce and the cooked pasta, squeeze in the mentaiko, add the mayonnaise, egg yolk, soy sauce and mirin and mix well.

Drain the clam juices, oil and butter into a medium pan (the one used for cooking the pasta could be used here), heat it through and fry the drained pasta for 30 seconds, season the pasta with the shichimi pepper.

Transfer the fried pasta into the bowl with the mentaiko sauce, mixing it well into the sauce. Next, add the grated Parmesan cheese, the chopped chives and the clams (reserving a few clams for garnishing) and mix gently again.

Using a fork and spoon, divide the pasta and clams onto each of the serving dishes in a tight circular mound (this shape will help the pasta retain its heat for longer), place a couple of clams over and around the pasta, sprinkle over some shichimi pepper and top with some kizami nori strands and toasted white sesame seeds. Serve immediately.

This chilled somen noodle was a favourite at our home – I remember my father getting through a fair few bowls of this on exceedingly hot summer days in São Paulo. In Japan, a similar dish known as zaru soba is enjoyed throughout the hot months, although that dish uses buckwheat noodles.

Limes and red chillies are abundant in Brazil and in this Nikkei recipe they bring freshness and a South American twist to a Japanese summer staple. The dashi stock needs to be clear and preferably home-made; I'm afraid that the instant variety will not work as well for this recipe. Every element of this dish will need to be chilled before it is put together and served – but your reward is one of the most refreshing dishes you will ever encounter.

CHILLED SOMEN NOODLES SERVED IN COLD DASHI WITH CHILLIES, LIME & ICE

SERVES 4

900ml (1 pint 10½fl oz/
  3½ cups) Primary dashi
  (see page 230)
4 tbsp soy sauce
4 tbsp mirin
2 tsp caster (superfine) sugar
4 small red chillies, deseeded
2.5cm (1in)-piece of root
  ginger
vegetable oil, for deep-frying
2 tbsp finely chopped chives,
  chilled
300g (10½oz) fine somen
  noodles
1 tbsp sesame seeds, to
  garnish
shichimi pepper, to garnish
2 limes, cut into 8 wedges,
  to serve

Make the dashi stock following the instructions for Primary dashi on page 230, then measure out 900ml (1 pint 10½fl oz/3½ cups).

In a large pan, put the dashi, soy sauce, mirin and sugar, and bring to the boil, then simmer for a few minutes until the flavours are well combined. Set aside to cool.

Fill 8 to 12 holes of an ice-cube tray with some of the cooled dashi broth and freeze.

Meanwhile, finely slice the chillies on the diagonal. Peel and grate the ginger, add this and the ginger juice (by squeezing the grated pulp) and half of the chillies to the remaining dashi broth. Let it infuse for at least an hour. Chill in a very cold fridge (the back and bottom of the fridge are the coldest).

Heat some vegetable oil in a medium pan until it reaches 160°C (310°F). Deep-fry the remaining chillies for 30 seconds and drain on kitchen paper (paper towels).

Cook the somen noodles for 2 minutes in a pan with plenty of boiling water (check the packet instructions). Drain and refresh completely under cold running water. Add the finely chopped chives and mix well. (Do not cook the noodles too far in advance as they will become soggy and sticky – the noodles will only retain their texture for 15 minutes or so if completely drained of water). Chill until needed.

To serve, place the noodles in the centre of each serving bowl. Carefully pour the chilled dashi broth around the noodles, add two or three dashi ice cubes, top the noodles with the deep-fried slices of red chillies and a little sprinkle of sesame seeds and shichimi pepper. Serve immediately with the lime wedges.

The fine and delicate Japanese somen noodles are flavoured here with shredded chicken and a nutty sesame dressing to create a light and refreshing salad, perfect for a summer's day. The flavoured Japanese egg, known as ajitsuke tamago, can be made a day or two in advance and kept in the fridge; these eggs will give the dish a wow factor.

SOMEN NOODLE & CHICKEN SALAD

FINE NOODLES, SHREDDED CHICKEN & FLAVOURED JAPANESE EGGS WITH A CREAMY SESAME DRESSING

SERVES 4

3cm (1¼in) piece of root
 ginger, skin left on, sliced
1 spring onion (scallion),
 roughly chopped
1 chicken breast (or 2 chicken
 thighs), skin off but reserved
½ small cucumber, skin on
10g (¼oz) chives, to garnish
1 red chilli, to garnish
200ml (7fl oz/¾ cup)
 sunflower oil, for deep-frying
½ portion of Sesame dressing
 (see page 238 or use the
 simplified version below)
150g (5½oz) somen noodles
2 Japanese flavoured eggs
 (ajitsuke tamago; see page
 242)
a handful of micro herbs or
 baby cress, to garnish
shichimi pepper, to garnish
a sprinkle of toasted white
 sesame seeds, to garnish

**For the simple goma-dare
 dressing:**
50g (1¾oz/¼ cup) light tahini
 (sesame seed paste)
1 tbsp light soy sauce
2 tbsp mirin
1 tbsp rice vinegar
1 tsp caster (superfine) sugar
salt, to taste
shichimi pepper, to taste

Put the sliced ginger and spring onion (scallion) in a pan, then add the skinned chicken along with enough water to cover. Simmer gently for 15 minutes or until the chicken is cooked through. Turn off the heat and let the chicken cool in the broth. Meanwhile, preheat the oven to 200°C/400°F/gas mark 6.

Scrape off any excess fat and feathers from the chicken skin with a knife without tearing the skin. Stretch it out on a flat baking tray (baking sheet) in a single layer. Place a smaller metal tray such as a roasting tin (pan) on top of the skin to keep it flat while roasting. Roast for 10 minutes until crisp and lightly golden. Remove from the oven and transfer to a cooling rack. When cool enough to handle, break the skin into four triangular pieces.

Next, prepare the garnishes. Deseed the cucumber and, using a mandolin, cut it into juliennes. Finely chop the chives, deseed and slice the red chilli, deep-fry the chilli slices in sunflower oil at 160°C (310°F) for 30 seconds, then drain on kitchen paper (paper towels).

Once the chicken is cool enough to handle, remove it from the broth (keeping the broth) and shred it finely, season with salt and keep it covered to avoid it drying out.

Make the dressing by mixing all the ingredients together. Add a few tablespoons (one at a time) of the chicken broth until you get the correct consistency (something akin to single cream). Check for seasoning and add salt and a little shichimi pepper, to taste.

When you are just about to serve, cook the somen noodles according to the instructions on the packet – it shouldn't take more than 2–3 minutes. Then, drain and refresh thoroughly under cold running water. Let them drain for 2–3 minutes before adding the finely chopped chives and, using your hands, mix them into the noodles.

Carefully and very delicately, cut the Japanese flavoured eggs in half lengthways trying to keep any runny yolk from spilling along or outside the egg white.

To serve, use a flat bowl: make a tight but flattish mound of noodles per bowl, top with shredded chicken, spoon 2–4 tablespoons of dressing over the chicken, place some julienned cucumber on top, then the micro herbs and a slice of red chilli. Now, very carefully place a triangular piece of crispy chicken skin in the middle of the mound, sprinkle some chopped chives, a little shichimi pepper and sesame seeds over the chicken and garnishes. Carefully place half of the Japanese flavoured eggs by the noodle mound and serve.

Made using egg rather than buckwheat (soba) noodles, yakisoba is one of the most popular street food dishes in Japan and Brazil. In São Paulo it is ubiquitous; it is found in many Japanese, Nikkei and Brazilian restaurants, with countless variations. Here, crunchy vegetables, caramelised noodles and wok-fried pork and prawns (shrimp) come together as a meal in one pot.

SÃO PAULO-STYLE YAKISOBA

SERVES 4

400g (14oz) fresh or dried
   egg noodles (ramen noodles)
1 tbsp sesame oil, plus
   2 tsp for noodles
180ml (6¼fl oz/¾ cup)
   yakisoba sauce (ready-made
   Otafuku brand or see below)
½ tsp ground white pepper
2 tbsp sunflower oil
250g (9oz) pork belly, sliced
100g (3½oz) onion, sliced
2 garlic cloves, sliced
4 shiitake mushrooms, wiped
   and sliced
150g (5½oz) carrots,
   julienned
150g (5½oz) cabbage,
   chopped into 2cm (¾in)
   pieces
100g (3½oz) spring onions
   (scallions), sliced into 2cm
   (¾in) pieces
12 large prawns (shrimp),
   deveined, tail on
10g (¼oz/⅔ cup) bonito fish
   flakes
2 tsp green nori (aonori),
   to garnish
2 tsp red ginger pickle (beni
   shoga), to garnish
2 tsp toasted white sesame
   seeds, to garnish

For the yakisoba sauce:
3 tbsp Worcestershire sauce
1 tbsp oyster sauce
1 tbsp ketchup
2 tsp soy sauce
2 tsp sugar

Cook the noodles in a pan of salted boiling water according to the packet instructions, but lightly undercook them by about a minute, because later they will be stir-fried in a hot wok for a couple of minutes when the dish is being assembled. Refresh the noodles under cold running water, drain thoroughly and mix in a couple of teaspoons of sesame oil to stop them from sticking together.

As with any stir-fry, prepare all the ingredients meticulously before starting to cook the dish and put in separate bowls. Keep the pork and prawns (shrimp) in the fridge until needed. Add the ground white pepper to the yakisoba sauce (ready-made or home-made), mix well. Set aside until needed.

Heat a large wok with the sunflower and sesame oils until smoking hot, add the pork belly and fry until whitened but not coloured for about 2–3 minutes. Add the sliced onions and garlic, fry for another minute then add the mushrooms, carrots and cabbage and stir-fry until they are lightly softened, but not overcooked; this should only take a couple of minutes on a high heat. Now, add the sliced spring onions (scallions) and the prawns (shrimp), and stir-fry until the prawns (shrimp) are lightly pink and the spring onions (scallions) are beginning to wilt, about another minute. Finally, add the noodles along with the yakisoba sauce and, using cooking tongs or two salad forks, lift and drop the noodles as if tossing a salad to coat them evenly with the sauce. Sprinkle the bonito fish flakes into the noodles and continue tossing until the noodles are a uniform colour and you can smell the sauce starting to caramelise.

Divide the yakisoba noodles between four plates and then sprinkle with green nori seaweed, the red ginger pickle and the toasted white sesame seeds. Serve.

Cook's note For this dish, the ready-made Otafuku yakisoba sauce works very well and I recommend using it if possible. If you can't get hold of it, make your own yakisoba sauce by combining all the ingredients in a small bowl and whisking them well together.

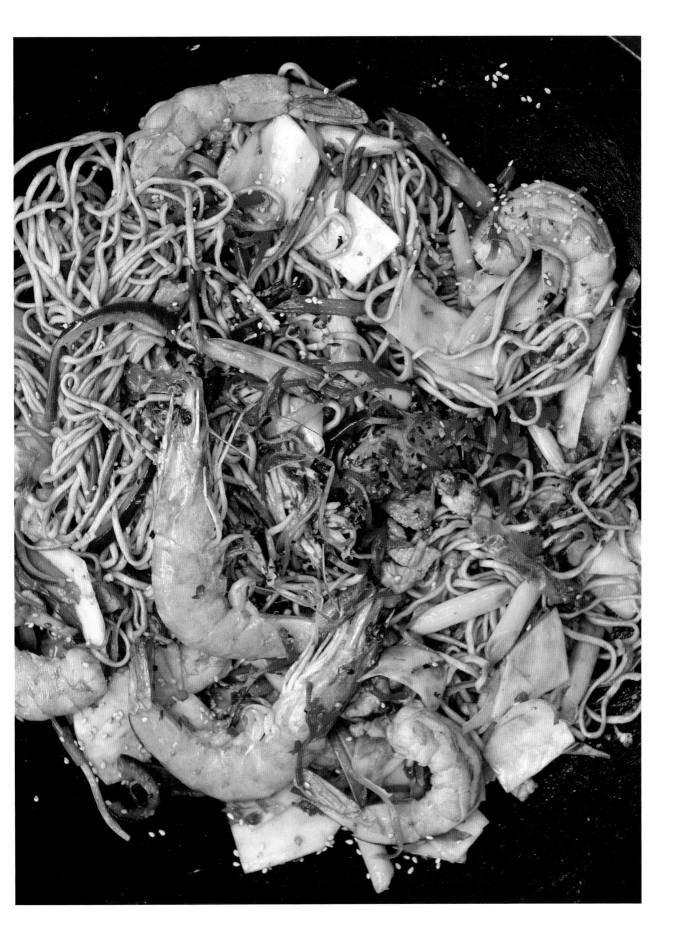

Sea urchin is a favourite, not only as 'uni' in Japan, but also in France and Italy. I wish sea urchin were as popular in the UK, but while you won't see it on your fishmonger's counter very often, it is possible to order it in advance; it is not nearly as rare or expensive as you might think. This wonderful ingredient is combined in this recipe to create a wafu pasta dish — a Western-style pasta with Japanese ingredients including yuzu juice and black tobiko eggs.

SEA URCHIN LINGUINE
WITH TOBIKO CAVIAR & YUZU CREAM

SERVES 4

100g (3½oz) fresh sea urchin sacs (about 500g (1lb 2oz) whole sea urchins in their shells), reserve 4–8 whole sacs, to garnish

400g (14oz) dried linguine (best Italian, preferably from Gragnano)

2 tbsp unsalted butter

2 tbsp extra virgin olive oil

2 tbsp black tobiko eggs (or lumpfish caviar)

4 tsp finely chopped chervil

Maldon sea salt flakes, to garnish

garlic flowers, to garnish (optional)

For the yuzu cream:

4 tbsp Japanese-style mayoneizu (see page 232) or ready-made Japanese mayonnaise

2 tbsp light soy sauce

2 tbsp mirin

1 egg yolk

1 tbsp yuzu juice

½ tsp Espelette or shichimi pepper, plus extra to garnish

½ tsp Maldon sea salt flakes

First, make the yuzu cream. Whisk all of the ingredients together in a bowl, cover and refrigerate until needed. Ideally the cream needs to be at room temperature when you mix it in with the pasta later, so remove from the fridge in good time.

To extract the sea urchin roe (known in Japanese as uni) from a live sea urchin you will probably need to wear protective latex gloves if the sea urchins are large and spiky; if they are small in size, a robust tea-towel (dish towel) will probably do the job. Be careful as the spines are sharp and exude a dark-purple ink. Make a brine of water and salt, and keep in a bowl beside you. Also have a separate clean plate ready to receive the cleaned uni sacs. The shell is covered with spines and at the centre of the animal's underside is its beak. Hold the sea urchin in one hand with the tea-towel (dish towel) and, using strong scissors in the other hand, snip the beak out of the shell, cutting a disc of about 5cm (2in) diameter (or smaller depending on the size of the shell). Grasp this disc firmly and pull it out. Tip any liquid into the sink and carefully scrape out the black guts using a teaspoon, then scrape the five sacs of uni out of the sides, using a firm motion from top to bottom. Extract all the uni, trying to keep the sacs as intact as possible; many uni will break up, but be really gentle at this stage to aim for intactness. Rinse the uni gently in the salt-water solution, delicately lifting away any black mucus or spines that may have stuck to the roe with your fingers or tweezers. Place the cleaned uni on the prepared plate. Continue until all the sea urchins are done.

In a large pan of boiling, salted water, cook the linguine until al dente according to the packet instructions then drain it. The pasta will be fried for a minute or so after this initial cooking, so err on the side of caution and do not overcook it at this stage.

Return the pan to a low heat, add the butter and olive oil, then add the drained pasta and stir to thoroughly coat the linguine. Add the sea urchin (except the reserved whole sacs) and mix it vigorously into the pasta for about 1 minute. The sea urchin should break into the pasta, but small pieces of it should be visible, do not mush it. Take the pan off the heat, add the yuzu cream, the black tobiko, half of the chervil and mix well but gently until the pasta is coated with the creamy sauce. Check for seasoning and adjust if necessary.

Divide the pasta between four bowls, top with one or two whole sea urchin sacs, a scattering of chopped chervil, Maldon sea salt and Espelette pepper, along with the garlic flowers, if using, and serve straightaway.

A refreshing rice noodle salad with meltingly tender aubergine (eggplant) and pork – this is one of my summer staples. 'Soboro' pork (or chicken) is the topping for one of Japan's most popular rice dishes: soboro gohan. Here, I borrow Othis delicious ingredient, slow-cooked in soy sauce, sugar and sake, to create my Nikkei noodle salad. Served at room temperature, all elements of this dish can be prepared in advance and put together just before serving.

AUBERGINE, PORK & RICE NOODLE SALAD
WITH A ZINGY SOY, CHILLI & GINGER DRESSING

SERVES 4

100g (3½oz) dried rice
  vermicelli noodles
1 tbsp finely chopped
  coriander (cilantro) leaves,
  plus a few extra to garnish
sunflower oil, for deep-frying
2 aubergines (eggplants)
  (about 250g (9oz) each)
2 tsp toasted white sesame
  seeds
a sprinkle of shichimi pepper

For the pork soboro:
2 tbsp sesame oil
300g (10½oz) pork, minced
  (ground)
50ml (2fl oz/¼ cup) sake
50ml (2fl oz/¼ cup) mirin
100ml (3½fl oz/½ cup) soy
  sauce
2.5cm (1in) piece of root
  ginger, skin on and grated
2 tsp sugar

For the dressing:
½ tsp Asian chicken stock
  powder, dissolved in
  4 tbsp of hot water
1 tbsp rice vinegar
1 tbsp toasted sesame oil
1 tbsp caster (superfine)
  sugar
2½ tbsp soy sauce
2 tsp finely chopped red chilli
2 tsp finely chopped root
  ginger

First, prepare the pork soboro. Heat the sesame oil in a small pan, add the pork, sake, mirin, soy sauce, ginger and sugar and simmer for about 20–30 minutes until most of the liquid has evaporated. Take off the heat and let it cool to room temperature. Next make the dressing. Mix the dissolved Asian chicken stock powder with all of the other ingredients and mix well until combined. Set aside until required.

Cook the noodles according to the packet instructions. You'll want the noodles al dente, so try them and stop them cooking when ready by plunging them into iced water. Drain them in a sieve (strainer) then add the chopped coriander (cilantro) leaves and mix well. Set aside.

You'll need a pan large enough to accommodate and deep-fry both whole aubergines (eggplants). Fill the pan no more than half full with sunflower oil and start heating the oil to 170°C (325°F) over a medium heat. While the oil is heating, wipe the aubergines (eggplants) thoroughly. Make a few incisions in the skin so that they do not burst during cooking. When the oil reaches temperature, carefully place the whole aubergines (eggplants) in the pan, one at a time and very slowly to avoid any oil spilling. Deep-fry the aubergines (eggplants) for 5–6 minutes, turning them around every minute or so to ensure all sides of the aubergines (eggplants) are cooked in the hot oil.

While the aubergines (eggplants) are cooking, place plenty of ice cubes and very cold water in a bowl large enough to take both whole aubergines (eggplants). When the aubergines (eggplants) have had their time, carefully remove them from the pan with a slotted spoon and plunge them into the iced water. The aubergines' (eggplants') skin will shrivel up immediately on contact with the chilled water. Leave them in the water for a few minutes until they're cool enough to handle. Take out of the water and peel off the skin – it should come off fairly easily with your fingers.

Cut one aubergine (eggplant) in half lengthways, then turn each half top to tail, cut side down. Cut the two halves diagonally into 1.5cm (½in) slices and transfer them onto a plate, with the slices close together in the original order to keep the appearance of unsliced half-aubergines (eggplants). Repeat with the other aubergine (eggplant) and another plate. Top each of the aubergine (eggplant) halves with the noodles and chopped coriander (cilantro), forming a line. Spoon some dressing over the noodles. Now, create another line of pork over the noodles and top with the remaining dressing. Scatter some coriander (cilantro) over the pork, finishing with a sprinkling of sesame seeds and shichimi pepper.

The origins of *Arroz con pollo* (literally, rice with chicken), as it is known throughout Latin America and Spain, are somewhat contentious with several different countries claiming it as their national dish. In its purest form, the rice and chicken are cooked in beer, which imparts a deliciously savoury quality to the dish.

In Japan, takikomi gohan (or flavoured rice) is a staple in every Japanese home with each family having its own recipe, and chicken is often used. For this Nikkei chicken rice, I blend elements of both Peruvian and Japanese cuisines into a delicious one-pot meal I am sure you will love serving up to family and friends.

ARROZ CON POLLO NIKKEI

SERVES 4–6

500g (1lb 2oz/2⅓ cups)
  short-grain white rice
500ml (18fl oz/2 cups)
  Japanese beer (Asahi or
  Kirin)
1 tbsp dashi powder
2 tbsp mirin
2 tbsp light soy sauce
1 tsp salt
500g (1lb 2oz) skin-on,
  boneless chicken thighs
8 shiitake mushrooms
50g (1¾oz/1 cup) shiso
  leaves, finely sliced, or
  coriander (cilantro), finely
  chopped
2 garlic cloves, finely sliced
2 tbsp finely sliced spring
  onions (scallions), to garnish

Wash the rice in a bowl with plenty of fresh water using a circular motion with your hand. Drain the water and repeat three or four times until the water runs clear. Then, transfer the rice to a sieve (strainer) and let it drain for 15 minutes.

Prepare the broth by combining the beer, dashi powder, mirin, light soy sauce and salt in a pan, mix well and set aside. Meanwhile, preheat the oven to 200°C/400°F/gas mark 6.

Remove the skins from the chicken thighs. Scrape off any excess fat and feathers from the skins with a knife. Stretch the skins out on a flat baking tray (baking sheet) in a single layer. Place a smaller metal tray, such as a roasting tin (pan), on top of them to keep them flat while roasting. Roast for 10–12 minutes until crisp and lightly golden. Remove from the oven and transfer to a cooling rack.

Meanwhile, cut the chicken thighs into 2.5cm (1in) pieces (they will shrink during cooking so don't cut them too small) and chill until needed.

Wipe the shiitake mushrooms, remove the woody stems and slice the caps.

Add the sliced shiso or chopped coriander (cilantro) to the cooking broth and mix well.

Rice cooker method: Add the drained rice to the cooking broth, transfer to the rice cooker and top with the pieces of chicken and the slices of mushroom and garlic (do not stir at this stage), close the rice cooker lid and turn on. It should take about 15–20 minutes to cook. Once the rice cooker's alarm beeps, let the rice sit for at least 15 minutes before opening.

Hob (stove) method: Choose a pan with a tightly fitting lid (preferably of glass). Add the drained rice and the cooking broth, top with all the other ingredients, place the lid on and bring to the boil. As soon as it boils (do not remove the lid at any stage during cooking or resting), turn the heat to its lowest setting and simmer gently for 15 minutes. Turn off the heat and let the rice rest for a further 15 minutes.

While the chicken and rice is cooking, cut up the crispy chicken skin into 1–2cm (½–¾in) squares. Then, stir half of the squares into the rice, mixing well, and scatter the remainder on top with the finely sliced spring onions (scallions). Serve immediately.

Nikkei lobster rice
(recipe overleaf)

If you are looking for a dish for a special occasion, then look no further – this is it! The lobster and saffron add a touch of luxury, although I find that crab (which is less than half the price) works really well, too. You will need a little time to make the lobster stock in which the rice is cooked, so plan ahead and start it a day in advance of when you'd like to serve it. I like to serve it with nothing more than a glass of chilled Champers!

NIKKEI LOBSTER RICE

CREAMY LOBSTER BISQUE, SAFFRON & WHITE MISO (illustrated on previous pages)

SERVES 4

2 x 500g (1lb 2oz) lobsters
0.5g packet of saffron
100ml (3½fl oz/½ cup) hot
    water
300g (10½oz/1⅓ cups)
    short-grain white rice
60g (2oz/4 tbsp) butter
1 large banana shallot,
    chopped
2 garlic cloves, crushed
100g (3½oz/½ cup) white
    miso
3 tbsp concentrated tomato
    purée (paste)
3 tbsp light soy sauce
90ml (3¼fl oz/⅓ cup) double
    (heavy) cream
6 tbsp cream sherry
Maldon sea salt flakes
coriander (cilantro) sprigs
shichimi pepper, to garnish

For the vegetable stock:
3 litres (5¼ pints/2.6 quarts)
    water
1 carrot, chopped
1 onion, chopped
1 celery stick, chopped
1 bay leaf
1 tsp salt

Wash the lobsters thoroughly then place them in the freezer for 1–2 hours; this freezing will render them comatose before being boiled.

Next, prepare a light vegetable stock by adding all the ingredients to a deep pan; choose a pan that is not too wide but that is deep enough for the lobsters to be totally submerged in the stock while cooking. Bring the stock to the boil then simmer for 20 minutes.

Meanwhile, prepare a bowl of iced water. Remove the lobsters from the freezer and place them in the simmering stock. Cook the lobsters for 5 minutes exactly, remove them from the hot stock and immediately dunk them into the iced water. Leave them in the iced water until they are cold. Cover the stock and turn off the heat.

Preheat the oven to 200°C/400°F/gas mark 6. Prepare the lobster, making sure not to throw away any of the lobsters' shells. Start by twisting off the claws, then breaking those into sections. Crack the claw shell with the back, blunt end of a heavy knife, then carefully remove the flesh. Using a pair of scissors, cut off the small legs from the body, flatten with the back of a knife and then using a pick or a teaspoon handle to remove the flesh. Remove the lobster heads, one of the smaller heads can be used as a garnish if you like. Next, using a pair of scissors, cut through the lower part of the shell of the lobsters tail, crack it open so that the meat is completely exposed. Carefully remove the whole tail meat from the shell. Devein the lobster tail by running a knife along the middle and over the top part of the tail to remove the dark intestinal thread. Cut the tail in half lengthways. From the body of the lobsters, remove and discard all gills (also known as dead men's fingers) and the pale stomach sac. The green liver (known as tomalley) is considered a delicacy and can also be added to the recipe together with the meat (the green colour will turn orange when cooked). Pick as much of the white meat as possible from the lobsters' bodies. If any coral-coloured roe is present, it can also be mixed with the meat for this recipe. Keep two lobster halves and two whole claws for presentation, and roughly chop the remaining meat. Refrigerate the lobster meat until needed.

Next place all the lobsters' shells into a roasting tray and into the oven for 30 minutes, mixing them halfway through to ensure the shells are browning evenly. Remove the roasted shells from the oven, place them in a plastic bag and, using a rolling pin, break up the shells into smaller pieces. Add the roasted lobster shell pieces to the vegetable stock and simmer for 45 minutes. Then strain using a very fine sieve (strainer), reserving the lobster cooking liquor. This liquor will be the base for cooking the rice.

While the lobster shell is roasting, place the saffron strands in a cup and add the measured hot water. Let it infuse for at least 20 minutes.

Wash the rice with plenty of water using a circular motion with your hand. Drain the water and repeat three or four times until the water runs clear. Let the rice drain in a colander.

Before you are ready to cook, bring the liquor to the boil then turn off the heat. Using a clay pot or a beautiful serving pan, melt the butter and sweat the banana shallot and garlic for 3 minutes or until translucent but not coloured. Add the drained rice and fry in the butter for a minute. Now start adding the liquor a ladleful at a time, stirring it gently into the rice, adding a ladleful of the liquor as soon as the rice starts to look a tad dry as you would when cooking risotto. The rice should be cooked in this way for exactly 15 minutes.

Ten minutes into the cooking process, add the roughly chopped lobster meat, the white miso, saffron strands and its water, the tomato purée (paste) and soy sauce into the rice and mix well. A minute or so before the 15 minutes are up, add the whole lobster halves and claws into the hot liquor to warm them through. Now, add the cream and sherry to the rice, mixing these in gently. Check for seasoning and add some Maldon sea salt flakes, if necessary. The lobster rice consistency should be creamy and runny, like a rich risotto; if it seems too dense, add a little more liquor until the desired consistency is achieved.

Before serving, place the whole lobster halves and claws in the middle of the rice pot with a few coriander (cilantro) sprigs. Finish off with a dusting of shichimi pepper and serve.

Tai gohan (sea-bream rice) is a classic of Japanese home cooking and is a dish I have always loved. It can be made in a rice cooker or in a clay pot or elegant pan to be served at the table for added wow. The fish is cooked over the rice, imparting a delicious flavour to the dish. Here I give my Nikkei interpretation, by adding a dressing of olive oil, yuzu juice and jalapeño green chillies, mixed into the rice just before serving. It's like traditional Japan embracing the spice of South America.

NIKKEI SEA BREAM WITH YUZU & GREEN JALAPEÑO RICE
COOKED IN A CLAY POT

SERVES 8–10

600g (1lb 5oz/2¾ cups) short-grain white rice
550ml (19fl oz/2½ cups) dashi (see page 230) or water
100ml (3½fl oz/½ cup) mirin
100ml (3½fl oz/½ cup) light soy sauce
2.5cm (1in) piece of root ginger, peeled and cut into fine julienne strips
4 sea bream fillets, scaled and pin-boned
a sprinkle of sansho pepper

For the yuzu & green jalapeño dressing:

1 green jalapeño chilli, deseeded and finely chopped
4 tbsp finely chopped spring onions (scallions)
4 tbsp yuzu juice
4 tbsp extra virgin olive oil

Wash the rice in a bowl with plenty of fresh water using a circular motion with your hand. Drain the water and repeat this rinsing three or four times until the water runs clear. Let the rice drain in a colander for at least 15 minutes.

Meanwhile, prepare the soaking and cooking broth. Combine the dashi or water, mirin and light soy sauce and set aside. Soak the drained rice in the cooking broth in a clay pot or a rice cooker (see below) for 30 minutes.

Rice cooker method: After the soaking and before cooking, scatter half of the ginger strips over the rice, lay the sea bream fillets on top and turn the rice cooker on. It should take about 15–20 minutes to cook. Once the rice cooker's alarm beeps indicating that the rice is cooked, let the rice rest for at least 15 minutes before opening the rice cooker.

Clay pot method: Tightly wrap a tea-towel (dish towel) over the lid of a Japanese clay pot (known as donabe) or if you do not have one you can use a heavy casserole pan (Dutch oven). After the soaking and before cooking, scatter half of the ginger strips over the rice, lay the sea bream fillets on the top (I like to arrange the fillets to look like an open flower), place the lid on top and bring to the boil. Once boiling, bring the temperature down to the lowest setting and cook for 15 minutes. Turn off the heat, and without opening the lid (don't open the lid at any stage of the cooking process), rest for a further 15 minutes.

Up to this stage, this rice is a traditional Japanese tai gohan or Japanese sea bream rice and can be served as it is – it will taste delicious. But for added va-va-voom, I like serving this with a yuzu and green jalapeño dressing, which I pour over the fish and rice just before serving. To make the dressing just put all the ingredients in a bowl and mix together well.

Take the unopened clay pot to the table, open it in front of your guests and, if desired, carefully remove the skin of the fish. Pour the dressing over the fish and rice then using a wide wooden spoon, fluff the rice well, breaking the fish into tiny pieces and mixing it together with the dressing into the rice. Mix thoroughly. If you are using a rice cooker, follow all the above steps but do not take the rice cooker to the table! Make all the necessary preparations and serve the rice in individual bowls at the table.

To serve, place the rice in individual rice bowls, top with the remaining julienned ginger in the centre of each bowl followed by a sprinkle of sansho pepper and serve immediately.

Autumn (fall) in Japan is the season for chestnuts, and people across the whole country go crazy for them. Kuri gohan is another classic of Japanese home cooking, and I love serving it in my supper club as an accompaniment to pork dishes, such as the Super-slow-braised pork belly on page 162 or the Iberian pork cheeks with daikon & foie gras on page 164. Cooked in a mixture of water and mirin (sweetened sake), the rice and chestnut combination is slightly sweet, which I find works a treat with unctuous pork dishes.

CHESTNUT RICE KURI GOHAN

SERVES 8

600g (1lb 5oz/2¾ cups)
  short-grain white rice
150g (5½oz/¾ cup) sticky
  rice (see Cook's note)
250g (9oz) ready-roasted
  and peeled chestnuts (see
  Cook's note)
960ml (1 pint 12fl oz/
  4¼ cups) water
240ml (8fl oz/1 cup) mirin
1 tsp salt
1 tbsp sake

Mix the two types of rice in a bowl. Wash the rice with plenty of fresh water using a circular motion with your hand. Drain the water and repeat this rinsing three or four times until the water runs clear. Place the washed rice in a rice cooker.

Roughly chop half of the chestnuts keeping the other half as whole as possible, these will be placed on top of the rice for serving.

Rice cooker method: Scatter the chestnuts over the uncooked rice in the rice cooker. Do not mix at this point. You want moisture to penetrate the rice grains evenly, and thereby cook evenly; mixing in the chestnuts will prevent that from happening. In a bowl, mix the water, mirin, salt and sake. Then pour this mixture on to the rice in the rice cooker. Close the rice cooker and turn it on. When it's done, remove some of the whole chestnuts from the surface of the rice and set aside (these will be used for garnishing. Then, fluff up the rice with a wet rice spatula, mixing in the chestnuts as you do so, and serve immediately into bowls with a few whole reserved chestnuts placed on top.

Hob (stove) method: If you do not have a rice cooker, choose a pan with a tightly fitting lid (preferably of glass) and with a small ventilation hole for some of the steam to escape. Add the rice, water, mirin, salt and sake to the pan then top with the chestnuts, place the lid on and bring to the boil (a glass lid will allow to see when the water comes to the boil). As soon as it boils, turn the heat to its lowest setting and simmer gently for 15 minutes. Do not remove the lid at any stage during cooking or resting. Take off the heat and let the rice rest for a further 15 minutes before fluffing it and serving as above.

Cook's note The sticky rice (also known as glutinous rice or mochi gome in Japanese) will give a denser texture to the final rice dish. If you prefer a lighter version, just replace it with another 150g (5½oz/⅔ cup) of short-grain rice. The ready-roasted and peeled chestnuts can be purchased in vacuumed foil bags in Korean food shops where they are sold as snacks. The Korean roasted chestnuts have a toastier and better flavour than the French variety found in supermarkets. Or, if you prefer, you can buy the chestnuts and roast and peel them yourself.

4 medium-sized dried shiitake
   mushrooms
800ml (1 pint 7fl oz/3½ cups)
   hot water
2 tsp caster (superfine) sugar
4 large eggs
200g (7oz/1 cup) short-grain
   white rice
2 tsp instant dashi powder
30g (1¼oz/⅛ cup)
   mascarpone cheese
30g (1¼oz/⅛ cup) brown
   miso
60g (2oz/4 tbsp) butter
½ tsp shichimi pepper, plus a
   little extra
6g (⅛oz/½ cup) bonito fish
   flakes

For the garnish:
a few strands of Caramelised
   konbu seaweed (see page
   240)
red, green and pink Japanese
   pickles (optional)
salt, to taste

Rehydrate the shiitake mushrooms by soaking them in the hot water and sugar for 1 hour.

If you have a *sous-vide* water oven, set it to 64°C (147°F). If you do not have a *sous-vide* oven, you can still make perfect *sous-vide*-style eggs. You'll need a medium pan and a food thermometer, ideally one with a temperature alarm. Set the thermometer's temperature alarm to a minimum of 63°C (145°F) and a maximum of 65°C (149°F). The alarm should sound whenever the temperature reaches either extreme; turn the heat up or add a little cold water to cool it down to keep it within the desired range. If you are pressed for time or do not have a food thermometer, you can poach the eggs instead. However, the *sous-vide*-style egg has a wonderfully creamy yolk, silken in texture and is quite different to a poached one, which is generally runny.

Carefully add the eggs to the *sous-vide* water oven or improvised water-bath pan and cook them for 50 minutes. When the time is up, remove the eggs and immediately plunge them into a bowl of iced water to stop the cooking. Set aside.

Wash the rice in a bowl with plenty of fresh water using a circular motion with your hand. Drain the water and repeat this rinsing three or four times until the water runs clear. Let the rice drain in a colander for at least 15 minutes.

Meanwhile, remove the mushrooms from their soaking liquid, reserving this stock for later to make the risotto. Squeeze out the excess liquid from the mushrooms, remove the stems and discard, slice the caps finely and set aside.

Transfer the soaking liquid to a pan, being careful to leave any mushroom residue or grit in the bowl. Measure 600ml (1 pint/2½ cups) of this mushroom liquid, warm it through and add the instant dashi powder, mix well to dissolve and keep warm.

Mix the mascarpone and brown miso until you get a light, homogeneous brown paste. In a separate pan, melt the butter and add the shichimi pepper. Keep warm.

Prepare the zosui by making a risotto – add a couple of ladles of the hot mushroom dashi into a pan, heat it through, add the rice and mix it thoroughly into the hot broth. Using a spatula to scrape the bottom of the pan, add more broth, a ladle at a time and stir. Continue this for exactly 15 minutes until the rice is cooked but slightly al dente. Then, add the miso-mascarpone mix and the sliced shiitake mushrooms to the rice and stir to mix well. Check for seasoning.

Gently break open the shell of the eggs and discard the shell and any uncooked white from around the yolks; place the yolks in a shallow bowl covering with hot water (not boiling) to warm them through for a couple of minutes.

To serve, place a couple of tablespoons of creamy risotto rice onto each of four shallow bowls followed by a handful of bonito fish flakes then one drained egg yolk over the rice. Drizzle 2 teaspoons of shichimi butter over the egg yolk, then place a couple of strands of caramelised konbu over the yolk and the red, green and pink Japanese pickles (if using) by the egg. Add a sprinkle of shichimi pepper over the dish and serve immediately.

Traditionally, zosui is a Japanese rice-porridge or soup, made in its simplest form with leftover cooked rice, water and chicken. Similar in concept to the Chinese congee, or a Brazilian *canja*, it is the kind of dish eaten when people are feeling under the weather or after a night on the tiles. For this Nikkei version, I jazz things up a bit: this dish is cooked like a risotto using shiitake dashi to cook the rice from scratch, is flavoured with miso-mascarpone then topped with a *sous-vide*-style egg. This is luxury comfort food, but on a shoe-string.

SHIITAKE ZOSUI

Bacalhau is the Portuguese name for salt cod, and luckily Brazil, a former colony, has taken a real shine to it. The salt-drying once used to preserve fish for feeding Portuguese sailors as they crossed the oceans imparts a umami flavour to the fish, as well as making for a firmer and more interesting texture than fresh cod. Growing up in São Paulo, *bacalhau* used to feature on our family table more often than not, and here I recreate one of my favourite Brazilian Nikkei dishes.

STIR-FRIED JAPANESE RICE WITH PORTUGUESE SALT COD (*BACALHAU*), YUZU KOSHO & LEMON

SERVES 6

400g (14oz) Portuguese salt-
  cod trimmings
400g (14oz/2 cups) short-
  grain white rice
400ml (13½fl oz/1¾ cups)
  water
1½ tsp instant dashi powder
12 mangetout (snow peas)
3 tbsp sunflower oil
2.5cm (1in) piece of root
  ginger, cut into fine juliennes
3 garlic cloves, finely sliced
1 tbsp soy sauce
3 tsp yuzu kosho
2 tbsp water
2 tbsp toasted sesame oil,
  plus a little more for coating
2 tbsp toasted white sesame
  seeds
salt to taste
4 spring onions (scallions),
  finely sliced
1 red chilli, deseeded and
  thinly sliced
6 lemon wedges, to serve

If the *bacalhau* is not already de-salted and rehydrated when purchased, you will need to do this first. Wash the *bacalhau* under fresh running water until all the salt crystals have been washed off. Place it in a large bowl and fill it two-thirds full with fresh, cold water. Cover and leave for 6 hours. Trimmings will require less time than fillets, which are normally soaked for 24 hours. After 6 hours, test the *bacalhau* to make sure it is ready to be used and is not too salty – cut a small slice and boil it in water for a couple of minutes. Taste it. In the unlikely event it is still too salty, let it soak in water for an additional 2–4 hours and test again. Cut the *bacalhau* into 2cm (¾in) pieces.

Prepare the rice following the instructions on page 225, but dissolving the instant dashi powder to the soaking water before adding the rice. Once the rice is ready, fluff the rice and cool it down as quickly as possible using a fan or by transferring it to a container and placing it in a bowl of iced water.

Next, as with any stir-fry, prepare and measure all the ingredients before you start wok-frying. Blanch the mangetout (snow peas) (off the heat) in boiling water for 30 seconds. Drain and plunge them immediately into a bowl of iced water. Let them cool completely, pat dry and cut diagonally into 2cm (¾in) slices (reserve eight slices for the garnish).

Using a large wok, add the sunflower oil and heat it up until smoking. Add the salt-cod pieces and fry them until lightly coloured for about 5 minutes. The *bacalhau* will break up into smaller pieces, but be gentle and try not to turn it into a mush.

Add the ginger, garlic and soy sauce and fry, stirring gently for another minute or so. Add the yuzu kosho and the water and stir until well combined.

Start adding the rice, a little at a time, stirring in the sesame oil and sesame seeds towards the end, continue adding until all the rice has been incorporated and the fish and other ingredients are thoroughly mixed in. Check for seasoning and add salt if needed. Take off the heat and fold the spring onions (scallions) and mangetout (snow peas) into the rice.

To serve, lightly grease a rice bowl with a tiny amount of sesame oil and fill it up with rice, pressing the rice down with a spatula or wide spoon. Place a serving plate over the mouth of the rice bowl and turn it over. Top with a couple of slices of mangetout (snow peas) and a slice of red chilli and add a wedge of lemon. Serve straightaway.

SOUPS &
HOTPOTS

If you have not tried *mandioquinha* yet, I beg you to – for this is one of the most delicious types of root vegetable on earth. *Mandioquinha* (man-deeo-keen-ya) is close to the potato family, originally from the Andes and is commonly used in everyday home cooking in Peru and Brazil. With a delicate flavour and natural sweetness, *mandioquinha* makes a great accompaniment to hearty meat dishes such as salt beef, its classic partner in Brazil. In soups and sauces, it imparts a uniquely rich, velvety texture. With this in mind, I partnered this wondrous root with Japanese miso to create a creamy soup spiked with crispy salt-beef for a Nikkei marriage of contrasting flavours and textures.

MISO & *MANDIOQUINHA* CREAM
WITH CRISPY SALT BEEF

SERVES 8

250g (9oz) Brazilian salted beef (available from Latin American food shops)
1 litre (1¾ pints/4 cups) dashi (see page 230; or use 1 tbsp instant dashi powder and 1 litre (1¾ pints/ 4 cups) boiling water if time is tight)
500g (1lb 2oz) *mandioquinha*, peeled (or substitute with ⅔ swede (rutabaga) and ⅓ carrots)
sunflower oil, for deep-frying
100g (3½oz/½ cup) white miso
2 tbsp finely sliced, on the diagonal, spring onions (scallions)
a sprinkle of shichimi pepper

Remove the salt and rehydrate the salted beef by running it under cold water. Place the beef in a pan and fill it with water. Bring to the boil and simmer uncovered for 45 minutes. Drain, pat dry and when cool enough to handle cut it finely; you can shred in a mini-food processor for a finer texture, but be careful not to grind it to a mush.

Meanwhile, make the dashi by following the recipe instructions on page 230 or opt for the instant version if you're pushed for time. Add the peeled *mandioquinha*, bring to the boil and simmer for 25–30 minutes or until very soft. (Please note: if you buy the precooked *mandioquinha* in a vacuum bag, you only need to warm it through for 5 minutes.) Transfer the cooked vegetable and dashi to a blender and whizz until you get a smooth consistency, pass it through a sieve (strainer), if necessary, keep warm and set aside.

Heat the sunflower oil to a temperature of 160°C (310°F). Deep-fry the shredded salt beef for 1 minute until crispy, transfer to a plate lined with kitchen paper (paper towels) and keep warm.

Just before serving, add the white miso to the warm *mandioquinha* dashi and whisk until the miso is thoroughly dissolved. Check for seasoning and add more salt if necessary.

To serve, add the *mandioquinha* miso cream to a bowl, carefully place a tablespoon of crispy salt-beef in the centre, top this with the spring onions (scallions) followed by a sprinkle of shichimi pepper. Serve immediately.

Cook's note *Mandioquinha* is also known as *batata baroa* in Brazil and *virraca* in Peru. It is available precooked in vacuum bags from Latin American food shops. See the list of suppliers on page 250.

A winter staple in many homes from Tokyo to São Paulo and Lima, this soup is a hearty miso soup made with sliced pork belly, chunky root vegetables and sake lees, a byproduct of sake making. The latter imparts a real depth of flavour to the soup; it may be a little tricky to find, but I assure you your efforts will be richly rewarded.

Ton kasu jiru works well as an accompaniment to a number of other dishes in a meal but I think it is also substantial enough to have as a one-pot supper.

A HEARTY JAPANESE MISO SOUP

WITH SAKE LEES, PORK BELLY & ROOT VEGETABLES

SERVES 6

1.2 litres (2 pints/5 cups) dashi (see page 230; or use 1 tbsp instant dashi powder and 1.2 litres (2 pints/ 5 cups) boiling water if time is tight)

150g (5½oz) white radish or daikon, cut into 1cm (½in) cubes

150g (5½oz) carrot, cut into 1cm (½in) cubes (pumpkin or sweet potato also work well)

300g (10½oz) thinly sliced pork belly, cut into 1cm (½in)-wide, 2cm (¾in)-long pieces

6 tbsp brown miso paste

100g (3½oz) sake lees (also known as sake kasu in most Japanese food shops)

2 tbsp finely sliced spring onions (scallions), to garnish

shichimi pepper, to garnish

Make the dashi by following the recipe instructions on page 230 or opt for the instant version if pushed for time. Transfer to a medium pan that is large enough to accommodate all of the other ingredients.

Add the white radish cubes to the dashi stock, bring to the boil then simmer for 10 minutes on a medium–low heat. Add the carrot and pork belly slices to the pan and cook for a further 10 minutes. Remove any scum from the surface from time to time.

Ladle some of the dashi into a separate bowl, add the brown miso and, using a whisk, mix well until the miso has completely dissolved. Return this mixture to the pan with the dashi, vegetables and pork belly.

Next, add the sake lees to the pan and stir well. Check for seasoning and add more of the brown miso paste if necessary.

Divide the soup between six Japanese soup bowls, sprinkle some sliced spring onions (scallions) in the middle of each bowl and dust with shichimi pepper before serving.

Every country has its rice and chicken soup. In Brazil and Portugal, *canja de galinha* is perhaps the most popular of soups; warming and delicious, it is home cooking at its best. This soup is easy to make and the ingredients are not expensive or difficult to find. In this Nikkei version, I make use of *chu-chu* or chow-chow, also known as chayote in the UK and US, which is native to Mexico but grown all over South America. Use the best-quality chicken on the bone for this dish if you can. I like to make a big pot to keep in the fridge to savour over a few days. It somehow tastes even better a couple of days later!

RICE & CHICKEN SOUP WITH CHAYOTE & A MINT, LEMON & GARLIC GREMOLATA *CANJA DE GALINHA* NIKKEI *COM CHUCHU*

SERVES 8

2 tbsp unsalted butter
1 tbsp extra virgin olive oil
4 corn-fed, skinless, bone-in
chicken thighs (about 600g
(1lb 5oz))
1 small white onion, chopped
1 chayote (about 200g (7oz)),
peeled and cut into 1cm
(½in) cubes (available in
South American, Chinese
and Turkish food shops)
2 garlic cloves, sliced
2cm (¾in) piece of root
ginger, peeled
2 litres (3½ pints/8 cups)
water
10cm (4in) square of konbu
1 tbsp instant dashi powder
100g (3½oz/½ cup) short-
grain white rice
2 tbsp Maldon sea salt flakes
¼ tsp ground white pepper

**For the mint, lemon & garlic
gremolata:**
25g (1oz/1 cup) parsley, finely
chopped
15g (½oz/1 cup) mint, finely
chopped
finely grated zest of 1 lemon
4 garlic cloves, very finely
chopped
1 tsp Maldon sea salt flakes

In a medium cast-iron pan, heat the unsalted butter and olive oil, add the chicken thighs and fry on a medium heat for a couple of minutes until the meat is whitened. Next add the chopped onion, the chayote (or potato), garlic, ginger and fry on a low heat until the onion is softened but not coloured, about 5 minutes. Add the measured water, the konbu and the instant dashi powder to the pan, bring to the boil and then gently simmer, partially covered, for 20 minutes. Skim off any scum from the surface.

Meanwhile, wash the rice in a bowl with plenty of fresh water using a circular motion with your hand. Drain the water and repeat three or four times until the water runs clear. Transfer the rice to a sieve (strainer) or colander and let it drain for 15 minutes.

Remove the chicken thighs from the cooking broth (reserving the stock) and, once it is cool enough to handle, roughly shred the chicken meat, discarding the bones.

Bring the chicken stock to the boil, add the drained rice and the salt and pepper, and simmer gently for another 12 minutes or until the rice has just gone soft. In the last 2 minutes of cooking the rice, return the shredded chicken to the pan to warm it through.

Before serving, discard the konbu and piece of ginger, remove any dark chicken meat or browned onions that float to the surface and adjust the seasoning.

The mint leaves will oxidise quickly once chopped, so make the gremolata just before serving the soup. To make the gremolata, mix all the ingredients together in a bowl then season with Maldon sea salt.

Ladle the soup into bowls, top with a scattering of gremolata and serve immediately.

At our Nikkei home in Brazil, perhaps reflecting our Portuguese background, we loved mixing pork and seafood, and spicing things up by adding chilli to the dashi stock to create our hotpots (hotchpotches). Many years later when I started my Japanese and Nikkei supper club in London, this was the very first hotpot (hotchpotch) I introduced, based on those same flavours. For this recipe, I make use of some wonderful Korean ingredients: gochujang or chilli-soybean paste is bright red and adds both colour and spice to the dashi. The hotpot (hotchpotch) also contains sweet potato noodles, which the Koreans use for their beloved stir-fried 'japchae', and toasted sesame oil for added flavour. The hotpot (hotchpotch) should be beautifully arranged before being taken to the table, with additional ingredients plated separately. As with any hotpot (hotchpotch), the ingredients should be picked out as they are cooked into individual bowls, with fresh ingredients added to replenish the hotpot (hotchpotch). Take your time, it's a lovely dish to get everyone eating and chatting around the table.

NIKKEI HOTPOT OF PORK BELLY, COD & SEAFOOD

WITH A SPICY GOCHUJANG-DASHI BROTH (illustrated on the previous pages)

SERVES 8

400g (14oz) cod loin, skinned and cut into 2cm (¾in) thick pieces
200g (7oz) pork belly, sliced into thin lardons (small pieces) of about 2cm (¾in) long and 1cm (½in) wide
Maldon sea salt flakes
12 prawns (shrimp), deveined, tail on (reserve a couple of whole prawns (shrimp) to garnish)
200g (7oz) baby squid, sliced into thin rings
200g (7oz) clams, washed under running water
100g (3½oz) baby asparagus spears, woody ends removed
200g (7oz) sweet potato noodles (known as dangmyeon, available from Korean food shops)
1 tbsp toasted sesame oil
250g (9oz/1 cup) firm tofu, cut into 2cm (¾in) cubes
200g (7oz) mixture of shiitake, shimeji and oyster mushrooms

For this dish, you'll need an earthenware Japanese nabe pot or heavy casserole pan (Dutch oven) about 25–30cm (10–12in) in diameter and a portable gas burner.

First, make the spicy broth. Add the dashi, gochujang paste, toasted sesame oil, light soy sauce and mirin to a medium pan, bring to the boil and then turn off the heat. Check the seasoning and adjust, if necessary, by adding more gochujang paste (for more heat), soy sauce or mirin. Set aside.

Keep all the prepared meat, fish and shellfish covered in separate bowls in the fridge until needed. Transfer the cod loin pieces to a container with a lid, coat them liberally in sea salt, cover and refrigerate for 2 hours. Then, rinse well under running water and drain.

Next, bring a large pan of water to the boil and blanch the baby asparagus spears for 1 minute, remove from the pan using a slotted spoon (reserving the water) and plunge them into a bowl of iced water to cool them down. Drain and pat dry.

Then, add the sweet potato noodles to the boiling water, cook for 1 minute, remove from the pan with tongs (reserving the water) and cool down under cold running water in a colander, then let the noodles drain for a few minutes. Transfer to a bowl, add a tablespoon of toasted sesame oil and mix well. You may like to cut the noodles at this point using a pair of scissors, which will help when serving it later. Cover and set aside.

Cook the tofu cubes in the reserved boiling water until they float up to the surface, drain, transfer to a bowl, cover and set aside.

Remove the stems of the shiitake mushrooms, carve out a cross on top of each cap, cut off and discard the woody end of the bunch of shimeji mushrooms, wipe all mushrooms with a damp cloth. If the oyster mushrooms are large, cut them into bite-sized pieces.

½ bunch shiso leaves, washed and spin dried

½ Chinese cabbage

1 carrot, peeled

½ bunch enoki mushrooms

100g (3½oz) watercress, washed and spin dried

½ bunch spring onions (scallions), washed and cut into 7–8cm (2¾–3¼in) lengths

For the spicy gochujan-dashi broth:

2 litres (3½ pints/8 cups) dashi (see recipe on page 230; or use 2 tbsp instant dashi powder and 2 litres (3½ pints/8 cups) boiling water if time is tight)

4 tbsp gochujang paste (Korean chilli-soybean paste)

4 tbsp toasted sesame oil

90ml (3¼fl oz/⅓ cup) light soy sauce

50ml (2fl oz/¼ cup) mirin

Place the shiso leaves one on top of the other, roll them tightly like a cigar and then slice very thinly. Next, prepare the Chinese cabbage. Remove the outer leaves, cut in half lengthways then cut a handful of 7–8cm (2¾–3¼in)-long pieces, cut the remaining cabbage into 3cm (1¼in) pieces.

Using a flower cutter, cut 1cm (½in) thick flowers from slices of carrots, precook them in boiling salted water for a couple of minutes. Set aside until needed.

Once you've prepared the ingredients and made the broth, you are ready to assemble your hotpot (hotchpotch). Do not overcrowd the pan or the broth will overflow when cooking the ingredients in the pot. Any leftover ingredients can be arranged on plates and placed around the pot so that they can be added to the hotpot (hotchpotch) as other ingredients are taken out during eating.

Start assembling the hotpot (hotchpotch) by layering the bottom of the earthenware nabe pot or casserole pan (Dutch oven) with the 3cm (1¼in) cabbage pieces to create a raised bed for the remaining ingredients. Next, scatter the thin strips of shiso leaves around the pot. Place the sweet potato noodles in the middle of the pot. Now, all the other ingredients will be placed around and between the noodles and the walls of the nabe pot or casserole (Dutch oven). Arrange the tofu, mushrooms, watercress, baby asparagus spears, spring onions (scallions) and 7–8cm (2¾–3¼in) cabbage pieces around the noodles, spacing them out so that the entire circumference of the pot is covered, use any remaining cabbage pieces to prop up the ingredients. Place the rinsed and drained cod cubes, pork belly, squid and prawns (shrimp) over the noodles, finishing with the clams and precooked slices of carrots.

Bring the gochujang-dashi broth nearly to the boil, set the portable gas burner on the table, place the pot over the burner and carefully pour the broth into the pot, without overfilling it; more broth can be added later if needed. Bring it to the boil, ensuring that all the seafood is submerged, then reduce the heat to a simmer and cook for about 5 minutes. Serve immediately.

Cook's note To finish off the hotpot (hotchpotch), once all the ingredients are eaten but there is still a highly flavoursome broth left over, add more sweet potato noodles. Known as 'shime' this is the traditional way of finishing off a hotpot (hotchpotch) in most Nikkei or Japanese homes. Other possible shime options are udon or soba noodles or a cracked egg with white rice.

Monkfish & seafood nabe hotpot with a creamy white miso & soya milk broth (recipe overleaf)

Hotpots (hotchpotches) are a celebration of social eating; they should be beautifully presented and enjoyed in a leisurely fashion with friends or those close to you. This version has meaty monkfish in a creamy broth of soya milk and white miso, yam noodles (known as shirataki) as well as seafood and vegetables.

As with any hotpot (hotchpotch), the ingredients should be picked out as they are cooked into individual bowls with some of the broth, with fresh ingredients added to replenish the hotpot (hotchpotch). This is a heartwarming all-in-one meal that I hope you will enjoy.

MONKFISH & SEAFOOD NABE HOTPOT
WITH A CREAMY WHITE MISO & SOYA MILK BROTH (illustrated on the previous pages)

SERVES 6

600g (1lb 5oz) monkfish fillet, cut into 2cm (¾in) cubes

12 prawns (shrimp), deveined, tail on (reserve a couple of whole prawns (shrimp) to garnish)

2 fresh squid, cleaned and cut into thin rings

200g (7oz) live clams, washed under running water

100g (3½oz) fine French (green) beans, topped

200g (7oz) shirataki yam noodles (available from Japanese food shops)

400g (14oz/1½ cups) firm tofu, cut into 2cm (¾in) cubes

300g (10½oz) mixture of shiitake, shimeji and oyster mushrooms

a few shiso leaves, washed and spin dried

½ Chinese cabbage

75g (2¾oz) baby spinach leaves, washed and spin dried

1 bunch spring onions (scallions), cut into 7–8cm (2¾–3¼in) lengths

12 slices of narutomaki (Japanese fishcake with a pink spiral within)

For this dish, you'll need an earthenware Japanese nabe pot or heavy casserole pan (Dutch oven) about 25–30cm (10–12in) in diameter and a portable gas burner.

Keep all the prepared fish and shellfish covered in separate bowls in the fridge until needed.

Next, bring a large pan of water to the boil and add the fine French (green) beans. Cook for 1 minute, remove from the pan using a slotted spoon (reserving the water) and plunge them into a bowl of iced water to cool them down. Drain and pat dry.

Then add the shirataki noodles to the boiling water, cook for 1 minute, remove from the pan with tongs (reserving the water) and drain in a colander. Transfer the noodles to a bowl, cover and set aside.

Cook the tofu cubes in the reserved boiling water until they float up to the surface, drain, transfer to a bowl, cover and set aside.

Remove the stems of the shiitake mushrooms, carve out a cross on top of each cap, cut off and discard the woody end of the bunch of shimeji mushroom, wipe all mushrooms with a damp cloth. If the oyster mushrooms are large, cut them into bite-sized pieces.

Stack the shiso leaves one on top of the other, roll them tightly like a cigar and then slice them very thinly. Next, prepare the Chinese cabbage. Remove the outer leaves, cut in half lengthways then cut a handful of 7–8cm (2¾–3¼in)-long pieces, cut the remaining cabbage into 3cm (1¼in) pieces.

Make the broth just before assembling and serving the hotpot (hotchpotch). In a large pan, add the soya milk, white miso, dashi stock and fish sauce, check the seasoning and adjust if necessary by adding more fish sauce or salt, if desired.

Once you've prepared the ingredients and made the broth, you are ready to assemble your hotpot (hotchpotch). Do not overcrowd the pan or the broth will overflow when cooking. Any leftover ingredients can be arranged on plates and placed around the pot so that they can be added to the hotpot (hotchpotch) as other ingredients are taken out during eating.

For the broth:

1 litre (1¾ pints/4 cups) soya
  milk (preferably an Asian
  brand for a higher soybean
  content)
150g (5½oz/½ cup plus
  2 tbsp) white miso
500ml (18fl oz/2 cups) dashi
  (see page 230; or use
  ½ tbsp instant dashi powder
  and 500ml (18fl oz/2 cups)
  boiling water if time is tight)
3 tbsp fish sauce
Maldon sea salt flakes

Start assembling the hotpot (hotchpotch) by layering the bottom of the earthenware nabe pot or casserole pan (Dutch oven) with the 3cm (1¼in) Chinese cabbage pieces to create a raised bed for the remaining ingredients. Next, scatter the thin strips of shiso leaves around the pot. Place the shirataki noodles in the middle of the pot over the cabbage pieces. Now, all the other ingredients will be placed around and between the noodles and the walls of the nabe pot or casserole (Dutch oven). Arrange the tofu, mushrooms, baby spinach, fine French (green) beans, spring onions (scallions) and 7–8cm (2¾–3¼in) cabbage pieces around the noodles, spacing them out so that the entire circumference of the pot is covered, use any remaining cabbage pieces to prop the ingredients. Place the monkfish cubes, squid and prawns (shrimp) over the noodles, finishing with the clams and slices of narutomaki.

Bring the broth nearly to the boil, set the portable gas burner on the table, place the pot over the burner and carefully pour the broth into the pot, without overfilling it; more broth can be added later. Bring it to the boil, ensuring that all the seafood is submerged, then reduce the heat to a simmer and cook for about 5 minutes. Serve immediately.

Cook's note To finish off the hotpot (hotchpotch), once all the ingredients are eaten but there is still a highly flavoursome broth left over, you can add more yam noodles. Known as 'shime' this is the traditional way of finishing off a hotpot (hotchpotch) in most Nikkei or Japanese homes. Other possible shime options are udon or soba noodles or a cracked egg with white rice.

Sukiyaki is a Japanese hotpot (hotchpotch) enjoyed all over the world, but particularly in the Nikkei households of Brazil where we have a real fondness for beef. Sake was hard to come by when I was a kid, so we substituted dark beer, which gave an extra richness to the broth, like a good carbonade of beef. To enjoy sukiyaki, we sit around the pot and pick out the ingredients as they are ready and take them into individual serving bowls. It's a great social event and fresh ingredients are added back to the hotpot (hotchpotch) until everyone is satisfied.

NIKKEI BEEF SUKIYAKI

HOTPOT OF BEEF, MUSHROOMS, NOODLES, GRILLED TOFU & GREENS IN A RICH DARK BEER & SOY BROTH

SERVES 4

200g (7oz) white shirataki
   yam noodles (available in
   most Japanese food shops)
250g (9oz/1 cup) tofu, cut
   into 2cm (¾in) cubes
1 large bunch stalky spinach
250g (9oz) mixture of
   shiitake, shimeji and oyster
   mushrooms
2 tbsp toasted sesame oil
2 tbsp beef suet
½ onion, thinly sliced
400g (14oz) sirloin (or top
   round) beef, very thinly
   sliced
6 spring onions (scallions),
   cut into 2–3cm (¾–1¼in)
   pieces on the diagonal
4 eggs

For the broth:
300ml (10fl oz/1¼ cups) soy
   sauce
75g (2¾oz/⅓ cup) sugar
200ml (7fl oz/¾ cup) stout or
   other dark beer
2 tsp instant dashi powder
200ml (7fl oz/¾ cup) mirin
200ml (7fl oz/¾ cup) water

For this dish, you'll need a heavy cast-iron Japanese sukiyaki pan or another heavy shallow casserole (Dutch oven) about 25–30cm (10–12in) in diameter and a portable gas burner.

Start by making the broth. In a small pan, add the soy sauce, sugar, stout or other dark beer, dashi powder, mirin and water and bring to the boil. Turn off the heat and set aside.

Boil plenty of water in a medium pan and cook the noodles for 1 minute. Drain the noodles, reserving the water. Place the noodles in a bowl and, using a pair of scissors, cut them up roughly. Set aside. Return the reserved boiling water to the pan, bring back to the boil and cook the tofu pieces until they rise to the surface. Drain the tofu pieces into a colander and leave there for 30 minutes. Next, place the tofu in a metal bowl and blow-torch them until lightly browned, about 30 seconds; or lightly brown under a hot grill (broiler) for a couple of minutes.

Cut off and discard the end of the spinach stalks (keeping most of the stalks) and wash it. Cut into 5cm (2in)-long pieces, stacking the leaves together to make a tight bunch. Remove the stems of the shiitake mushrooms and carve out a cross on top of each cap. Cut off and discard the woody end of the bunch of shimeji mushrooms. Wipe all mushrooms with a damp cloth. Cut any large oyster mushrooms into bite-sized pieces.

1 Set the gas burner on the table, heat the sukiyaki pan with the oil and suet until hot, and fry the onion and a few slices of beef until a beef crust forms on the bottom of the pan and the onion is softened.

2 Carefully pour the broth (using a measuring jug (cup) or ladle) into the pan, without overfilling it; more broth can be added later. Bring it to the boil then start adding the ingredients. **3–6** Place the noodles in the middle of the pan then the grilled (broiled) tofu, mushrooms, spinach, spring onions (scallions) and the slices of beef. Do not overcrowd the pan or the broth will overflow when cooking the ingredients in the pan. Any leftover ingredients can be arranged on plates and placed around the pan, so that they can be added to the hotpot (hotchpotch) as other ingredients are taken out during eating. Once the broth boils again, reduce the heat to a gentle simmer and cook for a couple of minutes.

Pick bite-sized portions from the pan as the ingredients cook. If you like, you can break and lightly stir an egg into a serving bowl and dip the ingredients in the raw egg before eating. Or each diner can add their own egg to the sukiyaki pan and lightly poach it before eating; this will thicken and flavour the sauce. Over time, the sauce will evaporate and become saltier, you may add more fresh broth and some hot water, if you wish.

Cook's note If your butcher cannot cut the sirloin finely (about 2mm (⅛in) thick), you can buy a piece of sirloin beef, partially freeze it then cut it yourself at home. Alternatively, find a Japanese or Korean supermarket or butcher and buy the beef already cut for sukiyaki.

MAINS

If Nikkei cuisine refers to the cooking of Japanese migrants and their descendants, it should not be limited to Brazil, Peru or the USA. As a Brazilian Nikkei chef living in the UK for most of my life, I take inspiration from local ingredients and dishes. Here, I take one of Britain's national dishes — the much-loved fish and chips (fries) — to create my own Nikkei version. This uses monkfish cheeks, deep-fried in a light tempura batter and accompanied by cassava chips (fries).

NIKKEI FISH & CHIPS

TEMPURA OF MONKFISH CHEEKS, CASSAVA CHIPS & WASABI MAYO

SERVES 4

500g (1lb 2oz) cassava
500g (1lb 2oz) monkfish
  cheeks
1 tbsp sake
1 tbsp soy sauce
sunflower oil, for deep-frying
freshly ground sea salt

For the wasabi mayo:
50g (1¾oz/¼ cup) Japanese-
  style mayoneizu (see
  page 232) or ready-made
  Japanese mayonnaise
15g (½oz/1 tbsp) wasabi
  paste
a few drops of lemon juice

For the tempura batter:
100g (3½oz/1 cup) Showa
  tempura flour (or use the
  basic tempura batter recipe
  on page 229)
160ml (5½fl oz/¾ cup) chilled
  water

Peel the cassava and cut into halves (or quarters if the cassava is very thick) and then into 10cm (4in)-long pieces. Place in a pan, cover with fresh cold water and bring to the boil. Reduce the heat and simmer for 1 hour or until the cassava is very soft. Drain and let the cassava cool. Once cold, cut the cassava into chunky chips (fries).

Remove the membrane from each monkfish cheek and discard. Wash the cheeks well, pat dry, transfer to a bowl and add the sake and soy sauce. Cover and refrigerate until needed.

Next, mix together the Japanese mayonnaise, wasabi paste and lemon juice in a bowl. Cover and refrigerate until needed. Then, preheat the oven to 80°C/175°F/gas mark ¼.

Fill a deep pan with enough oil to deep-fry the cassava chips (fries). Heat the oil to 160°C (310°F) and deep-fry them until golden, 5–8 minutes. Transfer the chips (fries) to a plate lined with kitchen paper (paper towels), season them with sea salt and keep warm.

Now, top up (top off) the pan with a little more sunflower oil to deep-fry the monkfish cheeks, the depth of oil in the pan should roughly be twice or more than the thickness of the food items being deep-fried. Now, heat the oil in the pan to 170°C (325°F).

While the oil is heating up, quickly prepare the tempura batter. In a bowl, add the tempura flour, then the chilled water, mix gently just until they are loosely combined. The batter should be very lumpy. If you over-mix, the batter will be sticky and the coating will turn out oily and heavy, not light and airy as you'd like. The goal is to achieve a lacy, golden effect with the deep-fried coating and not a thick, pancake-like casing. To avoid a heavy, oily-tasting coating, do the opposite of what you would do to make good pancakes — make the tempura batter just before deep-frying, do not mix it well and do not let it stand.

Coat the monkfish cheeks one by one in the batter and add a few at a time to the hot oil. Do not overcrowd the pan as the oil temperature will drop too fast and the fish will be stewed in the oil rather than fried. Fry for about 2–3 minutes or until a crispy, lightly golden colour is achieved. Transfer to a plate lined with kitchen paper (paper towels) and season it with freshly ground sea salt. Serve the tempura monkfish cheeks with the cassava chips (fries) and wasabi mayo. As with any other tempura dish, the monkfish cheeks should be served immediately; they will need to be served soon after being fried — don't wait to serve them all together as the initial batches will have lost their crispness.

Yuzu kosho is a Japanese condiment made from the rind of the yuzu fruit, green chillies and salt. The yuzu fruit is one of Japan's most characteristic ingredients and is a citrus fruit unlike any found in Europe or North America, with flavours and aromas reminiscent of tangerine, lime and grapefruit. Yuzu kosho is left to ferment over a few months giving it an even more intense citrus flavour and heat.

Cooking *en papillote* (oven-baked in a greaseproof (wax) paper bag) is one of the best ways to prepare fish and seafood – the delicate texture and moisture remain inside the bag – and here the flavours and aromas are intensified by the addition of shiso herb, yuzu kosho and lime. There are many variations on this theme in Japan but my Nikkei version is a gutsier, more robust interpretation, bringing together the flavours of the regional Japanese cuisine I grew up eating in São Paulo. But I think that the best part of this dish is the element of surprise as each guest tears open their own paper bag at the dinner table!

Needless to say, a little yuzu kosho goes a long way to season grilled (broiled) fish, meats and soups. It is one of the most popular exports of Kyushu Island, the westernmost island of Japan, from where my family emigrated to Brazil.

MONKFISH, SEAFOOD & YUZU KOSHO COOKED EN PAPILLOTE

SERVES 4

8–12 mussels
1 tbsp oil
60g (2oz/4 tbsp) butter
500g (1lb 2oz) monkfish
4 large prawns (shrimp),
 tail on
4 baby squid with tentacles
12 fine green beans
12 oyster or shiitake
 mushrooms
2 spring onions (scallions)
4 x 30cm (12in)-square
 pieces of baking parchment
1 lime, quartered, to serve

For the yuzu kosho marinade:
1½ tbsp Yuzu kosho (see
 page 232)
3 tbsp sake
3 tbsp mirin
8 shiso leaves, finely chopped

Clean the mussels, cook with the oil and 20g (¾oz/1½ tbsp) of the butter within a lidded pan over medium–high heat for 3 minutes or until the mussels have opened; discard any mussels that remain closed after cooking. Strain the mussel juices into a bowl and reserve. Cover the mussels in their shells in a bowl and chill.

Next, make the yuzu kosho marinade – mix together the Yuzu kosho, sake and mirin in a bowl (use one large enough to fit in all the fish and seafood during marinating), tip in the mussel juices and mix well. Lastly, add the shiso.

Now, you'll need to prepare the fish and seafood or ask your fishmonger to do this for you. Fillet and skin the monkfish, then cut it into large cubes. Devein the prawns (shrimp) (I sometimes peel the prawns (shrimp) to make for easier serving, but it's up to you) and clean and slice the baby squid into rings, keeping the tentacles whole.

In a bowl, mix the yuzu kosho marinade with the fish and seafood and mix so that everything is well coated. Marinate for at least 2 hours in the fridge or overnight.

Nearer the time you want to cook, preheat the oven to 230°C/455°F/gas mark 8 and prepare the vegetables – top the fine green beans, wipe the oyster or shiitake mushrooms, and wash and slice the spring onions (scallions).

Fold the pieces of baking parchment in half and then fold each opened end over twice very firmly. Next, divide all of the ingredients – fish, seafood, vegetables and marinade – between the four paper bags along with 10g (3 tsp) butter per bag and close them tightly. Bake in a preheated oven for 10–15 minutes.

Serve each closed bag on a plate with a lime wedge and let your guests open their parcels.

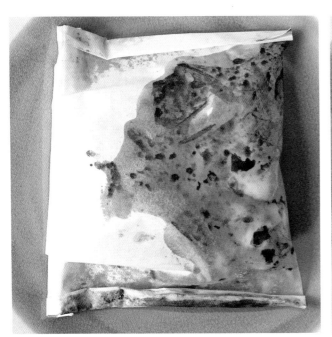
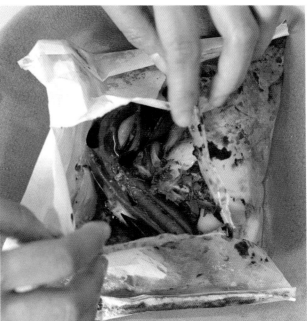
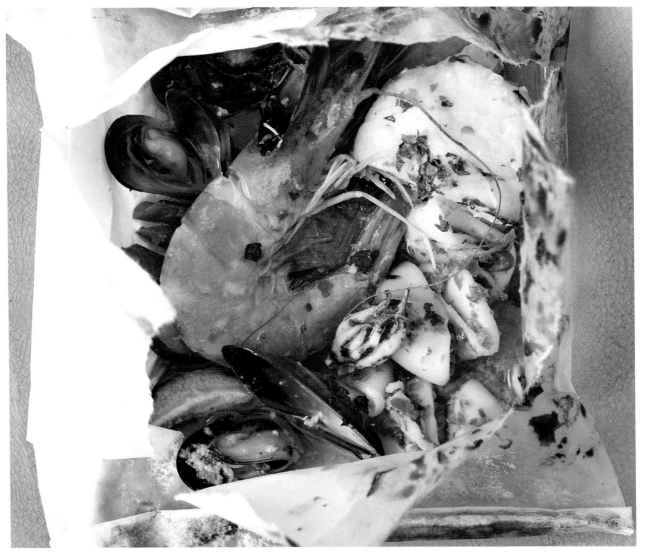

Moqueca is a quintessentially Brazilian dish, with nearly every seaside town having its own variation on this fish or seafood stew. In Bahia, they add an African element to the dish in the form of dendê oil. Derived from the palm tree, this bright orange oil has a very special flavour for which there is no substitute. *Moqueca* is very easy to prepare, and you can substitute prawns (shrimp) with small fillets of fish or other types of seafood. I love serving this *moqueca* over Japanese rice that's flavoured with coriander (cilantro) and lemon, as in this donburi recipe.

MOQUECA DE CAMARÃO & CORIANDER RICE DONBURI

SERVES 4

750g (1lb 11¾oz) large fresh
    prawns (shrimp), peeled and
    deveined (reserve 2 whole
    prawns (shrimp) to garnish)
½ tsp freshly ground black
    pepper
2 tbsp light soy sauce
juice of 1 lemon
2 garlic cloves, crushed
400g (14oz) tinned Italian
    tomatoes, including juice
2 tbsp olive oil
1 medium onion, finely
    chopped
1 tsp paprika
2 tsp Maldon sea salt flakes
400ml (13½fl oz/1¾ cups)
    coconut milk
1 red chilli, deseeded and
    finely chopped
1 tbsp dendê oil (it's a palm
    oil available from Brazilian or
    African food shops)
sunflower oil, for greasing
2 tbsp coriander (cilantro)
    cress, to garnish

For the coriander rice:

1½ portions of Steamed rice
    (see page 225)
2 tbsp extra virgin olive oil
1 tbsp Maldon sea salt
finely grated zest and juice of
    ½ lemon
2 garlic cloves, crushed
8 tbsp finely chopped
    coriander (cilantro)

First, prepare the Japanese steamed rice by following the instructions on page 225. Once the rice is cooked and before fluffing it, make a green coriander (cilantro) salsa by mixing in a bowl the extra virgin olive oil, salt, lemon zest and juice, garlic and coriander (cilantro). Fold the coriander (cilantro) salsa well into the cooked rice and set aside.

In a bowl, mix together the prawns (shrimp), freshly ground black pepper, light soy sauce, lemon juice and garlic well, cover and let marinate for 15 minutes. Meanwhile, blend the tomatoes with their juice in a food processor and pass through a sieve (strainer), discarding any seeds or skin. Set aside this tomato purée (paste).

In a medium cast-iron pan, heat the olive oil over a low heat and fry the onion until just beginning to soften, about 5 minutes. Add the paprika, salt and the tomato purée (paste) and simmer, stirring occasionally, until most of the liquid has evaporated and the mixture is thick; this should take about 10 minutes.

Meanwhile, in a separate pan, fry the reserved whole prawns (shrimp) in a little olive oil until pink, about 3 minutes. Turn off the heat and cover the pan to keep the prawns (shrimp) warm.

Next, stir the coconut milk and chopped chilli into the thickened tomato sauce, bring to the boil and then add the prepared prawns (shrimp) as well as the marinade. Cook over a medium heat until the prawns (shrimp) have gone lightly pink, about 1 minute. Then, stir in the dendê oil, turn off the heat and check for seasoning.

A classic Japanese donburi is a bowl of steamed rice with a topping of meat, fish or vegetables. For this Nikkei dish, however, I like serving the *moqueca de camarão* placed around the rice rather than over it. So, lightly grease a medium bowl with a little sunflower oil, fill it with the coriander rice and press it down so that the rice is lightly compressed. Up end the bowl and turn out the rice in the middle of a serving plate and then remove the bowl. Spoon the prawn (shrimp) stew (moqueca de camarão) around the mound of coriander rice adding plenty of sauce, place the whole prawns (shrimp) on the plate and finish off with a scattering of coriander (cilantro) cress. Serve immediately.

Tempura of courgette flowers stuffed with a scallop,
tofu & lemon mousse
Tempura of soft-shell crab & vegetables

The love for deep-frying vegetables and fish was introduced to Japan by the Portuguese in the 16th century. One of the simplest of Japanese dishes, but also one of the hardest to get right, I recommend reading Tempura Ins & Outs on page 228 before attempting this recipe. You can make tempura out of most fish and vegetables (meat is not used), so try to get a selection of different coloured and textured vegetables. Some of my favourites are broccoli, mushrooms and kabocha pumpkin. I also love filling courgette (zucchini) flowers when they are in season, for a Nikkei version of an Italian classic, stuffed with a mousse of scallop, tofu and lemon rather than with ricotta.

Soft-shell crabs are caught immediately after moulting their shell, in the few days before the new one has hardened up. In fact, their skin hardens into a new larger shell only 5 to 10 hours after moulting if they remain in water so timing is crucial. There are only two seasons in the year when crabs moult their shells, and as the season is so short-lived, most soft shell crabs available all year round are frozen. They are delicacies in Venice, New England and in many Asian countries including Japan where they are served as crispy tempura or in maki sushi, and yes, you do indeed eat the whole thing!

A TEMPURA NIGHT IN

TEMPURA OF COURGETTE FLOWERS WITH A SCALLOP, TOFU & LEMON MOUSSE & TEMPURA OF SOFT-SHELL CRAB & VEGETABLES (illustrated on the previous pages)

SERVES 4

1 portion of Yuzu kosho mayonnaise (see page 233)
8 courgette (zucchini) flowers
sunflower oil for deep-frying

For the scallop mousse:
100g (3½oz) firm tofu
100g (3½oz) sushi-grade scallops
finely grated zest and juice of ½ lemon
½ tsp Maldon sea salt flakes
½ egg (beaten and weighed to measure out half)
100ml (3½fl oz/½ cup) double (heavy) cream
¼ tsp ground white pepper

For the dipping sauce:
90ml (3¼fl oz/⅓ cup) dashi (see page 230 or use instant dashi powder)
25ml (¾fl oz/2 tbsp) soy sauce
25ml (¾fl oz/2 tbsp) mirin
50g (1¾oz) daikon radish, grated (optional)

Before attempting this recipe, have a quick read of Tempura: the ins & outs (see pages 228–229) in the Basics section. You'll also need a couple of sushi mats.

Prepare a portion of Yuzu kosho mayonnaise as instructed on page 233. Set aside.

The tofu will need to be drained of most of its water before being used – this will take a couple of hours. Place one sushi mat over a bowl, then put the tofu block in the middle of the mat. Now top the tofu with another sushi mat. Place a heavy (non-breakable) object, such as the lid of a pan, over the mat to compress the tofu and extract water from it for at least an hour or two.

In the meantime, make the dipping sauce by combining the dashi, soy sauce and mirin in a small pan and bringing to the boil. Turn off the heat and let it cool. If using the daikon: grate it, squeeze out and discard any excess water from it before adding the grated flesh to the dipping sauce – do this just before serving the tempura.

To make the scallop mousse, blend the scallops, with the lemon juice and Maldon sea salt in a food processor. Add the drained tofu and egg and blend further until very smooth. Add the lemon zest, cream and white pepper. Check the seasoning. Set aside in the fridge.

Using a piping (pastry) bag or teaspoon, stuff the courgette (zucchini) flowers one-third full with the scallop mousse, as gently as possible so as not to tear the petals. Twist the end of the petals together to close the flower and place on a plate until all the flowers are stuffed. Cover with clingfilm (plastic wrap) and chill until you are ready to deep-fry them.

4 large soft-shell crabs
  (available from Oriental
  supermarkets)
100g (3½oz) mixed oyster
  and shiitake mushrooms
100g (3½oz) Japanese
  kabocha pumpkin, skin on
  and cut into 4 slices about
  1cm (½in) wide
100g (3½oz) broccoli florets
100g (3½oz) red (bell)
  peppers, deseeded and cut
  into 10cm (4in)-long and
  1.5cm (½in)-wide slices

For the tempura batter:
300g (10½oz) tempura
  batter mix (or see recipe
  on page 229)
420ml (14fl oz/1¾ cups)
  chilled water
6 or 8 ice cubes

Soft shell crabs are available already cleaned and frozen from most Oriental supermarkets. They should be thoroughly washed and defrosted over a rack placed inside a tray and covered in the fridge for a few hours. Pat them dry thoroughly after defrosting.

In a medium pan, heat enough sunflower oil for deep-frying to 170°C (325°F). Just before you are ready to fry the tempura, prepare the tempura batter. In a bowl, add the tempura batter mix to the chilled water and 3 or 4 ice cubes, mix gently with chopsticks until you get a lumpy batter that has the consistency of double (heavy) cream.

Gently coat the soft-shell crabs and a few pieces of vegetables in this batter and carefully place in the pan (only do a few items at a time, if you crowd the pan the oil temperature will fall too much and the tempura will be stewed in the oil rather than crisply fried). Leave them undisturbed for 1 minute so that a crispy batter is formed on the outside before turning them over. Cook for 2–3 minutes until lightly golden (different vegetables will require more or less cooking time but none should be in the hot oil for more than about 3 minutes), drain on a wire rack.

While the crab and vegetables are draining, now gently coat a couple of stuffed courgette (zucchini) flowers in the batter (without overloading the pan) and very carefully place them in the oil, that way they won't open and release their mousse into the pan. Leave it undisturbed for 1 minute, so that a crispy batter forms on the outside before turning it over. Cook for 2 minutes, drain on kitchen paper (paper towels), let rest for 1 minute and serve immediately with the remaining tempura, the dipping sauce and yuzu kosho mayonnaise. As with any other tempura dish, the courgette (zucchini) flowers, soft-shell crab and vegetables should be served immediately; they will need to be served soon after being fried – don't wait to serve them all together as they will have lost their crispness.

Cook's note You could, if you prefer, use other combinations of vegetables in this recipe including aubergines (eggplants), okra and onions but it's worth trying a selection of differently coloured vegetables for a nice presentation.

For this Nikkei dish I use British halibut marinated in miso, sake and *aji amarillo*, served with a velvety mashed potato. For best results, let the fish marinate for a day or two – the miso will infuse the flesh with wonderful umami flavours, while the *aji amarillo* and lemon add a gentle heat and refreshing acidity. This dish makes an elegant main course for any supper.

GRILLED HALIBUT WITH WHITE MISO, *AJI AMARILLO* & LEMON ON POTATO MASH

SERVES 4

4 halibut loin fillets (about 150g (5½oz) each; or another white fish, such as monkfish, hake or cod)
2 large potatoes (800g (1lb 12¼oz)), quartered
200g (7oz/¾ cup) unsalted butter
100ml (3½fl oz/½ cup) whole milk
freshly ground salt and pepper
2–3 tsp sunflower oil, for greasing
2 tsp black tobiko eggs (you could use black lumpfish caviar instead)
a drizzle of extra virgin olive oil, to garnish
4 lemon wedges, to serve
2 tbsp finely chopped chives, to garnish
freshly ground black pepper, to serve

For the miso marinade:
50ml (2fl oz/¼ cup) sake
50ml (2fl oz/¼ cup) mirin
50g (1¾oz/¼ cup) sugar
150g (5½oz/½ cup plus 2 tbsp) white miso paste
finely grated zest and juice of 1 lemon
1 tbsp ready-made *aji amarillo* paste (available from Peruvian food shops)

First, make the miso marinade. Pour the sake and mirin into a small pan, bring to the boil and simmer uncovered for 30 seconds to burn off the alcohol. Add the sugar, mix well until the sugar has dissolved, then add the miso paste. Using a whisk, mix thoroughly ensuring no miso lumps are left. Turn the heat to low and cook the miso mixture for 10 minutes, stirring often with a spatula, scraping the bottom of the pan to make sure that the marinade does not burn. Keep your eye on the marinade, stirring until you get a firmer, paste-like consistency. Remove from the heat and let it cool completely. Once cool, add the lemon zest and juice along with the *aji amarillo* paste, and mix until well combined. Transfer to a lidded container and pop it in the fridge until needed; the marinade should be chilled before applying it to the fish.

Rub the marinade gently but firmly, into the halibut fillets, place them in a sealable container with the marinade and marinate for 12–48 hours. You'll need to remove the halibut from the fridge 30 minutes before grilling (broiling).

Make the potato mash by cooking the potato quarters in a pan filled with water. Bring to the boil and simmer for 20 minutes or until the potatoes are soft. Drain and, while hot, pass them through a drum sieve (strainer) (for a finer texture) or a potato ricer. Return to the pan, warm through, add the unsalted butter and milk until you achieve a creamy consistency. Season with freshly ground salt and pepper and keep warm.

Preheat the grill (broiler). Line a roasting tray with foil and grease it lightly with oil.

Using your hands, remove any excess marinade from the fish fillets and place them on the prepared tray. When the grill (broiler) is very hot, grill (broil) the halibut for 5 minutes on each side (10 minutes in total) or until they are cooked through, but not overcooked – this will depend on the size and thickness of the fillets. The marinade should be golden brown in colour.

Just before the halibut fillets are ready, spoon enough mashed potato onto each plate to create a base for the fish. Transfer the fillets of fish onto the serving plates over the mashed potato mounds. Place half a teaspoon of black tobiko eggs over each fillet then a drizzle of extra virgin olive oil over the fish with a lemon wedge by it. Finish with a sprinkle of finely chopped chives and some freshly ground black pepper, and serve immediately.

In our household, tofu was an important part of nearly every meal. Having grown up eating it, I love the clear flavour of soy and the different textures you can get from this much under-rated ingredient. In the West, tofu may not be everyone's cup of tea, but in this recipe I top slices of silken tofu with fresh crab, avocado and chervil, and a refreshing yuzu ponzu dressing to tempt you. I have yet to find a diner at my supper club who does not love it.

CRAB, AVOCADO & CHERVIL SALAD

ON SILKEN TOFU WITH A YUZU-PON DRESSING

SERVES 4

200g (7oz) silken tofu
25g (1oz) chervil
1 ripe avocado
juice of ½ lemon (optional)
¼ red onion
16 white seedless grapes
120g (4oz) freshly dressed
  crab meat
1–2 tsp toasted sesame
  seeds, to garnish

For the yuzu-pon dressing:
1 portion of Yuzu-pon sauce
  (see page 235)
5 tsp toasted sesame oil
⅛ onion, very finely chopped

To make this salad, you'll need two sushi mats to help extract water from the tofu before it is used. Place one sushi mat over a bowl, then put the tofu block in the middle of the mat. Now top the tofu with another sushi mat. Place a heavy (non-breakable) object, such as the lid of a pan, over the top mat to compress the tofu and aid the draining for at least an hour or two.

In the meantime, prepare the Yuzu-pon sauce following the instructions on page 235. To this, add the toasted sesame oil and the very finely chopped onion. Mix well and set aside.

Wash and spin-dry the chervil. Chop two-thirds of the leaves, keeping one-third whole for garnishing. Cover with clingfilm (plastic wrap) and refrigerate until needed, to stop them from wilting.

Peel and stone (pit) the avocado and cut the flesh into 1.5cm (½in) cubes; coat the avocado cubes in a little lemon juice, placing them with the stone (pit) to help prevent the flesh from going brown. Refrigerate until needed. Cut the red onion into thin 2cm (¾in)-long slices. Just before assembling and serving, halve the grapes lengthways.

Ensure that the meat from the dressed crab has no traces of shell; run your fingers gently through it. In a bowl, gently mix the crab, onions, chopped chervil, avocado, two-thirds of the grapes and the yuzu-pon dressing. Check and adjust the seasoning if necessary.

Cut the tofu into squares 1cm (½in) thick and about 5cm (2in) wide, interleaving the slices in a row over a rectangular plate. To serve, place the salad mixture over the tofu squares in a line, place the reserved chervil leaves over it and scatter the remaining grape halves around the plate, with a sprinkle of toasted sesame seeds to finish. Serve immediately.

Nikkei chef Diego Oka was born and raised in Lima, Peru, and his cooking draws influences ranging from his Japanese grandmother's cooking to his personal experiences and the food he discovered while living in Mexico and Colombia. He worked for many years with celebrated Peruvian chef Gastón Acurio, at his restaurant Astrid & Gaston in Lima. Now in Miami as the Executive Chef at the Mandarin Oriental's restaurant La Mar by Gastón Acurio, Oka focuses on Peruvian cooking such as *ceviche* and *causa*, as in this contributed recipe, in addition to other Nikkei dishes.

Causa is one of the most popular dishes in Peru – it combines flavoured potato mash with fish or seafood and is found throughout the country, from the simplest café to the most refined restaurant. Here, Diego Oka gives his Nikkei version of this classic dish, which can easily be made at home, and is a deliciously refreshing dish.

CAUSA NIKKEI

SERVES 4

For the rocoto potato dough:
450g (1lb) potatoes, for mashing
80ml (3fl oz/⅓ cup) canola oil (or vegetable oil)
a pinch of salt
juice of 2 limes
120g (4oz/½ cup) ready-made rocoto chilli paste (see Cook's note)

For the tuna tartare filling:
240g (8½oz) sushi-grade tuna
30g (1¼oz/1¾ tbsp) ready-made sweet chilli sauce
¼ tsp shichimi pepper
a dash of sesame oil
¼ tsp salt
30g (1¼oz/2 tbsp) Japanese mayonnaise
50ml (2fl oz/¼ cup) lime juice
30g (1¼oz) red onions, cut into 5mm (¼in) cubes

For the garnish:
½ avocado, roughly crushed with a fork
a generous sprinkle of nori strips (known as kizami nori)
2 tbsp Huancaína sauce (see page 235)
baby coriander (cilantro) cress
a sprinkle of shichimi pepper

Cook the potatoes in a pan of boiling water. Drain and put them through a potato ricer or pass through a fine sieve (strainer) into a clean bowl and while warm mix in the oil. When the mixture is cold, add the other ingredients and mix well until you have a lovely smooth mixture.

Cut the tuna into 1cm (½in) cubes and transfer the cubes to a medium bowl. Next, add the sweet chilli sauce, shichimi pepper, sesame oil, salt, Japanese mayonnaise, lime juice and cubed red onions, and mix well but gently until combined.

Make a cylinder with the rocoto potato dough and cut it into 12 bite-sized pieces. To serve, place three of these pieces on each plate, top with some crushed avocado followed by the tuna tartare filling. Garnish with the nori strips, the Huancaína sauce and a sprinkle of shichimi pepper and serve.

Cook's note The level of heat in ready-made rocoto chilli paste varies considerably from brand to brand – try using just 30g (1¼oz/⅛ cup) to start, then test for heat. Add more if desired in small increments; once it's added, you can't take it away! This paste is available in Peruvian food shops, see the list of suppliers on page 250.

In Japanese, tataki refers to the technique of searing the outside of the fish or meat, while keeping the flesh juicy and semi-raw. For this dish to work, you will need the best quality tuna you can get hold of, and time is also of the essence. The tuna blocks should be seared in a smoking hot pan for only a few seconds on each side, before being plunged into the chilled truffle ponzu dressing.

If you prefer a different dressing, the Sesame-ponzu sauce on page 234 also works brilliantly. This dish makes for a perfect summer lunch – slices of seared tuna in a truffle dressing served with a green salad and toasted hazelnuts. You could also serve this in a smaller quantity as an elegant little starter (appetizer).

TUNA TATAKI WITH TRUFFLE PONZU & TOASTED HAZELNUTS

SERVES 4

1 portion of Truffle ponzu
   sauce (see page 234)
½ banana shallot, finely
   chopped
1 tbsp sunflower oil
300g (10½oz) sushi-grade
   tuna
50g (1¾oz) mixed baby leaf
   salad, washed and spin dried
2 tbsp hazelnuts, toasted and
   roughly chopped
2 tbsp finely chopped chives,
   to garnish

Make a portion of Truffle ponzu sauce following the instructions on page 234. Then, add the finely chopped shallot and refrigerate for a couple of hours or overnight. This marinating time will soften the shallot and lightly sweeten the ponzu.

Forty-five minutes before you are ready to serve, heat the sunflower oil in a non-stick frying pan (or skillet) until very hot. While the pan is heating up, remove the truffle-onion ponzu sauce from the fridge and place it in a small but deep bowl – the bowl has to be big enough to take the whole piece of tuna; the tuna should ideally be submerged in the dressing.

Once the pan is hot and smoking, add the tuna piece to the pan and sear it for a few seconds on each side being careful not to overcook it at this stage. When the tuna is seared on all sides, quickly dunk it into the chilled truffle ponzu sauce, cover and let it marinate at room temperature for a minimum of 30 minutes and no longer than 2 hours. If the tuna is not completely submerged in the truffle ponzu sauce, you will need to turn it halfway through the marinating.

When you are ready to serve, remove the tuna from the sauce (reserving the sauce) and cut it into 5mm (¼in) slices. Share the tuna slices equally between four serving plates; I like to arrange the tuna slices in an open fan shape towards the side of each plate or in a line, as pictured. Spoon the truffle ponzu sauce and the chopped shallots over the tuna.

Now, in a bowl, dress the baby leaf salad with a couple of tablespoons of the truffle ponzu sauce and half of the chopped hazelnuts and combine well. Place a mound of salad at the end of the fan (or line) of slices of tuna on each plate, sprinkle the remaining hazelnuts and the chopped chives over the fish and salad and serve.

In Brazil, *churrasco* (the name for the national barbecue) and *picanha* are almost synonymous, but what is a Brazilian *picanha*? This beef cut comes from the cap lying above the top sirloin and rump (top round) areas; it is a triangular cut and just like our British rump (top round), it has a beautiful layer of fat. The *picanha*'s thick blanket of fat lends the meat flavour and succulence while protecting it from human error that may occur during grilling. And because it is little known in Europe, a *picanha* is still relatively cheap. In Brazil, *picanha* is grilled encased in a thick layer of rock salt and nothing else. In my childhood Nikkei home in São Paulo, we tended to use rather less rock salt, but basted the meat in a mixture of soy sauce, lime, garlic and olive oil instead during grilling.

I also give recipes for grilled corn-fed chicken in a Peruvian Nikkei *aji amarillo anticucho* sauce and another for lamb cutlets (chops) marinated in green miso – a spicy mixture including white miso, green jalapeño chillies, garlic, ginger and coriander (cilantro). Combined, these will give you a good spread for an authentic Nikkei barbecue experience.

BRAZILIAN *CHURRASCO* WITH NIKKEI FLAVOURS

1.3kg (2lb 14oz) Brazilian
  beef *picanha*, whole piece
150g (5½oz/1 cup) rock salt
  (do not use table, cooking
  salt or sea salt flakes)
sunflower oil, for brushing

For the soy & lime dressing:
120ml (4fl oz/½ cup) soy
  sauce
60ml (2½fl oz/¼ cup) extra
  virgin olive oil
60ml (2½fl oz/¼ cup) lime
  juice
6 garlic cloves, crushed
1 red chilli, deseeded and
  finely diced

For the Brazilian *farofa*:
4 tbsp extra virgin olive oil
4 garlic cloves, crushed
400g (14oz/3¼ cups)
  cassava flour for *farofa*
  (known as *farinha de
  mandioca*, available from
  Brazilian food shops)
Maldon sea salt flakes, to
  taste
freshly ground black pepper,
  to taste

PICANHA OF BEEF IN SOY & LIME WITH *FAROFA* (illustrated on the previous pages)

Score the fatty blanket on the *picanha* by making criss-cross cuts into the thick layer of fat covering one side. Cut the piece of *picanha* into four or five thick steaks of about 250–300g (9–10½oz) each and 2.5–5cm (1–2in) thick, keeping the fat covering the upper surface of each steak. Place the steaks on a tray and cover them thoroughly in the rock salt, this will help to seal in the juices of the meat. Table or cooking salts are too fine and more of them will be needed to do the same job resulting in a very salty barbecued *picanha*, so do stick to rock salt for this recipe. In addition, rock salt does not penetrate nearly as much as finer salts, giving a delicious and lightly salty crust to the meat.

Next, make the dressing by mixing together the soy sauce, olive oil, lime juice, crushed garlic cloves and red chilli. Half of this dressing will be used for basting the meat while on the grill and the other half will be used as a dipping sauce to serve with the slices of beef.

Get your barbecue hot and ready for the *picanha* and generously brush the grill plates with oil. Grill the steaks fat-side up for a few minutes until a little juice leaks out of the steaks. Turn the steaks onto their sides to grill for a few minutes more on each side. Using a brush, baste the meat with the reserved half of the soy and lime dressing every time you turn the steaks. Finally, grill fat-side down, moving the steaks away from the hottest part of the fire to avoid overcooking and to reduce the chance of the fire flaring up from the dripping fat. Grill to your desired doneness; anything from 15 to 25 minutes depending on the thickness of the steaks and how fierce the barbecue is. I like to use the 'finger poke method' to know when the meat is done – I like my *picanha* rather pink, so the meat should feel bouncy but firm (cooked for about 15–20 minutes in total). Alternatively, take one steak out of the grill and cut a small piece of it from its thickest part to check for doneness.

If you don't have a barbecue you can still cook the *picanha* under a hot grill (broiler) in your kitchen. Place the steaks over a rack within a roasting tin (pan); this is important as the *picanha*'s fat will drip into that and not your oven. Grill (broil) the steaks for 7 minutes flesh-side up, then turn them over and grill (broil) fat-side up, on a lower rack, for 8–12 minutes; baste the beef with the reserved dressing 2 minutes before the end of cooking. If using the kitchen grill (broiler) (rather than the barbecue), you can use a meat thermometer for doneness – the internal temperature of the meat should be 60°C (140°F) for rare, 63°C (145°f) for medium rare, 71°C (160°F) for medium and 77°C (170°F) for well-done. If you don't have a thermometer, just use the finger poke method described earlier (see above).

While the meat is cooking, prepare the Brazilian *farofa* – no Brazilian Nikkei barbecue would be complete without this classic accompaniment. To prepare it, heat the olive oil in a non-stick frying pan (or skillet) over a medium heat, add the crushed garlic and fry for a few seconds then add the cassava flour and fry, scraping the bottom of the pan and stirring the flour constantly for about 5–10 minutes or until it is lightly golden. Season to taste. Set aside until ready to eat – the *farofa* is served at room temperature.

Don't worry about serving the *picanha* all at once – in a Brazilian *churrasco*, the idea that 'that is my steak and this one is yours' is really non-existent. Let the *picanha* rest for

12 lamb cutlets (chops)
sunflower oil, for brushing

For the green miso marinade:
150g (5½oz/½ cup plus
  2 tbsp) white miso
30g (1¼oz/⅔ cup) coriander
  (cilantro) leaves, chopped
4 green jalapeño chillies,
  deseeded and chopped
4 garlic cloves, crushed
2.5cm (1in) piece of root
  ginger, peeled and grated
1 tsp Maldon sea salt flakes
1 tsp ground white pepper
4 tbsp rice vinegar
juice of 1 lime
3 tbsp olive oil
1 tbsp toasted sesame oil

a couple of minutes before serving. The meat should be sliced thinly and served in a sharing manner, accompanied by the obligatory *farofa* and, at our Nikkei home, also with the reserved soy and lime dressing. In this way, guests can choose the slices they want, some will prefer more rare, others more well-done so everyone is happy!

LAMB CUTLETS WITH A SPICY GREEN MISO (illustrated on the previous pages)

In a food processor, make the marinade by whizzing all the ingredients together until you get a smooth, green paste. Marinate the lamb in two-thirds of this green miso paste for at least 4 hours or overnight. Serve the remaining third as a sauce with the barbecued lamb.

Preheat the barbecue to hot and make sure the grill bars are clean and brushed with oil. Remove the lamb from the marinade, brushing off excess. Reserve the marinade for basting the lamb. Cook the cutlets (chops) on the grill for 3–4 minutes on each side, basting both sides of each cutlet (chop) with the marinade before and after flipping them over. Remove from the grill and let the lamb rest in a warm place for 5 minutes.

If you prefer, you can cook the lamb cutlets (chops) in your kitchen under a grill (broiler) preheated to high, and follow the instructions and timings above as in the barbecue method. You can check doneness by cutting a small piece from one of the cutlets (chops). Rest the lamb for 5 minutes and serve with the reserved marinade as a sauce alongside.

8 large corn-fed chicken
  thighs (skin on and bone-in),
  ask your butcher to cut each
  thigh in half so that you have
  16 smaller pieces (about
  1.2kg (2½lb) in total)
1½ portions of *Anticucho*
  marinade for chicken (see
  page 241)
sunflower oil, for brushing

ANTICUCHO OF CHICKEN IN *AJI AMARILLO* (illustrated on the previous pages)

Marinate the chicken thighs in half of the marinade for at least 8 hours or overnight, if possible. Serve the other half of the marinade as a sauce alongside the cooked meat.

To cook on the barbecue, preheat the grill and generously brush the grill plates with oil. Remove the chicken from its marinade, brushing off any excess. Reserve the marinade for basting the chicken while grilling. Reduce the heat to medium and place the chicken pieces on the grill, skin-side up and cook for 12 minutes. Before turning the chicken, baste them with some of the reserved marinade. Flip the thigh pieces over and baste the other side with the remaining marinade, then cook for another 12 minutes. Check for doneness by piercing the thicker part of the chicken, if the juices run clear the chicken is done; if there's any blood in the juice, then cook a little longer and retest.

If you prefer to cook the chicken under a hot grill (broiler) in your kitchen, place them skin-side down over a rack in a roasting tin (pan). Grill (broil) for 8 minutes and baste the chicken with the reserved marinade before turning them over. Flip the chicken pieces, baste their other side with the remaining marinade and grill (broil) for another 7 minutes or until the skin is lightly charred and crispy and the meat is cooked. Check this by piercing the thickest part of the chicken and seeing whether the juices that run from it are clear; or use a thermometer, the internal temperature of the chicken should read 75°C (167°F). However you've cooked the chicken, let it rest for 5 minutes before serving with the sauce.

SERVES 6

1.5 litres (2 pints 10fl oz/6⅓
  cups) dashi (see page 230;
  or use 1 tbsp instant dashi
  powder and 1.5 litres
  (2 pints 10fl oz/6⅓ cups)
  boiling water if time is tight)
150ml (5fl oz/⅔ cup) sake
200ml (7fl oz/1 cup) soy
  sauce
150ml (5fl oz/⅔ cup) mirin
75g (2¾oz/¼ cup plus
  2 tbsp) brown sugar
5 garlic cloves, lightly crushed
1 star anise
2 red chillies, each cut into
  4 segments
200g (7oz) daikon radish,
  peeled and cut into 2cm
  (¾in) irregular chunks
50g (1¾oz/¼ cup) short-
  grain white rice
sunflower oil
1kg (2¼lb) boneless beef
  short ribs, cut into 6 pieces
150g (5½oz) carrots, peeled
  and cut into 2cm (¾in)
  irregular chunks
1 medium onion (about 150g
  (5½oz)), cut into quarters
150g (5½oz) ready-roasted
  and peeled chestnuts (see
  Cook's note, page 110)
50g (1¾oz) mangetout
  (snow peas)
1 tbsp cornflour (cornstarch)

Make the dashi by following the recipe instructions on page 230 or opt for the instant version if pushed for time. Then get on with the cooking broth. In a large bowl, mix together the dashi stock, sake, soy sauce, mirin, brown sugar, garlic cloves, star anise and chillies. Stir well until the sugar has dissolved and set aside.

In a small pan, cover the daikon and the rice with water and bring to the boil. Simmer for 5 minutes. Drain and discard the rice. This process softens the daikon and eliminates its strong daikon odour.

In a pressure cooker or heavy ovenproof casserole (Dutch oven) (that has a lid), add a little sunflower oil and brown the pieces of short ribs on all sides, for about 5 minutes; do not overcrowd the pan or the beef will stew rather than brown, you may need to do this in batches. Then, remove the beef and discard any excess oil from the pan.

Return the browned pieces of beef to the pressure cooker or casserole (Dutch oven), add the carrots, daikon, onion and roasted chestnuts. Cover with the cooking broth, reserving any leftover. Close the pressure cooker and cook for 25 minutes once high pressure is reached. Alternatively, preheat the oven to 170°C/325°F/gas mark 3, put the lid on the casserole (Dutch oven) and bring to the boil on the hob (stove). Once the liquid has boiled, transfer the casserole (Dutch oven) to the oven and cook for 2–2½ hours; the meat needs to be supremely tender. Do not be tempted to braise for much longer as the meat can overcook and become tough and fibrous.

Once the pressure-cooking time is up, turn off the heat and let the pressure die down naturally as the pan cools; this will take about 30–60 minutes and is known as the natural pressure release. If you are pressed for time, release the pressure by lifting the pressure valve, this will speed up the process but it is not recommended as the sudden change in pressure and temperature can make the beef fibres contract, making the ribs tougher.

Cook the mangetout (snow peas) in salted boiling water for 30 seconds, plunge them into chilled water until tender, drain and pat dry.

After all the pressure has been released from the pressure cooker, open it, and carefully skim off the layer of melted fat on the surface of the broth. Sieve (strain) two-thirds of the broth into a clean pan, keeping the meat warm in the remaining juice. Reduce the broth by half to get a lovely concentrated flavour; if it's over-reduced or salty, just add a little water. Bring the reduced broth to the boil and meanwhile dissolve the cornflour (cornstarch) in a little cold water. Add the cornflour (cornstarch) mixture little by little until it thickens; not all of the cornflour (cornstarch) mix may be needed. Check for seasoning and adjust.

Place a piece of short rib in the centre of a serving bowl, a few pieces of daikon, carrots, onions and chestnuts around it as well as some mangetout (snow peas) pieces. Pour the thickened sauce over the meat and vegetables and serve immediately.

I love using beef short ribs for this Nikkei dish. The meat should be meltingly tender, in a richly flavoured sauce, served with root vegetables, green mangetout (snow peas) and chestnuts. You can make this ahead of time; in fact, it tastes even better a day or two after it's made. A great warming dish for the colder months, all you need is a bowl of white rice to go with it!

BRAISED BEEF SHORT RIBS
IN SAKE, SOY SAUCE & BROWN SUGAR

Few dishes symbolise the marriage of Japanese and South American flavours better than this mouth-watering steak! Beef eating is a relatively recent custom in Japan, where it was prohibited until the end of the 19th century. In South America, on the contrary, particularly in places such as Brazil and Argentina, meaty barbecues locally known as *churrascos* are deeply ingrained in the national psyches.

There is so much more to miso than the ubiquitous miso soup – this wondrous ingredient is umami-laden and so incredibly versatile. In the recipe below, I use it alongside the smokiness of *aji panca*, a popular Peruvian chilli, to marinate some top-quality rib-eye beef. I suggest marinating the steaks overnight, or if time allows for up to 48 hours, to get the most out of this delicious marinade. A medley of crunchy green vegetables served with a sweet nutty dressing (see page 183) is a great accompaniment to these pan-fried steaks and would work well with any cooked on the barbecue, too.

PAN-FRIED RIB-EYE STEAK MARINATED IN MISO & *AJI PANCA*

SERVES 4

2 x 400g (14oz) rib-eye steaks
2 tbsp vegetable oil, for shallow-frying

For the miso marinade:
50g (1¾oz/¼ cup) red miso
1 tbsp ready-made *aji panca* paste (available from Peruvian food shops)
1 tbsp sake
2 tbsp mirin
1 tbsp sugar

For the miso & *aji panca* cream:
100g (3½oz/½ cup) brown miso
250ml (8½fl oz/1 cup) double (heavy) cream
60ml (2½fl oz/¼ cup) mirin
30ml (1fl oz/2 tbsp) water
½ tsp dashi powder
10g (¼oz/2 tsp) ready-made *aji panca* paste
10g (¼oz/2 tsp) preserved crispy chilli sauce
30ml (1fl oz/2 tbsp) rice vinegar
1 tbsp cornflour (cornstarch)

First, make the marinade. Mix together all the ingredients in a pan and cook, stirring with a spatula to avoid it burning at the bottom of the pan for 10–15 minutes, to burn off the alcohol and concentrate the marinade flavours. Set aside to let it cool. Pop the steaks and the cooled marinade into a big zip-lock bag and refrigerate overnight or for up to 48 hours.

Next, make the miso and *aji panca* cream. Mix the miso, double (heavy) cream, mirin, water, dashi powder, *aji panca* paste and preserved crispy chilli sauce in a pan over a medium heat, and stir well with a whisk until the miso has dissolved and all the elements are well combined and warmed through. Remove from the heat, let it cool and then add the rice vinegar. Check for seasoning and adjust if required. Refrigerate until needed.

Remove the rib-eye steaks from the fridge 2 hours before cooking.

Bring the miso and *aji panca* cream to the boil, dissolve the cornflour (cornstarch) in a little water and add it little by little, stirring vigorously with a whisk, until the sauce is thickened to the consistency of double (heavy) cream; ensure there are no lumps. Keep it warm.

Before cooking the steaks, heat a non-stick frying pan (or skillet) with the oil until very hot. Wipe off any excess marinade from the steaks and fry the steaks for about 2 minutes on each side for medium-rare. Transfer to a chopping (cutting) board and let them rest for 1 minute.

To serve, cut five slices of steak per person and place them over a bed of crunchy green vegetables, overlapping them in a criss-cross pattern, pour 2 tablespoons of the miso and *aji panca* cream over the meat and serve immediately.

Known in Japanese as buta no kakuni, this dish is a Chinese import that the Japanese have embraced wholeheartedly. I use this meltingly tender pork belly in My Nikkei hakata buns (see recipe on page 44). Cooking in brown rice softens the meat beyond recognition, while keeping it succulent. Start preparing at least a day before serving or use a pressure cooker.

SUPER-SLOW-BRAISED PORK BELLY
COOKED IN BROWN RICE & CARAMELISED IN SOY SAUCE, SAKE & SUGAR

SERVES 4

1 tbsp sunflower oil
900g (2lb) boneless pork
  belly, in 1 piece
250g (9oz/1¼ cups) brown
  rice
750ml (1 pint 6fl oz/3 cups)
  dashi (see page 230)
120ml (4fl oz/½ cup) sake
60ml (2½fl oz/¼ cup) mirin
80g (2¾oz/½ cup) soft dark
  brown sugar
120ml (4fl oz/½ cup) soy
  sauce
1–2 star anise
100g (3½oz) root ginger (80g
  (2¾oz), peeled and cut into
  thin slices, plus 20g (¾oz)
  cut into fine julienne, to
  garnish)
1 tbsp cornflour (cornstarch)
100ml (3½fl oz/½ cup) cold
  water
1 tbsp Japanese mustard,
  to garnish

Preheat the oven to 120°C/250°F/gas mark ½. Meanwhile, heat the oil in a heavy casserole (Dutch oven) (that has a lid) just big enough to hold the pork over a medium–high heat. Add the pork belly, skin side down, and sear until golden brown, about 5 minutes. Turn over and brown on the other side, about 5 minutes more. Transfer to a plate so that you can pour off the fat from the casserole (Dutch oven) and discard.

Return the pork to the casserole (Dutch oven) and sprinkle the rice over the meat. Pour in enough cold water to cover by 2.5cm (1in) and bring to a simmer over a high heat. Pop the lid on and transfer to the preheated oven. Let the pork braise gently until it is tender when pierced with a knife, about 6–8 hours. Once done, remove from the oven, uncover and let the pork cool for a couple of hours in its rice crust. Then, carefully remove the pork, keeping it in one piece, and discard the rice and any cooking liquid. Cover in clingfilm (plastic wrap) and refrigerate the pork belly for at least 8 hours and for up to 2 days.

When you're ready to cook the dish, take the pork out of the fridge and cut it crosswise into four pieces about 6cm (2½in) wide. In a clean, heavy pan, add the dashi, sake, mirin, sugar, soy sauce, star anise and ginger slices and stir over a high heat until all the ingredients are mixed. Add the pork to the pan and return to the boil. Then, reduce to a simmer and cook, turning occasionally for 1–2 hours or until the pork is very tender.

Carefully strain the cooking liquid into a pan, reduce over a high heat until lightly syrupy and concentrated. Be careful not to over-reduce the sauce as it will become too salty; if you need some thickening help, dissolve the cornflour (cornstarch) in the cold water and whisk in, little by little, until the sauce thickens to a coating consistency. Check for seasoning and adjust.

To serve, top each piece of pork with about 2 tablespoons of the reduced sauce, and garnish with the julienned ginger and a dollop of Japanese mustard.

Cook's note Pressure cooking is a quicker method for this dish, although the pork will not be quite as tender as the traditional method. Pressure cooker method: Cover the pork in water and 100g (3½oz/½ cup) of brown rice (note: much less rice here) and cook it for 1 hour in the pressure cooker. Once the time is up, turn off the heat and let the pressure die down naturally as the pan cools; this will take 30–60 minutes. Refrigerate the pork as above then return the pork with the cooking broth ingredients to the pressure cooker and cook for 1 hour, letting the pressure be released naturally once again. Serve as above.

Iberian pigs are among the most flavoursome in the world; the most prized are fed exclusively on acorns, giving a deliciously marbled meat. For this dish, if you cannot get hold of Iberian (see the list of suppliers on page 250), use top-quality local pork cheeks. The daikon fondant should be very soft and buttery and combined with the creamy foie gras, this dish is a fitting one for a special occasion.

IBERIAN PORK CHEEKS WITH DAIKON & FOIE GRAS

SERVES 4

For the daikon:
500ml (18fl oz/2 cups) dashi (see page 230)
500g (1lb 2oz) daikon
1.5 litres (2 pints 10fl oz/ 6⅓ cups) water
50g (1¾oz/¼ cup) short-grain white rice
125g (4¼oz/½ cup) unsalted butter, melted
50ml (2fl oz/¼ cup) soy sauce
50ml (2fl oz/¼ cup) mirin
1 tbsp caster (superfine) sugar

For the Iberian pork cheeks:
sunflower oil, for frying
1kg (2¼lb) Iberian pork cheeks, cut into 8 pieces
700ml (1¼ pints/3 cups) dashi (see page 230)
150ml (5fl oz/⅔ cup) sake
150ml (5fl oz/⅔ cup) soy sauce
150ml (5fl oz/⅔ cup) mirin
50g (1¾oz/¼ cup) brown sugar
2.5cm (1in) piece of root ginger, washed and sliced
1 star anise
1–2 tbsp cornflour (cornstarch)

For serving:
6 mangetout (snow peas)
100g (3½oz) lobe of foie gras liver, cut into 4 slices

Make 1.2 litres (2 pints/5 cups) of dashi following the recipe on page 230; this stock is used both for the cooking broth for the pork and for cooking the daikon.

In a pressure cooker or heavy ovenproof casserole (Dutch oven) (that has a lid), add a little sunflower oil, and brown the pieces of pork cheeks on all sides, for 2–3 minutes. Remove the pork, letting it drain in a colander and discard the excess oil from the pan.

Next, make the cooking broth for the pork. In a bowl, mix the dashi, sake, soy sauce, mirin, sugar, ginger slices and star anise together until well combined.

Return the pieces of pork to the pressure cooker or casserole (Dutch oven), add the cooking broth, close the pan and cook for 60 minutes. If you don't have a pressure cooker, you can cook it in the oven at 150°C/300°F/gas mark 2 in a lidded casserole (Dutch oven) for 3 hours.

Meanwhile, peel the daikon, cut it into 4cm (1½in)-high pieces, bevel all the edges (using a potato peeler) and, using a toothpick, make a 1cm (½in) incision in the middle of each piece on both sides. Bring the measured water and rice to the boil, add the daikon pieces and simmer for 5 minutes. Then, remove the daikon pieces and set aside, and discard the rice mixture; this process helps to remove the odour and soften the daikon.

Once the pressure-cooking time is up, turn off the heat and let the pressure die down naturally as the pan cools; this will take about 30–60 minutes and is known as the natural pressure release. Ensure all pressure has been released before opening the pressure cooker. Whether using the pressure cooker or pan and oven method, carefully transfer the cooked pork and its cooking juices to a lidded container, let it cool down naturally and refrigerate until needed; the pork can be cooked a couple of days before it is served.

Next, make the cooking broth for the daikon. In a pan, mix the dashi, the melted butter, soy sauce, mirin and sugar until well combined and add to the pressure cooker along with the daikon pieces. Cook for 30 minutes or until very soft. If you do not have a pressure cooker, cook the daikon in a heavy ovenproof casserole (Dutch oven) for about 1½ hours in the oven, preheated to 200°C/400°F/gas mark 6, or until very soft. Then, transfer the cooked daikon and cooking broth to a pan and keep warm.

Scrape off the layer of fat from the top of the cooking broth containing the pork pieces.

Transfer the pork cheeks and the broth to a pan and reheat. Once hot, strain off the liquid into a clean pan and reduce over a high heat until lightly syrupy and concentrated. If not enough cooking broth is left, add some cooking broth from the daikon. Do be careful not to over-reduce the sauce as it will become too salty; if you need some thickening help, dissolve the cornflour (cornstarch) in a little cold water and whisk in, little by little, until the sauce thickens to a coating consistency. Check for seasoning and adjust.

Meanwhile, pop the mangetout (snow peas) in boiling water for 30 seconds, drain and plunge them into very cold water. Cut each mangetout (snow pea) in half diagonally.

Place the slices of foie gras in a frying pan (or skillet) and blow-torch them on both sides until golden brown and drain on kitchen paper (paper towels). If you do not have a blow-torch, fry the slices in a very hot, non-stick frying pan (or skillet) for 30 seconds on each side. Drain on kitchen paper (paper towels).

In a serving bowl, place one or two pieces of daikon, top with a couple of pork cheek slices then pour 2–3 tablespoons of the sauce over the pork. Place a slice of foie gras on top of the pork cheek. Place three mangetout (snow peas) halves beside the daikon, pork and foie gras tower and serve immediately.

A summertime favourite in Japan, this delicious salad is topped with thin slices of fried pork belly marinated in a rich mixture of ginger and soy, known in Japanese as buta no shoga yaki. It is an all-in-one meal – and with its zingy and intense ginger flavours, it's a very refreshing one, too.

PAN-FRIED PORK BELLY & GINGER WITH GREEN LEAVES & AVOCADO SALAD IN A WASABI VINAIGRETTE

A NIKKEI BUTA NO SHOGA YAKI SALAD

SERVES 4

400g (14oz) pork belly, thinly sliced
1–2 tbsp sunflower oil
1 large onion, thinly sliced
1 garlic clove, crushed
toasted white sesame seeds, to garnish

For the pork marinade:
4 tbsp soy sauce
2 tbsp mirin
1 tbsp grated ginger
freshly ground black pepper

For the wasabi vinaigrette:
3 tbsp soy sauce
2 tbsp rice vinegar
1 tbsp grated ginger
2 tsp sugar
1 tbsp wasabi paste
2 tbsp sunflower oil
1 tsp sesame oil

For the salad:
100g (3½oz) iceberg lettuce leaves
25g (1oz) baby rocket (arugula) leaves
25g (1oz) spring onions (scallions)
15g (½oz/⅓ cup) coriander (cilantro)
50g (1¾oz) sugar snaps
½ avocado
juice of ¼ lemon

Start by preparing the marinade. Mix all of the ingredients in a bowl, then add the pork belly and allow to marinate for about 10–15 minutes. Cover and set aside.

Now onto the wasabi vinaigrette. Add the soy sauce, rice vinegar, grated ginger, sugar and wasabi paste to a jar, close it and shake to mix. Ensure all the sugar and wasabi have dissolved in the liquid, then add the sunflower and sesame oils, mix vigorously again. Check for seasoning and adjust if required.

To prepare the salad ingredients, wash and spin-dry all the salad leaves separately (iceberg lettuce, rocket (arugula), spring onions (scallions) and coriander (cilantro)), keep them covered in a bowl in the fridge (do not wash the leaves too far ahead – maximum 1 hour or so before serving so that they do not go soggy). Blanch the sugar snaps in boiling water for 2 minutes, refresh in cold water, pat dry and cut into 1cm (½in) slices. Peel the avocado and cut it into 1cm (½in) cubes, place them in a container with the avocado stone (pit) and a good coating of lemon juice to stop the flesh from going brown. Roughly chop the iceberg lettuce leaves and slice the spring onions (scallions).

Before serving, mix all the salad leaves (greens) together in a large bowl. Arrange the salad leaves (greens) onto four rectangular plates, add a few cubes of avocado and sugar snaps around and over the leaves, then add 1–2 teaspoons of wasabi vinaigrette on each plate.

Heat a non-stick frying pan (or skillet) with the sunflower oil, add the thinly sliced onion and fry until translucent, then add the crushed garlic and fry for another minute. Add the pork belly slices and its marinade to the pan, making sure the slices do not curl up, fry on each side for 2–3 minutes until cooked through; do not overcook.

To serve, divide the fried pork belly and onion slices between the plates over the salad, add another 1 or 2 teaspoons of wasabi vinaigrette over the pork, sprinkle with toasted white sesame seeds and serve immediately.

When I started to write this cookbook, one of the first recipes that came to mind was my brother's barbecued pork ribs, and this book would not be complete without it. A professional photographer by day and an avid foodie by night, my brother Ricardo Hara is also the family's official barbecue chef in São Paulo. He loves to invite his mates around for a few beers and a Nikkei *churrasco*, and I have been lucky enough to attend his barbecues on many occasions when visiting Brazil.

For best results, marinate the pork for a day or two ahead and barbecue the ribs slowly to ensure that they are thoroughly cooked but not burnt on the outside. The miso will partially cure the meat, rendering it flavoursome and tender, while the sugar will give a glossy caramel to the finished ribs. I can tell you they're finger-licking good!

These ribs can be part of a larger barbecue spread – see Brazilian *churrasco* with Nikkei flavours on page 154, and My Nikkei piri-piri poussin on page 171.

RICARDO'S BBQ PORK RIBS IN A BROWN MISO & LIME MARINADE

SERVES 4

2kg (4½lb) meaty pork ribs,
  cut into individual ribs
2 limes, cut into wedges,
  to serve

For the miso marinade:
500g (1lb 2oz/2 cups) brown
  miso
50g (1¾oz/¼ cup) sugar
2 tbsp toasted sesame oil
juice of 5 limes
finely grated zest of 2 limes

Make the marinade. In a large bowl, mix the brown miso with the sugar, sesame oil, juice and zest of limes until well combined. Add the pork ribs to the bowl and, using your hands, coat each rib liberally with the marinade. Cover and refrigerate for a minimum of 2 hours and up to 48 hours.

The ribs can be barbecued or cooked under a hot grill (broiler). On the barbecue, ensure the coals are very hot. Place the ribs on the barbecue (bone side down) and grill for 10–15 minutes, flipping the ribs every 2 minutes or so and brushing with more marinade after each turn. The ribs should be cooked through and lightly charred from the caramelisation of the miso and sugar, with the bones sticking out. Check for doneness by making a small incision in one of the ribs: the meat should be white in colour and juicy with no pink. Let the ribs rest for 2 minutes before serving with a few lime wedges.

If you prefer to cook using a hot grill (broiler), start cooking with the bone side up for 6 minutes; the bone will protect the meat from burning. Turn the ribs over and cook for a further 6 minutes. Repeat this a couple of times at 4-minute intervals so that the total cooking time is about 20 minutes (this will depend on the thickness of the pork rib, how far it is from the grill (broiler) and how hot your grill (broiler) is). Check for doneness as suggested above; once ready, let the ribs rest for 2 minutes and then serve with a few lime wedges.

Piri-Piri is a classic Portuguese marinade and sauce mostly used for poultry. It makes use of hot chillies, garlic and vinegar (real trademarks of Portuguese cooking) to create a lip-smacking sauce for the meat. In this Nikkei version, my piri-piri marinade blends Peruvian rocoto chillies with some Japanese flavours.

I like marinating the poussin overnight and if I am making this at the weekend and the weather is fine, I cook it on the barbecue rather than under the grill (broiler). It makes a great addition to any barbecue, together with Ricardo's BBQ Pork Ribs on page 168 and the Brazilian *churrasco* with Nikkei flavours on page 154. Half the marinade, not used for marinating or basting the poussins, should be combined with coconut milk to make a delicious sauce for serving with the finished dish.

MY NIKKEI PIRI-PIRI POUSSIN

SERVES 4

4 small poussins (or 8 small chicken thighs, skin on, bone in)
Maldon sea salt flakes
1 tbsp sugar
40ml (1½fl oz/3 tbsp) coconut cream
1 tbsp coriander (cilantro) cress
4 lemon wedges

For the Nikkei piri-piri marinade:

6 tbsp ready-made *aji rocoto* paste
6 tbsp rice vinegar
6 tbsp soy sauce
8 tbsp extra virgin olive oil
120g (4oz/¾ cup) red onion, very finely chopped
6 garlic cloves, crushed
2 tsp ground cumin
1 tsp freshly ground black pepper
2 tsp Maldon sea salt flakes
2 tsp caster (superfine) sugar

First, prepare the Nikkei piri-piri marinade by mixing all the ingredients together in a bowl until well combined. Check for seasoning and add more *aji rocoto* paste or salt, if desired. Half of this marinade will be used for the piri-piri and coconut cream sauce while the other half will be used to marinate the poussins.

Coat the poussin (or chicken thighs, if using) thoroughly in half of the Nikkei piri-piri marinade, leaving them to marinate for at least 6 hours or overnight in the fridge.

Preheat the oven to 200°C/400°F/gas mark 6 and line a roasting tray with foil.

Remove the excess marinade from the poussin but reserve for basting it during its cooking. Place the pieces on the tray, skin side up, and coat them liberally with Maldon sea salt flakes. Cook in the preheated oven for about 20 minutes basting the poussin or chicken thighs every 5 minutes or so with the remaining marinade. Check the doneness of the poussin or chicken thighs by piercing a knife in the thickest part of the thigh, the juices should run golden and clear. If you have a meat thermometer, the internal temperature should be between 75°C and 80°C (167°F and 176°F). When ready, place the poussin or chicken thighs under a very hot grill (broiler) for 5 minutes to crisp up the skin. Remove the tray from the grill (broiler) and let the meat rest for a couple of minutes.

Meanwhile, quickly bring the reserved half marinade to the boil with the sugar then add the coconut cream and heat it through, mixing well. Remove from the heat.

Plate the poussin or chicken thighs on serving plates, drizzle some of the piri-piri and coconut cream sauce over them and around the plate, finishing with a scattering of coriander (cilantro) cress. Serve with the lemon wedges.

Probably the best known Nikkei restaurants outside of Brazil and Peru, SUSHISAMBA has been instrumental in bringing top-quality Nikkei cooking to a wider audience in the US and in Europe. Pedro Duarte was born in the Peruvian Andes and has a strong culinary background, helping both his parents to run their family restaurant. He moved to the US in 2001 and is now Executive Chef for SUSHISAMBA New York; here he presents one of his signature Nikkei recipes.

DUCK BREAST ROBATA WITH PICKLED PEARL ONIONS & SANSHO PEPPER VINAIGRETTE

SERVES 4

4 duck breasts (about 140g (5oz) each in weight)
4 lime wedges, to garnish
15g (½oz) micro shiso herb, to garnish

For the duck marinade:
400ml (13½fl oz/1¾ cups) soy sauce
400ml (13½fl oz/1¾ cups) mirin
1 garlic clove, finely chopped
13g (⅓oz/1 tbsp) finely chopped ginger

For the sansho pepper vinaigrette:
35ml (1¼fl oz/2 tbsp) soy sauce
12ml (2½ tsp) sake
16g (½oz/⅛ cup) shallots, very finely chopped
12ml (2½ tsp) yuzu juice, salted
12ml (2½ tsp) mirin
¼ tsp sesame oil
16g (½oz) pickled sansho pepper

For the pickled pearl onions:
48ml (2fl oz/¼ cup) sherry vinegar
48ml (2fl oz/¼ cup) red wine vinegar
3g (⅛oz/1 tsp) pink peppercorns
10g (¼oz/2 tsp) sugar
4 pearl onions (50g (1¾oz total weight)

First, make the marinade for the duck breasts. In a stainless-steel mixing bowl, combine the soy sauce, mirin, garlic and ginger.

Place the duck breasts in a shallow bowl that fits them all in one layer. Pour over the marinade and let the duck marinate for at least 2 and up to 8 hours.

Next, make the vinaigrette by combining the soy sauce, sake, shallots, yuzu juice and mirin in a stainless-steel bowl. Whisk the sesame oil into this mixture and, lastly, add the pickled sansho pepper. Transfer to an airtight container and keep in the fridge until needed.

Now, for the pickled pearl onions. In a pan, combine the vinegars, peppercorns and sugar and bring to the boil. Once it's reached boiling point, remove from the heat. Put the pearl onions in a bowl and cover with the hot vinegar mixture. Let the onions cool in this liquid and set aside.

Remove the duck breasts from the marinade and grill (broil) them on each side as you like them; I like to keep them quite pink. For medium rare, cook for about 4 minutes each side over a medium heat; for medium, cook for about 6 minutes each side over a medium heat; for medium/well done, cook for about 7 minutes on each side; for well done, cook for about 8 minutes on each side.

Transfer the duck breasts to a warmed plate to rest for 5 minutes. Thinly slice the breasts, keeping the slices together so that the breast still appears as a whole.

To serve, set a bamboo leaf on a plate and arrange the duck breast along the leaf, together with the lime wedges and pickled pearl onion. Spoon the sansho pepper vinaigrette over the duck breast and garnish with micro shiso.

One of the simplest meat recipes in this book, this is a delicate but flavoursome dish with three main components – chicken, dashi stock and kabocha pumpkin. For this dish to work, all three should be fresh and of the highest quality. If the budget stretches, I recommend corn-fed, preferably free-range chicken, and the dashi should be primary, crystal-clear and freshly made (see primary dashi recipe on page 230). This is an elegant chicken dish that is sure to impress.

CHICKEN & KABOCHA PUMPKIN STEW WITH CARAMELISED KONBU

SERVES 4

1 litre (1¾ pints/4 cups) Primary dashi (see page 230)
½ small kabocha pumpkin
100ml (3½fl oz/½ cup) mirin
1½ tbsp caster (superfine) sugar
5cm (2in) piece of konbu
5 tbsp light soy sauce
4 corn-fed chicken thighs, skin on, bone in
1 tsp sansho pepper, to garnish
1 tsp toasted white sesame seeds, to garnish
2 tbsp Caramelised konbu seaweed (see page 240), to garnish

Prepare the Primary dashi by following the recipe on page 230; this dish is all about the quality of the dashi and the chicken.

Start by preparing the kabocha pumpkin. First, cut the kabocha in half and remove the seeds. Then cut each half in half again: the quarters will have a thicker top part and a thinner bottom part. Then cut each quarter in half again so that you have eight pieces of roughly the same weight and size, for even cooking. Bevel the edges of each slice using a potato peeler (I do this to stop the sharp edges breaking off into the dashi and making it cloudy, which would also spoil the presentation). Finally, tap the heel of the knife blade into the kabocha's skin to cut small nicks into it, so when the kabocha cooks and the flesh expands, the harder skin will be able to expand with it and the slice will not crumble.

Put the kabocha in a medium pan, skin side down. Add the dashi, mirin, sugar and konbu piece. Bring to the boil over a medium heat. When the liquid boils, reduce the heat so the kabocha gently simmers. Cook until the kabocha is just cooked through but firm, about 7 minutes; test for doneness by sticking a toothpick through it. Do not overcook at this stage, as the kabocha will be cooked again. When the kabocha is ready, turn off the heat and add the soy sauce. Let the kabocha steep in its cooking liquor for at least 1 hour (more is fine, even a few hours but don't refrigerate). Now, carefully remove the kabocha from its liquor, setting it aside but reserving the liquid in the pan.

Next, preheat a heavy griddle pan over a high heat. When the pan is very hot, add the chicken, skin side down, and brown for a minute or so. Turn the pieces of chicken over and brown the other side for 2 minutes. Transfer the chicken to the pan of cooking liquor and bring it to the boil. Reduce the heat, so the liquid simmers gently, and continue to cook for 12 minutes. When the chicken is done, remove it from the pan and keep it warm.

Now, return the kabocha pumpkin pieces to the cooking liquid, bring to the boil then turn the heat down and simmer gently for a couple of minutes to heat the pumpkin through.

To plate, place one chicken thigh in a shallow serving bowl followed by two pieces of kabocha pumpkin alongside, then add a ladleful of the cooking broth. Finish off with a sprinkle of sansho pepper, the toasted sesame seeds and a few strands of caramelised konbu over the chicken. Serve immediately.

VEGETABLES, SALADS & TOFU

Persimmon is a native fruit of Japan and was introduced by Nikkei farmers to Brazil, where it is known by its Japanese name kaki. We love persimmon in Brazil, and it grows abundantly to give very sweet fruit. I remember my father used to cure the fruit in vats of sake for the grown-ups to enjoy as an after-dinner treat. I used to look on with envy!

This salad combines a selection of raw root vegetables and persimmon to create a multicoloured and textured dish that will taste delicious and look amazing. If you can't find round white radish, it can be substituted by daikon (mooli).

All elements of this salad can be prepared in advance, though the vegetables should be kept separate from each other and put together just before serving. The wasabi lemon cream should be zingy and have a kick of heat.

PERSIMMON, CANDY BEETROOT & WHITE RADISH SALAD
WITH WASABI LEMON CREAM

SERVES 4

½ portion of Wasabi lemon cream (see page 237)
150g (5½oz) persimmon
100g (3½oz) candy beetroot (beet)
100g (3½oz) round white radish
a sprinkle of Maldon sea salt flakes
1 tbsp finely chopped chives
4 tbsp micro herbs (optional)
1 tsp toasted black sesame seeds

Make ½ a portion of Wasabi lemon cream following the instructions on page 237.

Peel and wash the persimmon, candy beetroot (beet) and white radish; take quite a bit of peel off the white radish as the outer part of the flesh can be a tad tough and bitter. Cut all of the vegetables into 1cm (½in) cubes.

In a bowl, mix together the cubed vegetables and 3 tablespoons of wasabi lemon cream, followed by a sprinkle of Maldon sea salt and the chopped chives. Check for seasoning.

Place the vegetable salad in four serving bowls topped with a small bunch of micro herbs (if using) and a sprinkle of toasted black sesame seeds. Serve straightaway.

There is so much more to Japanese miso paste than its ubiquitous soup. Miso is a umami-laden but relatively undiscovered ingredient in the UK; it is made from fermented soya beans, is easy to use and adds tons of flavour to just about anything you cook – it's great as a marinade for grilled fish or meat; mix it with some sugar and lime to create a scrumptious rub for BBQ pork ribs (see page 168). Or why not spread it thinly over fried aubergine (eggplant), top with mozzarella cheese and finish off under a hot grill (broiler) as in this recipe?

GRILLED AUBERGINES WITH MISO DENGAKU & MOZZARELLA

SERVES 4

2 medium aubergines
   (eggplants)
4 tbsp vegetable oil
4 tbsp sesame oil
100g (3½oz/1 cup) ready-
   grated mozzarella cheese
1 tsp toasted white sesame
   seeds, to garnish

For the dengaku miso paste:
4 tbsp brown miso paste
4 tbsp mirin
2 tbsp water
4 tsp sugar

First, prepare the dengaku miso paste by mixing all the ingredients in a pan, warm it through until the sugar has dissolved and all the ingredients are well combined. Then set aside. This sauce can be made days in advance and keeps for weeks in an airtight jar in the fridge.

Wash the aubergines (eggplants) and pat them dry. Cut them lengthways, without removing the stems, into equal halves. Using a sharp knife, make criss-cross incisions into the flesh of each half without tearing through the skin.

Preheat the oven to 180°C/350°F/gas mark 4 and preheat the grill (broiler) to hot.

Meanwhile, in a large frying pan (or skillet) (with a lid), heat the oils until smoking hot. Lower the temperature to medium, place the four aubergine (eggplant) halves on the pan (flesh side down), cover with a lid and fry for 5 minutes. Turn the aubergines (eggplant) over, re-cover the pan and fry for a further 10 minutes. The aubergine (eggplant) halves should be very soft by this stage; use a wide spatula to transfer them to a roasting tray (this time, skin side down).

Apply a thin layer of the dengaku miso paste over the cut side of the aubergine (eggplant) halves using a knife or teaspoon. Cover the aubergine (eggplant) halves with the grated mozzarella and reheat them in the oven for 5 minutes.

Remove the aubergine (eggplant) halves from the oven and transfer straight underneath the hot grill (broiler) for 3–4 minutes or until the cheese is completely melted and lightly browned. Serve immediately with a sprinkle of toasted white sesame seeds.

I'd serve these as a side dish, a starter (appetizer) or as part of a selection of small dishes; that said, it's delicious on its own but could be equally nice eaten with a salad for a light vegetarian option to any meal.

This simple yet tasty dish of crunchy green vegetables in a nutty dressing is packed with flavours and textures. It is my favourite accompaniment to Pan-fried rib-eye steak marinated in miso & *aji panca* (see page 161) but also goes well with any grilled meat or fish recipes in this book – see, for example, Brazilian *churrasco* with Nikkei flavours on page 154.

The vegetables should be super-fresh and cooked in 10 times the volume of water to vegetables; this way, they retain their beautiful and vibrant green colour. Plunging them into iced water immediately after cooking is also important, since it will ensure the vegetables do not overcook as they cool.

Because this dish is served at room temperature, both the vegetables and the dressing can be made well in advance and combined just before you want to serve it. Put together a stunning platter of these bright-green vegetables with the black sesame dressing at any barbecue or picnic gatherings.

BROCCOLI, SUGAR SNAPS, FINE BEANS & ASPARAGUS
IN TOASTED BLACK SESAME DRESSING

SERVES 4

75g (2¾oz) broccoli, cut into
  small florets
75g (2¾oz) fine green beans,
  tailed
75g (2¾oz) asparagus tips
75g (2¾oz) sugar snaps,
  strings removed

For the black sesame dressing:
40g (1½oz/¼ cup) toasted
  black sesame seeds
4 tsp sugar
2 tsp mirin
4 tsp soy sauce

First, make the black sesame dressing. Roughly grind the toasted black sesame seeds in a pestle and mortar, then add the other ingredients and mix well.

Next, prepare the vegetables. Fill a very large pan with plenty of salted water and bring to the boil. Cook the broccoli florets for 3 minutes, the fine green beans and asparagus for 2–3 minutes and the sugar snaps for 1 minute in various small batches – you want them to be al dente. Refresh the vegetables in cold water, drain well and dry on a clean tea-towel (dish towel).

Before serving ensure all the vegetables are dry. Cut the green beans in half. In a serving bowl, mix all the vegetables with the black sesame dressing but do so gently, coating all the vegetables in the dressing. Then, set aside at room temperature until needed.

Chotto Matte is one of London's most talked about restaurants in recent times. One of the pioneers of Nikkei cooking in the UK, it is also a gorgeous restaurant with a great Soho location. I really enjoyed eating at Chotto Matte and meeting the Executive Chef Jordan Sclare (former head chef at Aqua Kyoto and Nobu) and his right-hand man, Head Chef Michael Paul.

One of the most memorable dishes I have eaten there is the paper-thin salad *El Peruano*, which Jordan and Michael kindly share here. This is a refreshing salad with some great flavours and it is visually stunning.

You will need a spiraliser, and not a mandolin, as this recipe requires the vegetables to be cut to a flat sheet.

PAPER-THIN SALAD *EL PERUANO*

SERVES 4

100g (3½oz) beetroot (beet)
80g (3oz) mooli (or daikon)
100g (3½oz) butternut squash
100g (3½oz/⅔ cup) quinoa
40g (1½oz) red onion, thinly sliced
30g (1¼oz) physalis (cape gooseberries) slices
50g (1¾oz) cherry tomato, skin on and diced
3g (⅛oz) coriander (cilantro) cress
40g (1½oz) broccoli florets, cooked
20g (¾oz/¼ cup) *choclo* corn, boiled

For the *aji* dressing:
7 tsp ready-made *aji amarillo* paste
40ml (1½fl oz/3 tbsp) rapeseed (canola) oil
20ml (⅔fl oz/4 tsp) yuzu juice
20ml (⅔fl oz/4 tsp) Chardonnay vinegar
a pinch of salt, to taste

For the physalis sauce:
40g (1½oz) mango purée (about ¼ mango blended)
40g (1½oz) physalis (cape gooseberries), chopped
1 tsp ready-made *aji amarillo* paste
40ml (1½fl oz/3 tbsp) lime juice

Make the *aji* dressing by mixing all of the ingredients together in a bowl until well combined.

Next, make the physalis (cape gooseberry) sauce. Whizz all of the sauce ingredients in a food processor and blend until smooth. Then, pass through a fine sieve (strainer) into a sterilised airtight jar and refrigerate until needed.

To prepare the vegetables, separately peel and wash the beetroot (beet), mooli (daikon) and butternut squash. Using a spiraliser, slice each vegetable thinly (check the manufacturer's instructions). Keep the slices together in stacks of six slices and keep each type of vegetable in a separate container. Cover the vegetable slices in their containers with the *aji* dressing. Place a weight on top of the vegetables and cover, leaving them to marinate for 4–6 hours; this can also be done under vacuum, if you have this facility for 3–4 hours. The vegetables will 'cook' in the acidity of the dressing.

Once the sliced vegetables have had their time, prepare the quinoa. Place the quinoa in a fine-mesh strainer and rinse well under running water. Rub and swish the quinoa with your hand while rinsing and rinse for at least 2 minutes. Drain. In a pan, cook the quinoa in twice the volume of water and simmer over a medium heat for 10 minutes. Then, pour into a baking tray (baking sheet), cover with clingfilm (plastic wrap) and let it rest for 10 minutes.

To plate the dish, season the quinoa with some of the marinating juices from the beetroot (beet). Roll the beetroot (beet), butternut and mooli (daikon) slices into equal sized cigars.

Spoon some of the dressed quinoa and physalis (cape gooseberry) sauce into the vegetable cigars. Sprinkle the red onion, physalis (cape gooseberry) slices and tomatoes around the plate. Add the physalis (cape gooseberry) sauce and beetroot-marinating liquor (which here is the *leche de tigre*) to the plate. Finish with a scattering of coriander (cilantro) cress, broccoli florets and *choclo* corn. Serve.

Cook's note Rinsing the quinoa before cooking removes its natural coating, called saponin, which can make it taste bitter or soapy. Although boxed quinoa is often pre-rinsed, it doesn't hurt to give the seeds an additional rinse.

Chinese century-old eggs, despite their name, are eggs preserved in a mixture of rice husks, clay and salt among other ingredients for about six months. The yolk becomes creamy and takes on a dark-green colour, while the white hardens into an amber-coloured jelly. Many people are wary of trying a century-old egg, as it looks quite odd, but I hope my Nikkei interpretation of this flavoursome dish will encourage you to experiment with a new ingredient. This is a rich dish and a small quantity goes a long way. It can be served as a side dish to a meal or as a canapé, perhaps in a Chinese soup spoon.

CENTURY-OLD EGG ON SILKEN TOFU
WITH SICHUANESE GREEN MUSTARD PICKLES, SESAME & SHICHIMI PEPPER

SERVES 4

2 Chinese century-old eggs, chopped into 1cm (½in) cubes (see Cook's note)
40g (1½oz) spring onions (scallions), finely chopped
6 tbsp Sichuanese green mustard pickle, finely chopped (see Cook's note)
2 tbsp toasted sesame oil
½ tsp sea salt flakes
½ tsp shichimi pepper, plus a little extra to garnish
250g (9oz) silken tofu, cut into 4 equal squares
1 tsp toasted white sesame seeds, to garnish

Gently mix all of the ingredients, except for the tofu, together in a bowl.

Place the tofu squares in separate serving bowls and top with the century-old egg mixture. Alternatively, you can serve 'family style' by placing all the slices of tofu on one large serving platter, then topping with the century-old egg mixture.

Finish off with a dusting of shichimi pepper and a sprinkle of sesame seeds before serving.

Cook's note Sichuanese green mustard pickle (known as zha cai in China or zasai in Japan) is a salt-fermented pickled vegetable. Depending on the brand, it can be rather salty, so go easy on any additional seasoning. Both zha cai and century-old eggs are available in most Chinese supermarkets.

Kyushu, the westernmost island of mainland Japan, is where my family came from before migrating to Brazil. Slightly off the beaten track, most visitors to Japan will only travel between Tokyo and Kyoto, sadly missing out on this part of the country. Kyushu is definitely worth a visit, not only for its hearty dishes but also for its natural hot springs or onsen. Jigoku Mushi is a method of cooking developed in Kyushu using the natural steam of the hot springs and the constant hot water temperature. One example is tamago onsen or onsen egg – when eggs are cooked at a constant temperature, they have a deliciously creamy yolk and a slightly sulphurous flavour that has made these eggs very popular. Egg and truffle is a classic combination and here I use truffle ponzu for a Nikkei twist.

ONSEN DUCK EGG ON SILKEN TOFU WITH TRUFFLE-PONZU SAUCE

SERVES 4

½ portion of Truffle ponzu
   sauce (see page 234)
4 duck eggs
200g (7oz) silken tofu

For the garnish:
5g (⅛oz/⅓ cup) bonito fish
   flakes
1 tbsp finely chopped chives
1 tsp toasted black sesame
   seeds
a sprinkle of shichimi pepper

Prepare half a portion of the Truffle ponzu sauce following the instructions on page 234.

If you have a *sous-vide* water oven, set it to 64°C (147°F). If you do not have a *sous-vide* oven, you can still make perfect *sous-vide*-style eggs. You'll need a medium-sized pan and a food thermometer, ideally one with a temperature alarm. Set the thermometer's temperature alarm to a minimum of 63°C (145°F) and a maximum of 65°C (149°F). The alarm should sound whenever the temperature reaches either extreme; turn the temperature up or add a little cold water to cool it down to keep it within the desired range. If you are pressed for time or do not have a food thermometer, you can poach the eggs instead. However, the *sous-vide*-style egg has a wonderfully creamy yolk, silken in texture and is quite different to a poached one, which is generally runny.

Carefully add the eggs to the *sous-vide* water oven or improvised water-bath pan and cook them for 50 minutes. When the time is up, remove the eggs and immediately plunge them in a bowl of iced water to stop the cooking. Set aside.

Gently cut the silken tofu block into four squares about 1.5cm (½in) thick and 5cm (2in) wide, each square roughly weighing 35g (1¼oz). Using a teaspoon, gently scrape out a little of the tofu from the middle of each square to create an indentation on which the egg will sit; this dent will help the egg from sliding off after being plated. Place each tofu square in the middle of a serving shallow bowl.

Take the truffle ponzu sauce out of the fridge to allow it to come up to room temperature.

Gently break the eggs, remove some of the uncooked white from around the yolk, place the yolks in a shallow bowl covering with hot water (not boiling water) to warm them through for a couple of minutes.

To serve, place a drained duck egg in the centre of each silken tofu square then pour a couple of tablespoons of the truffle ponzu sauce over the egg. Finish off by topping with a little of the bonito fish flakes and a sprinkle each of finely chopped chives, black sesame seeds and shichimi pepper and serve.

This is my Nikkei take on Brazil's number one salad – tomato and palm hearts. Like bacon and eggs or fish and chips (fries) in the UK, tomato and palm hearts always go together in Brazil; they are found on nearly every restaurant menu in the country, as well as in every home. Palm heart (known as *palmito* in Portuguese) is an interesting vegetable with an unusual texture and flavour – it's like a cross between bamboo shoot, artichoke heart and asparagus. When served fresh, it is one of the most sublime things I can remember eating as a child in Brazil.

Palm trees are grown commercially in Brazil to supply the locals' never-ending craving for palm hearts. They are mostly found preserved in jars or tins; I always advise buying them in jars rather than tins, as the flavour is far superior.

I like using heritage tomatoes of different colours to create this salad and it makes for an interesting presentation.

SALAD OF HEIRLOOM TOMATOES & PALM HEARTS
WITH A YUZU-PON DRESSING

SERVES 6

½ portion of Yuzu-pon sauce
   (see page 235)
500g (1lb 2oz) tomatoes of
   various colours, including
   1 yellow, 1 orange, 1 light
   green, 1 dark green and
   about 8 small red vine
   tomatoes
150g (5½oz/1 cup) palm
   hearts (preferably from a jar,
   avoid tinned ones)
½ banana shallot, finely sliced
2 tbsp coriander (cilantro)
   cress, to garnish
Maldon sea salt flakes and
   freshly ground black pepper

First, make half a portion of the Yuzu-pon sauce following the instructions on page 235; here we'll use this sauce as a dressing.

Cut the tomatoes into 5mm (¼in)-thick slices and place the slices flat on a large, white serving plate, arranging them so that the different colours are evenly spread. Drizzle the yuzu-pon dressing over the tomatoes.

Prepare the palm hearts. If you can't locate jarred palm hearts and have to use tinned ones then be sure to wash them under fresh water for a minute or so, taking care not to break them up. Cut the palm hearts into similarly sized slices and centre them on the plate.

Scatter the sliced shallot over the tomatoes, place the coriander (cilantro) cress on top of the palm hearts and finish off with a generous dusting of Maldon sea salt flakes and freshly ground black pepper. Serve.

Cooking food in parcels – be it *en papillotte* as in the recipe for Monkfish, seafood and yuzu kosho on page 138 or in foil as here – will ensure that the food is cooked perfectly without losing its moisture or flavour. Better still, you can avoid washing up (cleaning the dishes) afterwards since the foil can double up as the serving dish!

I like using a selection of Japanese mushrooms to produce a fabulous-looking dish that has a number of flavours. Shimeji and enoki mushrooms are beautiful, while shiitake offer some meatiness as well as a great texture. Oyster mushrooms are delicate and add yet another layer of flavour.

If you cannot get hold of yuzu juice for the yuzu-pon dressing, any other variation of the Ponzu sauces on pages 234–235 will work well as a substitute. And do be careful as you open the bag, as the steam will escape and may burn.

JAPANESE MUSHROOMS BAKED IN FOIL

WITH YUZU-PON BUTTER

SERVES 4

½ portion of Yuzu-pon sauce
  (see page 235)
200g (7oz) shiitake
  mushrooms
200g (7oz) oyster mushrooms
200g (7oz) shimeji
  mushrooms
100g (3½oz) enoki
  mushrooms
4 tbsp finely sliced spring
  onions (scallions)
8 tbsp unsalted butter, cubed
Maldon sea salt flakes
1 tsp toasted white sesame
  seeds, to garnish

Make half a portion of Yuzu-pon sauce following the instructions on page 235.

Preheat the oven to 200°C/400°F/gas mark 6, and cut or tear a 1m (39in) piece of foil into four rectangles, to make the four parcels.

Wipe all the mushrooms with a damp cloth, then remove and discard the shiitake mushroom stems. If the shiitake mushrooms are large, cut them in half. Cut off the woody, end stem from the shimeji and enoki mushrooms.

In a bowl, add the oyster and shiitake mushrooms, the yuzu-pon sauce and half of the sliced spring onions (scallions), gently mix together until all the mushrooms are coated.

Divide the seasoned mushrooms equally placing them in the middle of each of the foil pieces and topping each mound with a small bunch each of shimeji and enoki mushrooms. Scatter 2 tablespoons of the cubed butter over each parcel of mushrooms as well as a generous sprinkle of Maldon sea salt flakes. Now, carefully, fold one end of the foil over the other and pinch the sides tightly to create and close four neat pouches.

Transfer the pouches to a roasting tray and bake in the oven for about 15 minutes. Remove the parcels from the oven. Carefully open one of them slightly to check the doneness of the mushrooms, being careful not to scorch yourself with the escaping steam. If they are still a bit firm, re-close the pouch and return to the oven for a further couple of minutes.

Transfer the pouches to serving plates, carefully open them, scattering the remaining finely sliced spring onions (scallions) and a sprinkle of toasted white sesame seeds before serving.

Tokyo-ites are crazy about these peppers – there, they eat a variety from East Asia known as shishito but they're similar to those from the Spanish town of Padrón (*pimientos de Padrón*) – they are a popular snack served in many Japanese pubs, known as izakayas. This Nikkei version is flavoured with British Maldon sea salt flakes and red miso powder; this intense, earthy, Marmite-like seasoning (full of umami savouriness) complements the delicious flavours of the peppers perfectly.

I love eating these on their own or as an accompaniment to any of the grilled (or broiled) meats or fish in this book. Despite their name, they are not hot although around one in ten will have a bit of a kick.

PIMIENTOS DE PADRÓN NIKKEI
WITH MALDON SEA SALT FLAKES & RED MISO POWDER

SERVES 4

1–2 tsp Red miso powder (see page 241), plus extra to garnish
400g (14oz) *pimientos de Padrón* (green Padrón peppers)
1 tbsp sunflower oil
2 tbsp toasted sesame oil
Maldon sea salt flakes
4 lime wedges, to serve

To make the red miso powder, follow the instructions on page 241.

Wash the Padrón peppers, drying them well afterwards with a tea-towel (dish towel).

In a large wok or frying pan (or skillet), heat the sunflower and sesame oils until hot and smoking. Add the Padrón peppers and fry, tossing them from time to time, for about 3 minutes or until they are blistered and lightly golden. Season with sea salt then transfer them to a plate lined with kitchen paper (paper towels).

To serve, place the fried peppers around the edge of a plate, dust them with some of the red miso powder, beside it place a small mound of red miso powder and sea salt flakes and serve immediately with the lime wedges.

DESSERTS

This cake, although not Nikkei in its own right, is a rich, chocolatey dessert that works a treat with Japanese green tea ice cream (see page 201). There is something about green tea and dark chocolate that together create an alchemy only a few desserts can claim. This cake can be made a couple of days in advance, making it a great dessert with minimal fuss.

FLOURLESS CHOCOLATE CAKE WITH ARMAGNAC PRUNES

SERVES 10–12

200g (7oz) ready-to-eat, stoneless prunes
6 tbsp Armagnac or brandy
300g (10½oz) good-quality dark (semisweet) chocolate (minimum 55% cocoa solids but no more than 70%)
140g (5oz/⅔ cup) unsalted butter
5 large eggs, separated
140g (5oz/¾ cup) golden caster (superfine) sugar
300g (10½oz/2 cups) mixed berries (blackberries, raspberries and strawberries), to serve
icing (confectioners') sugar, for dusting

You'll need to soak the prunes preferably overnight in Armagnac. Before soaking, place the prunes in a pan along with 275ml (9½fl oz/1¼ cups) of water or until they are completely covered. Bring them to a simmering point and simmer for 20–30 minutes. Pour the prunes and their cooking liquor into a bowl and stir in 4 tablespoons of the Armagnac while they are still warm. Leave to cool. Once cool, cover the bowl with clingfilm (plastic wrap) and chill overnight (or for a few hours if you forget to start a day earlier).

When you are ready to make the cake, preheat the oven to 170°C/325°F/gas mark 3 and grease and line a 23cm (9in) springform cake tin (pan) with baking parchment. Start by breaking the dark (semisweet) chocolate into small pieces into a bowl, add the butter and melt them over a bain-marie or an ovenproof bowl set over a pan of simmering water; it will only take a few minutes. I place two to four sheets of kitchen paper (paper towels) in the water to stop the bowl having direct contact with the heat and burning the chocolate. Stir until you have a smooth, glossy mixture. Off the heat, add the remaining Armagnac, mix well and leave to cool.

Meanwhile, in a large bowl and using an electric hand whisk, whisk the yolks and sugar for a few minutes until the mixture has partially whitened and once the whisk is lifted it leaves a ribbon-like trail, what's known as ribbon stage.

Cut the soaked prunes in half and add to the melted chocolate (this will help to reduce the temperature of the chocolate), and then mix the chocolate and prunes into the whisked egg yolk and sugar mixture. In another large bowl, whisk the egg whites to soft peaks (use the electric hand whisk but ensure that it is clean and with no trace of water or yolks or your egg whites will not form soft peaks). Then, fold it into the egg and chocolate mixture.

Spoon the cake mixture (batter) into the prepared tin (pan) and bake it in the centre of the preheated oven for 25–30 minutes or until the centre feels springy to the touch. Allow the cake to cool in the tin (pan); it will deflate quite a bit so don't be alarmed. When it is completely cool, cover the tin (pan) in clingfilm (plastic wrap) and chill for several hours.

Take the cake out of the fridge a couple of hours before serving. Decorate the cake with the berries placing them on top in a haphazard but attractive sort of way. I like cutting most of the strawberries in half lengthways but keeping the green stems, they will go further this way and look prettier too. Make sure the fruit is dry otherwise the icing (confectioners') sugar will melt and you will not get a lightly dusted coating. Just before serving, dust the top with icing (confectioners') sugar. Cut the cake into small slices (it is rich) and serve.

One thing I miss from my days in Japan is the abundance of green tea; there, it's in everything from lattes to cheesecake, and pastries to chocolate. As popular in Asia as vanilla ice cream is in the West, this deliciously creamy and bitter-sweet green tea ice cream will guarantee any Japanese or Nikkei dinner ends on a high note. It will go down a treat accompanied by a little slice of the Flourless chocolate cake with Armagnac prunes (see page 198).

GREEN TEA ICE CREAM

MAKES ABOUT 1.8 LITRES (3 PINTS/2 QUARTS)

750ml (1 pint 6fl oz/3 cups) whole milk
600ml (1 pint/2½ cups) double (heavy) cream
2 tbsp green tea powder (matcha)
2 eggs
3 egg yolks
300g (10½oz/1½ cups) caster (superfine) sugar

The base of most ice creams is a light custard. But unlike the traditional custard recipes flavoured with vanilla, this ice cream base is flavoured with green tea powder, aka matcha.

In a pan, heat the milk and cream until it starts steaming, this will be around 65°C (149°F). In a separate container, add the green tea powder and a ladleful of the hot milk and cream mixture, whisking vigorously to ensure that there are no lumps. I find that a powerful hand-held blender is very useful for this step as green tea powder is rather tough to dissolve. Add this to the pan with the remaining hot milk and cream mixture.

While the cream and milk mix is heating, whisk the eggs, egg yolks and sugar in a large bowl using an electric hand whisk, until the mixture is paler in colour and frothy; this should take about 3 minutes.

Pour one-third of the heated cream into the egg yolk and sugar mixture, stirring well until completely combined. Pour this back into the pan with the remaining cream and milk mixture and cook over a low heat, stirring constantly with a spatula, scraping the bottom of the pan as you stir for about 5 minutes. The desired consistency is what we call a 'coating consistency' or, in other words, when a line remains clear as it is drawn on the back of the spatula. A word of warning – do not overheat the custard as it will curdle. The sugar in this recipe will help to stabilise the custard and stop it from curdling, but temperature control is essential as well; it should never reach boiling point.

Let the mixture cool down by placing the pan in an ice bath. Let this mixture rest covered in the fridge for a few hours or ideally overnight, but if you are pressed for time, you may skip this step and start churning the ice cream. Pour the green tea custard into the ice-cream maker and churn until frozen, following the manufacturer's instructions; this will take about 50 minutes from room temperature. Place it in an airtight container and freeze until required. (If you don't have an ice-cream maker, place the mixture in a bowl in the freezer, take it out every 2 hours and blitz it in a food processor to break up the ice crystals, repeat this three times.) Partially thaw for about 10 minutes before serving.

Like strawberries and cream, or rum and raisin, Oreo and green tea make for another great dessert combination. Thanks to the slightly bitter green tea powder and the soured cream, this New York-style baked cheesecake is deliciously creamy without being overly sweet or rich. Equally this makes a centrepiece for afternoon tea or a dessert at the end of a meal.

OREO & GREEN TEA CHEESECAKE

SERVES 12

700g (1lb 10oz/3 cups)
  cream cheese
300g (10½oz/1½ cups)
  caster (superfine) sugar
4 tbsp green tea powder
  (matcha)
240ml (8fl oz/1 cup) eggs
  (about 4 large eggs)
240ml (8fl oz/1 cup) soured
  cream at room temperature
2 tbsp unsalted butter, plus
  extra for greasing
a few raspberries, to decorate

For the Oreo crumble:
400g (14oz) Oreo cookies
50g (1¾oz/¼ cup) caster
  (superfine) sugar
120g (4oz/½ cup) unsalted
  butter, melted

**For the green tea & white
  chocolate ganache:**
200ml (7fl oz/¾ cup) double
  (heavy) cream
150g (5½oz) white chocolate,
  broken into pieces
50g (1¾oz) sugar
2 tsp green tea powder, plus
  a little extra for dusting

Preheat the oven to 180°C/350°F/gas mark 4, and grease a 23cm (9in) springform cake tin (pan) generously with butter and line the bottom and sides with baking parchment.

Make the crumble by whizzing the Oreos in a food processor until finely crushed. Transfer to a bowl, add the caster (superfine) sugar and melted butter, and mix to form a thick crumble. Tip into the tin (pan) and pack the mixture up the sides of the tin (pan) and across the bottom, about 5mm (¼in) thick. Use a flat spatula to compress the crumble firmly against the cake tin (pan), leaving the top flat and uniform. Refrigerate until ready to use.

In an electric food mixer using the paddle attachment, beat the cream cheese until smooth, scraping down the sides of bowl as needed. Combine the sugar and green tea powder then add this to the mix, whizzing until well incorporated and smooth. Next, add the eggs a little at a time, beating until smooth and scraping down the sides of the bowl. Finally, add the soured cream and blend until well combined.

Pour the cream cheese mixture into the chilled Oreo crumble, transfer it to the bottom of the oven and bake for 10 minutes. Open the oven door for about 30 seconds and turn the temperature down to 120°C/250°F/gas mark ½. Bake until just set (slightly puffed but not browned), about 1 hour. The initial high-temperature bake helps crisp up the crumble.

Remove the cheesecake from the oven and transfer to a cooling rack. Run a paring knife around the crumble to loosen it from the tin (pan), then slightly release the spring. Let the cheesecake cool to room temperature then chill thoroughly (6–8 hours, up to 48 hours).

A couple of hours before serving make the green tea and white chocolate ganache. Bring the cream to a gentle boil then add the white chocolate pieces and stir constantly with a spatula, ensuring that all the chocolate has dissolved. Mix the sugar and green tea powder in a separate bowl and whisk into the ganache little by little, stirring well until all the matcha has dissolved then turn off the heat. Carefully and evenly, spread it over the chilled cheesecake, returning it to the fridge for a further 1–2 hours. After chilling, carefully remove the cheesecake from its tin (pan) and dot with a few raspberries before serving.

Cook's note For the best results, please follow these important rules: all the ingredients must be at room temperature and beaten until very smooth; the oven temperatures should be followed exactly or you'll have cracks or a soggy bottom; loosen the crust after baking to prevent the cake from gaping and cracking as it cools. And if you do end up with the surface a little cracked or coloured, don't worry as the ganache covers a multitude of sins!

Matcha madeleines & Red bean ice cream (recipes overleaf)

Green tea is one of the most popular Japanese flavours – with red bean in close competition for the number one spot. The green tea powder – or matcha – gives these madeleines the most beautiful but subtle green hue. Enhance the greenness even more, if you like, with a wonderful dusting of matcha and icing (confectioners') sugar before you serve them alongside a scoop of Red bean ice cream (see opposite).

MATCHA MADELEINES (illustrated on the previous pages)

MAKES 24

125g (4¼oz/½ cup) unsalted
   butter, melted and cooled
   until tepid, plus extra melted
   butter for greasing
plain (all-purpose) flour, for
   dusting
4 eggs
125g (4¼oz/½ cup plus
   2 tbsp) caster (superfine)
   sugar
1 tbsp honey
125g (4¼oz/1 cup) plain
   (all-purpose) flour
1 tsp baking powder
1 tbsp green tea powder
   (matcha)
a pinch of salt
icing (confectioners') sugar
   mixed with a little matcha,
   for dusting

Start by brushing two 12-hole madeleine trays with plenty of melted butter. Pop into the fridge, allow to set and then apply a second layer of melted butter. Once set, dust with flour, shaking out any excess. Return the trays to the fridge until you're ready for them.

In a food mixer, whisk the eggs, sugar and honey until creamy and thick enough to leave a trail when the whisk is lifted, known as ribbon stage; this should take 5–10 minutes.

Sift the flour, baking powder, green tea powder and salt into a bowl and then sift again to ensure that the matcha is well combined with the other ingredients.

Carefully pour in half of the sifted flour mixture and half of the melted butter around the edge of the bowl of the food mixer and gently fold in until evenly incorporated. Repeat with the remaining flour and butter. Cover the bowl and chill for at least 45 minutes, and preheat the oven to 200°C/400°F/gas mark 6.

Using a tablespoon and a jug (pitcher) full of hot water, spoon out the batter mix, filling every hole two-thirds full. Dip the spoon into the hot water before using it again to spoon out more batter. Repeat to fill each tin (pan).

Bake in a preheated oven for 6–8 minutes or until well risen and golden. Ease the little sponges out of the tins (pans) and allow to cool on a wire rack.

Serve the madeleines dusted with a mix of icing (confectioners') sugar and matcha along with a simple scoop of Red bean ice cream (see opposite).

Japanese desserts are not very sweet and most are made from vegetables rather than fruit, which can seem odd to the Western palate. I love adding a French touch to my Japanese desserts and this has been a household favourite to challenge those who until now would not dream of trying red bean ice cream.

The ice cream should be creamy and nutty and have a beautifully light-pink colour, which is really set off by serving with the Matcha madeleines (see opposite). You can also serve some red bean paste over the ice cream for extra yumminess!

RED BEAN ICE CREAM (illustrated on the previous page)

MAKES 1.7 LITRES (3 PINTS/ 1.5 QUARTS)

For the red bean paste*:
250g (9oz/1⅓ cups) dried azuki beans
250g (9oz/1¼ cups) granulated sugar
a pinch of salt

For the red bean ice cream:
600ml (1 pint/2½ cups) whole milk
600ml (1 pint/2½ cups) double (heavy) cream
2 eggs
4 egg yolks
120g (4oz/½ cup) caster (superfine) sugar
250g (9oz) red bean paste

(*You can also buy the red bean paste, known as tsubushi-an, ready made in tins from most Japanese food shops. The paste and the ice cream can be made days in advance.)

First, make the red bean paste. Soak the azuki beans overnight in cold water. Drain them and rinse under running water. Place the beans in a pressure cooker with five times the amount of fresh water to beans and cook for 20–25 minutes; if you do not have a pressure cooker, cook the beans in a conventional pan for 1½–2 hours until soft. Carefully release the pressure from the pan, drain the beans and rinse under cold, fresh water. Transfer to a pan, add enough water to cover the beans and bring to the boil. Add the granulated sugar, mixing well. Simmer on a low heat, uncovered, for a further 30–45 minutes, stirring occasionally until the some of the beans start disintegrating. You want a thick paste in which the beans are half crushed. Add the salt and mix well.

Now, make the ice cream. The base of this ice cream is, like many ice creams, a *crème anglaise* or a light custard. In a pan, heat the milk and cream until it starts steaming, this will be around 65°C (150°F). While the cream and milk mix is heating, whisk the eggs, egg yolks and sugar in a large bowl until the mixture is whitened and frothy.

Pour one-third of the heated cream into the egg yolk and sugar mixture, stirring well until completely combined. Pour this back into the pan with the remaining cream and milk mixture and cook over a medium heat, stirring constantly with a spatula, scraping the bottom of the pan as you stir for about 5 minutes. The desired consistency is what we call a 'coating consistency' or, in other words, when a line remains clear as it is drawn on the back of the spatula. A word of warning – do not overheat the custard as it will curdle. The sugar in this recipe will help to stabilise the custard, but temperature control is essential as well; it should never reach boiling point.

Place the pan in an ice bath to cool it. Once at room temperature, mix in the red bean paste. Let this mixture rest covered in the fridge for a few hours or ideally overnight, but if you are pressed for time, you may skip this step and start churning the ice cream. Pour this mixture into an ice-cream maker and churn until frozen, following the manufacturer's instructions; this will take approximately 45 minutes from room temperature. Place it in an airtight container and freeze until required. (If you don't have an ice-cream maker, place the mixture in a bowl in the freezer, take it out every 2 hours and blitz it in a food processor to break up the ice crystals, repeat this three times.)

Partially thaw for about 10 minutes before serving with Matcha madeleines (see opposite).

Posset is a traditional English dessert dating back to medieval times, when cream was curdled with ale and then sweetened. Nowadays, the cream is curdled with lemon rather than ale, but in this Nikkei version I use Japan's aromatic citrus fruit – the yuzu – paired with raspberries and mint.

Once curdled, the cream will need to set in the fridge for a few hours, so the dessert is good to make a day or two in advance. Despite being mainly sweetened citrus cream, it is a refreshingly light dessert that will finish any meal elegantly.

Yuzu is a Japanese citrus fruit (*Citrus junos*) that is highly aromatic, with hints of tangerine, lime and grapefruit. If you cannot find Japanese yuzu juice, use a combination of these three citrus fruits. Yuzu has a very short season in the autumn (fall), and I was lucky to be in Tokyo for it a few years ago. I was blown away by the taste of this fruit and am delighted to have created a dessert that I think shows off its unique character.

YUZU POSSET WITH RASPBERRIES, MINT & CANDIED YUZU

SERVES 8

150g (5½oz/1¼ cups) raspberries, chopped
12 mint leaves, finely chopped
600ml (1 pint/2½ cups) double (heavy) cream
170g (6oz/¾ cup) caster (superfine) sugar
50ml (2fl oz/¼ cup) yuzu juice
50ml (2fl oz/¼ cup) lemon juice

For the candied yuzu zest:
200g (7oz) yuzu zest (it's available in the freezer compartments of Japanese food shops; alternatively, use the zest of 4 oranges)
200g (7oz/1 cup) sugar
200ml (7fl oz/¾ cup) water

Mix the raspberries and the mint leaves together, then divide this mixture equally into eight clear, glass ramekins.

Put the cream and caster (superfine) sugar in a pan large enough to allow the liquid to double in volume and bring to the boil, stirring to dissolve the sugar. This should take a few minutes but keep a close eye, as when it reaches boiling point, the mixture will expand really quickly.

Reduce the heat so that the mixture does not boil over and cook for 3 minutes, stirring constantly. Remove from the heat and stir in the yuzu and lemon juices; the mixture will thicken as the citrus juices curdle the cream, keep mixing well.

Divide the yuzu cream between the ramekins over the raspberry mixture. Tap the ramekins on a work surface (counter) to eliminate any air bubbles and transfer to the fridge. Chill for a few hours before serving. This dessert can be made one or two days in advance.

If you are using the frozen yuzu zest, defrost it thoroughly before using. In a pan, boil the sugar and water to make a syrup. Add the yuzu zest to the pan and poach it in the syrup until tender and translucent. Remove from the heat and let it cool. The zest can be stored in the syrup and drained as needed. (Alternatively, drain and pat off any excess syrup with kitchen paper (paper towels). Then, roll in caster (superfine) sugar and shake in a sieve (strainer) to remove excess sugar.)

If you are using oranges, peel the zest in strips using a vegetable peeler. Using a small sharp knife, remove the white pith. Square off the strips and then cut them into julienne. Boil the zest in a generous quantity of water until tender. Drain and discard the water. As per the candied yuzu zest, prepare a syrup of water and sugar, add the julienned orange zest and poach until tender and translucent. Store in its own syrup and use as needed.

Add a couple of strips of candied yuzu zest over each posset and serve.

Japanese immigration, although in smaller numbers, still takes place in South America. In São Paulo, I was charmed to meet chef Shin Koike at his restaurant Sakagura A1 and learnt of his arrival in the country as recently as 20 years ago. 'Brazil is my adopted home; I embraced its culture, people and food wholeheartedly', he said. His kids were born there and, like their parents, are truly integrated in Brazilian society – 'I will never live in Japan again', he concluded.

We shared a splendid Nikkei meal at Sakagura A1, ending it on a high note with his Rapadura ice cream with cachaça and coffee jelly. Here, chef Koike pays homage to two of the most popular of Brazilian flavours. Rapadura is Brazilian unrefined sugar cane in solid form, akin to Japanese muscovado (brown) sugar (kokuto), it was the perfect base for his Nikkei creation along with cachaça, the national spirit of Brazil, enjoyed in many caipirinhas across that nation and beyond.

RAPADURA ICE CREAM WITH CACHAÇA & COFFEE JELLY

SERVES 15

For the rapadura ice cream:
1 litre (1¾ pints/4 cups) good-quality vanilla ice cream
80g (2¾oz/⅓ cup) block of rapadura sugar (also known as jaggery) or dark muscovado sugar
40ml (1½fl oz/3 tbsp) cachaça (Brazilian cane-sugar spirit)

For the coffee jelly:
5g (⅛oz) gelatine powder or leaves
3 tbsp water
225ml (7½fl oz/1 cup) unsweetened black coffee
1 tbsp coffee liqueur

To prepare the rapadura ice cream, leave the vanilla ice cream at room temperature for 20 minutes to allow it to soften. Grate the rapadura into very small pieces and mix it well into the ice cream along with the cachaça. Then return the ice cream to the freezer.

Next, make the coffee jelly. Dissolve the gelatine in the measured water in a microwave for 30 seconds. Add the prepared coffee and coffee liqueur and mix well. Pour into a tray of about 20cm x 12cm (7¾in x 4½in) and refrigerate for 2 hours or until the jelly is firm. Cut the coffee jelly into small cubes, about 1.5cm (½in) in size.

Remove the ice cream from the freezer 10 minutes before serving so that it's slightly softened. Serve a scoop of the rapadura ice cream in individual bowls, with a scattering of the coffee jelly cubes on top.

In Brazil, pumpkin and coconut is one of the country's favourite desserts known as *doce de abóbora com coco*, sometimes flavoured with cinnamon and cloves. My version draws inspiration from my childhood but takes a different form, similar to those I have experienced in Asia. The Japanese kabocha pumpkin has a natural sweetness, which goes very well with this recipe. Once cooked, the skin is deliciously soft and can be eaten. The pumpkin should be sliced for serving, with some freshly grated coconut or, for those with a sweet tooth, a drizzle of sweetened condensed milk.

STEAMED JAPANESE KABOCHA PUMPKIN FILLED WITH COCONUT CUSTARD

SERVES 6

1.5kg (3lb 5oz) Japanese kabocha pumpkin
200g (7oz) egg yolks (about 12 egg yolks) at room temperature
200g (7oz/1 cup) caster (superfine) sugar
200g (7oz/¾ cup) thick coconut cream
a pinch of salt
100g (3½oz/1 cup) fresh coconut, grated
200ml (7fl oz/¾ cup) sweetened condensed milk (optional)

Cut a hole in the top of the pumpkin, large enough to allow a tablespoon inside. Scoop out all the seeds and then rinse well.

In my experience, a 1.5kg (3lb 5oz) pumpkin has a cavity large enough to take about 600ml (1 pint/2½ cups) of custard, which is the volume of the custard in this recipe. If your pumpkin needs more than this, adjust the quantity of egg yolks, sugar and coconut cream in equal measure for the desired total volume. A quick way to find out how much custard you need is to fill the pumpkin with water after removing the seeds and then pour out the water from the pumpkin into a measuring jug (cup) to measure the volume it can hold.

In a pan with a tightly fitting lid, place the pumpkin upside down, with the hole created on the top of the pumpkin facing down, and steam it for about 10 minutes until partially cooked. Remove it from the steamer and turn it to stand upright again.

Meanwhile, in a bowl, whisk the egg yolks, the sugar, coconut cream and salt well until the sugar has completely dissolved. Strain the mixture into a pan and heat it through until it starts steaming, stirring constantly and scraping the bottom of the pan as you do so. Pour the coconut custard into the pumpkin. Return the pumpkin to the steamer, still in its upright position, and steam gently for about 20–25 minutes until the custard is set.

To make sure the custard is set, insert a long skewer into the custard, it should come out completely clean. If you have a food thermometer, a better way to do this is to check the internal temperature of the custard – it should read 85°C (185°F) or more. If the custard is not set, steam it for a further 5–10 minutes before checking again.

When ready, take the pumpkin out of the steamer and carefully place it on a large plate. Leave it to cool completely then refrigerate it for at least an hour, or overnight. Cut into wedges of about 2.5cm (1in) thickness and serve with grated fresh coconut and the condensed milk (if using). You eat everything including the skin.

(from top to bottom)
Cupuaçu & white chocolate ice cream (left)
Graviola & cinnamon ice cream (right)
Lucuma & *dulce de leche* ice cream (left)
Sorbet of caju & cognac (left)
Sorbet of açaí & wild blossom honey (right/bottom)

When I left Brazil in 1992, I knew little about the Amazonian fruits that would soon become all the rage in the larger cities of the south. They are delicious and not nearly as hard to find as you may think – I bought their pulp right here in the UK (see my suppliers list on page 250 for more information).

Cupuaçu is a relative of the cocoa bean; it is a white-fleshed fruit with a delicious creaminess reminiscent of chocolate but with a refreshing tanginess. *Lúcuma* is one of the most interesting fruits of Peru – it is bright orange in colour, with flavours of pumpkin and maple syrup. Açai is perhaps Brazil's best-known fruit export – this little Amazonian berry has high levels of antioxidants and is thought to be a good hangover cure. Intriguingly, it has complex flavours of red wine, chocolate and olive oil! Everyone knows the cashew nut, but few are aware of the cashew fruit (also known as the cashew apple), from which a very popular juice is made in Brazil, presented here as a sorbet. Another interesting Brazilian fruit is the graviola (or soursop), with a creamy texture and flavours similar to banana, pineapple and strawberry. Here, I have created a graviola ice cream with a hint of cinnamon.

BRAZILIAN & PERUVIAN SUPER-FRUITS
(illustrated on the previous pages)

SERVES 12

600ml (1pint/2½ cups) whole milk
600ml (1pint/2½ cups) double (heavy) cream
1 large egg
5 egg yolks
200g (7oz/1 cup) caster (superfine) sugar
400g (14oz) white chocolate, melted
400g (14oz) *cupuaçu* pulp, thawed

CUPUAÇU & WHITE CHOCOLATE ICE CREAM

The base of this ice cream is, like many ice creams, a *crème anglaise* or a light custard. In a pan, heat the milk and cream until it starts steaming, this will be around 65°C (150°F). While the cream and milk mix is being heated, whisk the eggs, egg yolks and sugar in a large bowl until the mixture is whitened and frothy, this should take about 3 minutes.

Pour one-third of the heated cream into the whisked egg and sugar mixture, stirring well until completely combined. Pour this back into the pan with the remaining cream and milk mixture and cook over a low heat, stirring constantly with a spatula, scraping the bottom of the pan as you stir for about 5 minutes. The desired consistency is what we call a 'coating consistency' or, in other words, when a line remains clear as it is drawn on the back of the spatula. A word of warning – do not overheat the custard as it will curdle. The sugar in this recipe will help to stabilise the custard, but temperature control is essential; it should never reach boiling point.

While the custard is still hot, add the melted white chocolate and mix well. Let the mixture cool down, add the *cupuaçu* pulp and chill for a few hours or overnight. Pour the *cupuaçu* and white chocolate custard into the ice-cream maker and churn until frozen, following the manufacturer's instructions. Place it in an airtight container and freeze until required. (*If you don't have an ice-cream maker, place the mixture in a bowl in the freezer, take it out every 2 hours and blitz it in a food processor to break up the ice crystals, repeat this three times.) Partially thaw for about 10 minutes before serving.

LÚCUMA & DULCE DE LECHE ICE CREAM

SERVES 12

600ml (1 pint/2½ cups) whole milk

600ml (1 pint/2½ cups) double (heavy) cream

1 large egg

5 egg yolks

150g (5½oz/¾ cup) caster (superfine) sugar

500g (1lb 2oz) *lúcuma* pulp, thawed

300g (10½oz) *dulce de leche* (ready made or see recipe method using a 397g (14oz) tin (can) of sweetened condensed milk)

If you decide to make your own *dulce de leche*, this will need to be done ahead of the ice cream. So, remove the label from an unopened tin of sweetened condensed milk, place it in a pan with plenty of water (the water should always come up as high as possible up the side of the tin, so check periodically) and simmer for 2–3 hours – the longer it simmers, the more fudge-like the *dulce de leche* will be). Allow the tin to cool completely before opening it. The *dulce de leche* will firm up as it cools and can easily be reheated to a spreadable consistency; if you prefer it softer, just add a little milk and mix until the desired consistency is achieved. If you have a pressure cooker, you can cook the unopened tin covered in water at a high pressure for 30 minutes. Allow the pressure to release naturally by allowing the water and pan to cool down completely before opening the pressure cooker. Do not attempt to open the tin while it's still hot, as the hot *dulce de leche* may spit out because of the pressure inside.

To make the *crème anglaise*, follow the instructions opposite for the Cupuaçu & white chocolate ice cream but this time adding the *lúcuma* pulp and *dulce de leche* instead to the cool egg custard to flavour it. Mix well then chill it for a few hours before churning in an ice-cream maker, following the manufacturer's instructions or manually using a food processor (see opposite*).

GRAVIOLA & CINNAMON ICE CREAM

SERVES 10

600ml (1 pint/2½ cups) double (heavy) cream

600ml (1 pint/2½ cups) whole milk

1 large egg, plus 5 egg yolks

250g (9oz/1¼ cups) caster (superfine) sugar

500g (1lb 2oz) graviola pulp (soursop), thawed

2 tsp freshly ground cinnamon

To make the *crème anglaise*, follow the instructions opposite for the Cupuaçu & white chocolate ice cream but this time adding the graviola pulp and cinnamon instead to the cool egg custard to flavour it. Mix well, let the mixture cool down then chill it for a few hours before churning in an ice-cream maker, following the manufacturer's instructions or manually using a food processor (see opposite*).

SORBET OF CAJÚ & COGNAC

SERVES 6

200ml (7fl oz/¾ cup) water

200g (7oz/1 cup) caster (superfine) sugar

400g (14oz) *cajú* fruit (cashew fruit) pulp, thawed

2 tbsp lime juice

3 tbsp Cognac

Make a sugar syrup by heating the water and sugar in a pan until the sugar has completely dissolved. Then, let it cool down, add the thawed *cajú* fruit pulp, the lime juice and the Cognac then mix well. Leave it in the freezer until the mixture is extremely cold, then place it in an ice-cream machine and churn, following the manufacturer's instructions or manually using a food processor (see opposite*).

SORBET OF AÇAI & WILD BLOSSOM HONEY

SERVES 6

400g (14oz) açai pulp, thawed

75g (2¾oz/¼ cup) wild blossom honey

6 tbsp caster (superfine) sugar

juice of ½ lime

Combine all the ingredients in a large bowl, mix well and transfer to a freezer. Leave it there until the mixture is extremely cold, then place it in an ice-cream machine and churn, following the manufacturer's instructions or manually using a food processor (see opposite*).

Banana and Nutella – a combination made in heaven! Gyoza are normally prepared as a savoury snack, but my sweet Nikkei version of gyoza is inspired by the crêperies of Paris, where this pairing is a much-loved classic. I love serving them with a scoop of Sesame caramel ice cream (see page 221).

BANANA & NUTELLA GYOZA
WITH A DUSTING OF SWEETENED TOASTED SOYBEAN POWDER

SERVES 4

12 gyoza wrappers (fresh
   or frozen)
2 ripe bananas
6 tsp Nutella
2 tbsp sunflower oil

For the sprinkle mixture:
25g (1oz/¼ cup) icing
   (confectioners') sugar
50g (1¾oz) toasted soybean
   powder (known as kinako;
   available from Japanese food
   shops)

For the decoration:
1 ripe banana, cut into 12
   slices (3 slices per plate)
1 tsp caster (superfine) sugar

If you're using frozen gyoza wrappers, then take them out of the freezer 30 minutes before you need them but do not open the packet until you're ready to start, as they will dry out.

Cut the bananas in halves lengthways then cut each half into 1cm (½in) pieces. Put some cold water in a bowl and set aside.

When you are ready to start making the dumplings, open the gyoza packet, take one sheet and place over a work surface (counter); I like using a chopping (cutting) board. Using your index fingers, dip them in the bowl of water and wet the border of the wrapper. Place ½ teaspoon of Nutella in the middle of the wrapper, top it with 2 pieces of banana and fold over the wrapper. Make creases on one side of the wrapper, then pinch both sides firmly together to seal the wrapper to create a dumpling. Ensure the gyoza is completely sealed.

Line a tray or a plate with non-stick greaseproof (wax) paper, place the sealed dumplings on the paper and freeze them. Once frozen, carefully transfer them into a sealable bag. The dumplings can be made days in advance and kept in the freezer. Alternatively, if you are making these dumplings to be eaten straightaway, you will need to fry them soon after sealing or the bottom of the dumplings will become wet and sticky when fried.

To cook the gyoza, heat the sunflower oil in a non-stick frying pan (or skillet) (with a lid) until hot. Add the frozen (or fresh) gyoza and brown on one side for about 2 minutes. Turn them over, add 50ml (2fl oz/¼ cup) of cold water to the pan, be careful as it will splatter at this stage, and put the lid on. Turn the heat to low and cook for a further 4 minutes.

After 4 minutes, take the lid off – if water remains in the pan leave it for another minute until it evaporates, then turn off the heat. I prefer to have the gyoza drier for plating. Transfer the dumplings to a plate and rest for 2 minutes, the Nutella will be super-hot. Then, whizz up the decoration. Place three slices of banana on each serving plate, sprinkle caster (superfine) sugar over them and use a blow-torch (or transfer to a baking tray (baking sheet) under a hot grill/broiler) to caramelise them. Mix the icing (confectioners') sugar and kinako powder until combined and sprinkle some of this mixture over the gyoza. I like serving these gyoza dumplings with Sesame caramel ice cream (see page 221).

Cook's note Gyoza wrappers dry out easily so either keep them in their original packaging while preparing the dumplings or count the number of wrappers you need and place them on a plate topped with a clean, damp tea-towel (dish towel).

The sesame brittle in this recipe imparts a rich caramel flavour and toasty nuttiness to the ice cream. It is a great accompaniment to serve alongside the hot Banana & Nutella gyoza on page 218.

SESAME CARAMEL ICE CREAM

MAKES ABOUT 2.5 LITRES (4½ PINTS/2 QUARTS)

For the sesame caramel:
120g (4oz/¾ cup) toasted sesame seeds
300g (10½oz/1½ cups) granulated sugar

For the ice cream:
750ml (1 pint 6fl oz/3 cups) whole milk
600ml (1 pint/2½ cups) double (heavy) cream
2 eggs
4 egg yolks
160g (5¾oz/¾ cup) caster (superfine) sugar

Place the toasted sesame seeds in a non-stick frying pan (or skillet) over a medium heat and dry-fry them for a few minutes until lightly coloured. Be sure not to burn them or they will taste bitter. Remove from the heat and set aside until needed.

To make the sesame brittle, place a non-stick silicone baking mat inside a shallow baking tin (pan) (a Swiss/jelly roll tin/pan is ideal for this). Wash a heavy, preferably non-stick pan, well with hot water to remove any traces of grease and dry well – this will prevent the sugar from crystallising as it melts. Place the granulated sugar in the clean pan over a gentle heat and let it melt, tilting the pan occasionally to break up any lumps of sugar or very gently mixing it in with a spoon. Once all the sugar has dissolved, add the toasted sesame seeds and mix well. Pour this mixture onto the baking mat and let cool and harden.

The base of most ice creams is a light custard. In a pan, heat the milk and cream until it starts steaming, this will be around 65°C (149°F). While the cream and milk mix is heating, whisk the eggs, egg yolks and sugar in a large bowl using an electric hand whisk, until the mixture is paler in colour and frothy; this should take about 3 minutes.

Pour one-third of the heated cream into the egg yolk and sugar mixture, stirring well until completely combined. Pour this back into the pan with the remaining cream and milk mixture and cook over a low heat, stirring constantly with a spatula, scraping the bottom of the pan as you stir for about 5 minutes. The desired consistency is what we call a 'coating consistency' or, in other words, when a line remains clear as it is drawn on the back of the spatula. A word of warning – do not overheat the custard as it will curdle. The sugar in this recipe will help to stabilise the custard and stop it from curdling, but temperature control is essential as well; it should never reach boiling point.

Let the mixture cool down by placing the pan in an ice bath. Meanwhile, break up the sesame seed brittle into small pieces in a pestle and mortar, then crush them to a fine crumble. Add the crushed brittle to the cold custard, cover and chill for a couple of hours or preferably overnight.

Next, pour this mixture into the ice-cream maker and churn until frozen, following the manufacturer's instructions. Place it in an airtight container and freeze until required. (If you don't have an ice-cream maker, place the mixture in a bowl in the freezer, take it out every 2 hours and blitz it in a food processor to break up the ice crystals, repeat this three times.) Partially thaw for about 10 minutes before serving.

Cook's note Toasted black sesame seeds can also be used.

MASTERING
THE BASICS,
SAUCES, MARINADES &
CONDIMENTS

Rice is at the heart of Nikkei and Japanese cooking. The rice used in these cuisines is short grained and is very different in appearance and flavour to other varieties, such as jasmine, basmati or long-grained American rice. Cooking rice properly is the first step in attempting to cook any Japanese and Nikkei rice dishes, so it's worth taking the time to master this recipe.

Measuring the correct amount of water for the rice is important. The volume of water should be equal to the volume of rice; though, if you prefer your rice a little softer, you may add a tad more water (up to 10% more) to the rice. I measure both my rice and my water by volume, not weight. To do this accurately, I recommend you use the same cup for measuring the rice and the water. Below I've given you the weight of rice for four people but you might well want to use a cup to weigh it out so that you can gauge how much water to use.

STEAMED WHITE RICE

SERVES 4

300g (10½oz/1⅓ cups)
   short-grain white rice
370ml (12½fl oz/1⅔ cups)
   water

1–4 Wash the rice in a bowl with plenty of fresh water using a circular motion with your hand. Drain the water and repeat this rinsing three or four times until the water runs clear.

5–6 Tip the rice into a sieve (strainer) and let it drain for 15 minutes. Transfer the rice to a bowl and soak it in the measured water for a minimum of 30 minutes or up to 4 hours (the longer the soaking, the wetter and stickier the rice will be).

Rice cooker method: When the soaking time is up, add the rice along with its soaking water to the bowl of the rice cooker, close the lid and turn it on. It should take approximately 15–20 minutes to cook. Once the rice cooker's alarm beeps, let the rice rest in the unopened rice cooker for at least 15 minutes before fluffing it to serve.

Pan and hob (stove) method: Choose a pan with a tightly fitting lid (preferably of glass) and with a small ventilation hole for some of the steam to escape. When the soaking time is up, add the rice along with its soaking water to the pan, place the lid on and bring to the boil (a glass lid will allow you to see when the water comes to the boil). As soon as it boils, turn the heat to its lowest setting and simmer gently for 12–15 minutes. Do not remove the lid at any stage during cooking or resting. Take off the heat and let the rice rest for a further 15 minutes before fluffing it and serving. Cooking times may vary depending on the quality of the rice, the pan used and how hot the hob (stove) is.

Cook's note You can cook rice in advance and keep it warm in a rice cooker or reheat it in a microwave if time is tight, though the texture won't be the same.

Rice is the most important element in sushi – its quality, preparation and cooking will make or break any sushi dish you attempt. The sushi rice must be cooled and seasoned in an unvarnished wooden vessel – traditionally, a sushi barrel (known as hangiri or handai in Japanese), but if you don't have one, a large wooden chopping (cutting) board can also be used. The rice should never be placed in glass, stainless-steel or ceramic bowls as these materials will ruin the texture of the rice, making it too wet and sticky.

After preparing the sushi rice keep it at room temperature until served; putting it in the fridge will harden the grains, making it unpalatable. Sushi rice is vinegared, which will help to preserve it naturally. The rice should ideally be kept covered with a damp cloth to avoid drying and in a cool place for up to 8 hours. It must be eaten on the day it's made; leftover sushi rice can be frozen but the texture will be not quite the same when thawed.

SUSHI RICE

MAKES ABOUT 600G (1LB 5OZ)

300g (10½oz/1⅓ cups) short-grain white rice
370ml (12½fl oz/1⅔ cups) water
4–6 tbsp ready-made sushi seasoning (or make your own, see below)

To make the sushi rice, you'll need some essential equipment: an unvarnished wooden bowl, large wooden chopping (cutting) board or a sushi barrel (known as hangiri or handai); a plastic or wooden rice paddle (shamoji) or a large spatula; and a paper fan.

To prepare and cook the plain white rice to be used for sushi, first follow the instructions for making Steamed white rice on page 225.

Wet the inside of the wooden barrel (or the chopping/cutting board or bowl) and the spatula with fresh water to prevent the rice from sticking to them.

1 Transfer the steamed rice to the barrel and drizzle over the sushi seasoning a little at a time. **2–4** Use a fan and the rice paddle to fan the rice while folding it, cutting through the lumps of rice as you do so but being careful to avoid crushing the grains; this can be quite tricky – like rubbing your tummy while patting your head! **5–6** Fan the rice constantly to bring it down to room temperature as quickly as possible; this should take about 5 minutes. (Some chefs use an electric fan or a hairdryer on 'cool' to do this quickly.)

Finally, cover the finished sushi rice with a clean, damp tea-towel (dish towel) until you are ready to use it, otherwise it will dry out.

Make your own sushi seasoning
If you would like to make your own sushi seasoning, place 100ml (3½fl oz/½ cup) rice vinegar, 50g (1¾oz/¼ cup) caster (superfine) sugar, ½ tsp salt and ½ tsp instant dashi powder into a pan, warm it through while stirring to dissolve. Take off the heat and let it cool to room temperature.

TEMPURA – THE INS & OUTS

The classic 'batter-fried' food of Japan, tempura was introduced to the Japanese table by the Portuguese in the 16th century. When making tempura, there are three important rules to observe:

1 ingredients must be fresh

2 the oil should be at a constant temperature

3 a good batter is a lumpy one.

SUPER-FRESH INGREDIENTS

You can make tempura with a variety of seasonal fresh vegetables, fish and seafood – some of my favourites are: broccoli, aubergines (eggplants), mushrooms, onion rings, peppers, deveined prawns (shrimp), small fish fillets, pumpkin, okra, sweet potato slices and squid. By the way, chicken, pork and beef are considered too heavy for tempura.

Any ingredient must be prepared, thoroughly dried and preferably chilled before frying.

GETTING THE TEMPERATURE RIGHT

In terms of the right type of oil for tempura, I suggest pure sunflower oil blended with toasted sesame oil – I normally add 3 tablespoons of sesame oil to 2 litres (3½ pints/8 cups) of sunflower oil. Sesame oil is very strong and should not be the dominant flavour in tempura. Similarly, animal fats or olive oil are too flavoursome and would mask the natural flavour of the ingredients being fried, so they should not be used.

For the best results, different foods are fried at different temperatures. Generally speaking, fish is fried quickly at a high temperature to retain moisture and tenderness whereas vegetables are fried longer at a lower temperature. As a general rule, I say 150–160°C (300–310°F) for vegetables and 170–180°C (325–350°F) for fish and seafood. This guide may seem like there's not much difference in temperature, just 10°C (50°F) here or there, but if the oil is not hot enough, the food will absorb quite a lot of oil and become heavy, soggy and 'fatty'. Whereas, if the oil is too hot the outside frizzles black and the inside remains raw or too crunchy – I cannot overemphasise the importance of oil temperature here.

How do you know when the temperature is right? Well, you can test the temperature by dropping a tiny bit of batter into the oil; it should descend slightly beneath the surface of the oil, then float up to the surface with the oil gently bubbling round its edges. I find this method is good when you're starting off your first batch of deep-frying for tempura but it's not ideal for gauging the temperature for subsequent batches. So, if you're keen to make great tempura then I recommend investing in a cooking thermometer that can be clipped against the pan.

Once the oil has been heated to the right temperature, keep it at that level. To help maintain a constant oil temperature while deep-frying is taking place, do the following:

• deep-fry food in small quantities, so that the pan is never overcrowded

• never cover more than a third of the surface of the pan with deep-fried food

• the depth of oil in the pan should be twice or more than the thickness of the food items being deep-fried

• use a deep-fat fryer with a reliable thermometer or a heavy, thick-bottomed and flat pan (a wok is not adequate as the round shape results in different oil temperatures at the sides and in the centre).

A LUMPY BATTER IS BEST

MAKES ENOUGH FOR 500G (1LB 2OZ) OF INGREDIENTS

300ml (10fl oz/1¼ cups) iced water (preferably carbonated)

2 egg yolks

6 ice cubes

160g (5¾oz/1¼ cups) plain (all-purpose) flour, sifted

160g (5¾oz/1⅓ cups) cornflour (cornstarch) or potato starch

(Alternatively, you can buy a ready-made tempura batter mix – this is widely used in Japan, the most popular brand being Showa. If using Showa, use 100g (3½oz) batter mix to 160ml (5½fl oz/¾ cup) iced water, mix gently with chopsticks until you get a lumpy batter.)

Now, for the batter. Put the iced water and egg yolks in a bowl along with the ice cubes, break the yolks and mix together. Mix the flours together, add this to the iced water and egg mixture, then stir until the ingredients are loosely combined. The batter should be very lumpy. If you over-mix, the batter will be sticky and the coating will turn out oily and heavy.

The goal is to achieve a lacy, golden effect with the deep-fried coating and not a thick, pancake-like casing. To avoid a heavy, oily-tasting coating, do the opposite of what you would do to make good pancakes – make the tempura batter just before deep-frying, do not mix it well and do not let it stand.

The batter consistency, and consequently the deep-fried coating, can be adjusted according to personal taste – if a thicker batter is preferred, use less iced water and more flour and vice-versa if a lighter coating is desired.

DEEP-FRYING TEMPURA, STEP-BY-STEP

Prepare the food items to be deep-fried, ensure they are dry.

Make a dipping sauce – a classic one combines 120ml (4fl oz/½ cup) dashi (see page 230), 40ml (1½fl oz/3 tbsp) mirin and 40ml (1½fl oz/3 tbsp) soy sauce; prepare 50g (1¾oz/½ cup) grated daikon (white radish) just before serving and serve in a bowl. Good-quality salt (matcha salt is a personal favourite) is also often used instead of the dipping sauce.

Ensure fresh oil is heated to the right temperature, anywhere between 150°C (300°F) and 180°C (350°F) depending on what you're cooking.

Prepare the batter.

Dip individual pieces into the batter to coat and then slide the battered item into the oil.

Deep-fry for about 3 minutes or until lightly golden, turning in the oil for even cooking after 1–2 minutes.

Replenish the batter with more flour and ice cubes, as required, until everything is fried.

Briefly drain on a wire rack before transferring to a serving plate.

Just before serving the tempura, grate the daikon radish, squeeze out and discard any excess water from it before serving in a shallow bowl.

Serve immediately with the salt or dipping sauce, hot or at room temperature, with daikon on the side so that people can mix the daikon into the dipping sauce if they'd like.

Dashi is one of the pillars of Japanese and Nikkei cuisines, as well as being an all-purpose soup stock and seasoning. In its simplest form, dashi is made from air-dried bonito fish flakes, konbu (a type of seaweed; sometimes written as kombu) and water. The best dashi is home-made but you can also buy it in a granular form, rather like an instant stock cube (in Japanese this form is known as dashi-no-moto, and a popular brand is Hon Dashi by Ajinomoto); it is ready to use simply by dissolving in hot water. Instant dashi, although very practical, is not ideal when a delicate but subtle and crystal clear stock is needed. For these situations, I would always recommend making the primary dashi recipe below.

When you need a stock for a soup or noodle broth when clarity isn't an issue, then secondary dashi fits the bill. Primary dashi is the superlative dashi. It has a subtle flavour and is mainly used as a base for delicate clear soups and sauces accompanying fish, seafood, chicken and tofu. Secondary dashi is suitable for thick soups, noodle broths or as a cooking stock for vegetables and meat. It is a great way of using up konbu and bonito fish flakes leftover from primary dashi.

PRIMARY DASHI

MAKES ABOUT 1 LITRE (1¾ PINTS/4 CUPS)

1.2 litres (2 pints/5 cups) water
30g (1¼oz) konbu
30g (1¼oz/2 cups) dried bonito flakes

Fill a medium pan with the measured water, add the konbu and leave it to stand, covered, for 6–8 hours. Then, on a low heat, and now uncovered, bring the water to a near boil. If you are pressed for time, skip the soaking but heat the water and konbu very slowly for about an hour so that the konbu has enough time to flavour the stock.

Remove the konbu before the water reaches boiling point as it will give off a strong smell if boiled at this point. Press the fleshiest part of the kelp with your finger: if it is soft, sufficient flavour has been obtained; if still tough, return it to the pan for a few more minutes. Keep the water from boiling by adding a little cold water.

After removing the konbu, bring the stock to a full boil then immediately add the bonito flakes, removing the pan from the heat as you do so. Do not stir, allow the flakes to start to settle to the bottom of the pan; this should take only a few minutes. Skim and pass it through a muslin-lined sieve (cheesecloth-lined strainer) without pressing it.

Reserve the bonito flakes and konbu from the sieve (strainer) to make the secondary dashi (see right) and/or to make Caramelised konbu seaweed (see page 240).

SECONDARY DASHI

MAKES ABOUT 1 LITRE (1¾ PINTS/4 CUPS)

bonito fish flakes and konbu reserved from Primary dashi (see left)
1.5 litres (2 pints 10fl oz/6⅓ cups) water
15g (½oz/1 cup) dried bonito flakes

Place the bonito fish flakes and konbu reserved from making a primary dashi along with the measured water in a medium pan. Place the pan over a high heat until it just reaches boiling point, then reduce the heat to a gentle simmer until the stock is reduced by a third, or possibly half depending on the strength of flavour desired; this reduction should take about 20 minutes.

Add the dried bonito fish flakes and immediately remove the pan from the heat. Allow the flakes to settle to the bottom of the pan for a few minutes, skimming any foam from the surface. Strain the dashi through a muslin-lined sieve (cheesecloth-lined strainer) and discard the bonito flakes. The dashi keeps in the fridge for three days; if frozen it will keep for three months, though some of the flavour is lost, I find, once it's thawed.

Cook's note The leftover konbu can be used to make an excellent garnish; see the recipe for Caramelised konbu seaweed on page 240.

Below I share two vegetarian dashi recipes for those who don't eat fish – one using konbu only and another using shiitake mushrooms. These recipes are excellent as a base for cooking vegetables, making miso soup or to add flavour to rice dishes.

VEGETARIAN DASHI

KONBU DASHI

MAKES ABOUT 1 LITRE (1¾ PINTS/4 CUPS)

40g (1½oz) konbu
1.2 litres (2 pints/5 cups) water
a pinch of salt

Wipe the konbu lightly with a damp cloth. Add the konbu to the water in a medium pan and let it stand for 6–8 hours, or possibly overnight, so that the kelp has enough time to release its flavour into the stock. If you are pressed for time, skip the soaking and heat the water and konbu on a very low heat until nearly boiling.

Remove the konbu from the water and bring the dashi to a full boil. Take off the heat and add a little salt and the dashi is done. This dashi keeps in the fridge for one week or for up to three months in the freezer.

Cook's note The leftover konbu can be used to make Caramelised konbu seaweed (see page 240).

SHIITAKE MUSHROOM DASHI

MAKES ABOUT 1 LITRE (1¾ PINTS/4 CUPS)

1.2 litres (2 pints/5 cups) konbu dashi (see left) or water
30g (1¼oz) dried shiitake mushrooms
1 tsp caster (superfine) sugar
a pinch of salt

Reheat the konbu dashi until hot but not boiling. Turn off the heat, then add the shiitake mushrooms, sugar and salt and let the pan and its contents sit for 2–4 hours.

Remove the mushrooms and reserve them. You can transform them through caramelisation, as for Caramelised konbu seaweed (see page 240). Alternatively, you can chop the mushrooms and add them to the soaking water of steamed white rice before cooking it to make mushroom-flavoured rice (see page 225)

Strain the shiitake mushroom dashi into a bowl, avoiding any sediment or grit from the bottom of the pan, and it's ready to use. The dashi keeps in the fridge for one week or for up to three months in the freezer.

Ready-made Japanese-style mayoneizu is available in most Japanese food shops or online. Kewpie and Kenko are two of the most popular Japanese brands. For those who have no access to these options, below is a recipe that will give similar results.

JAPANESE-STYLE MAYONEIZU

MAKES ABOUT 400ML (13½FL OZ/1¾ CUPS)

1 tsp salt
1 tsp sugar
¼ tsp garlic powder
1 tbsp rice vinegar
1 tbsp apple vinegar
1 tbsp malt vinegar
½ tsp monosodium glutamate powder (see Cook's note)
½ tsp Japanese mustard (or English mustard)
¼ tsp instant dashi powder
3 large egg yolks
240ml (8fl oz/1 cup) sunflower oil

You'll need a food processor to make this mayo-like sauce.

In a food processor, whizz together the salt, sugar, garlic powder, all the vinegars, MSG, mustard and the instant dashi powder until the granules are thoroughly dissolved. Next, add the egg yolks and blend until well combined.

With the motor still running, slowly drizzle in the sunflower oil in a thin, steady stream. The mixture should emulsify to a creamy texture.

Check for seasoning, but do not add much more salt at this stage as any salt added after the oil has been incorporated will dissolve very slowly into the mixture and you might end up with a rather salty mayonnaise the following day. Transfer the mayoneizu to a sterilised, airtight jar and store in the fridge for up to a week.

Cook's note The use of monosodium glutamate is rather controversial, I personally do not use MSG in my recipes. I have included it here so as to be truthful to the original recipe found in Japan. You may leave it out if you prefer, but the flavour won't be the same.

Yuzu kosho is a salt-cured condiment made with yuzu citrus peel, chillies and salt. It's intensely fragrant and hot with a deliciously zesty undertone; it works excellently with grilled meats. Yuzu kosho originates from the westernmost Japanese island of Kyushu, an area that has traded with Korea and Southeast Asia for centuries; a connection that has produced some interesting cross-cultural influences, such as the alcoholic spirit shochu, as well as yuzu kosho.

YUZU KOSHO

MAKES ABOUT 300G (10½OZ)

200g (7oz) mixture of green bird's eye and jalapeño chillies
100g (3½oz) yuzu peel (or a mixture of lime, tangerine and grapefruit peels)
30g (1¼oz/¼ cup) Maldon sea salt flakes (or 10% of the total weight of yuzu and green chillies)

Remove the seeds from the chillies and chop them very finely; you may use a food processor for this but be careful not to blend the chillies to a pulp.

For the yuzu (or other citrus fruits), thinly peel the skin and chop it as finely as the chillies.

Add the finely chopped chillies and yuzu peel to a bowl and weigh the mixture. Add 10% of its total weight in sea salt.

Mix all of the ingredients well and transfer the mixture to a sterilised, airtight jar. The yuzu kosho needs to cure for at least one week in the fridge before it's ready to be used. It will keep in the fridge for one month; once it's cured, you can freeze it in an ice cube tray and then bag the cubes in the freezer, where it will last for up to one year.

Cook's note Ready-made yuzu kosho can be purchased from Japanese food shops.

Yuzu kosho and Japanese mayonnaise are perhaps two of my favourite flavours, so why not combine them? I use this as a dip for tempura of soft-shell crab (see recipe on page 144), or on steak, or even to dunk potato or cassava chips (fries).

YUZU KOSHO MAYONNAISE

MAKES ABOUT 100ML (3½FL OZ/½ CUP)

50g (1¾oz/¼ cup) ready-made Japanese mayonnaise or
  Japanese-style mayoneizu (see opposite)
50g (1¾oz/¼ cup) soured cream
1 tsp lemon juice
1 tsp yuzu kosho (ready-made or see opposite)
a pinch of Maldon sea salt flakes

In a bowl, mix all of the ingredients until well combined. Transfer to a sterilised, airtight jar and refrigerate. This flavoured mayonnaise keeps in the fridge for about a week.

Why pay big bucks for ready-made bottled teriyaki sauce, when it is so easy to make at home for a fraction of the cost, and with much better results? This sauce is a permanent fixture in my fridge, where it lasts for weeks. I like flavouring teriyaki sauce with lightly crushed cloves of garlic and using it in my Nikkei 'surf & turf' sushi trio (see recipe on page 52).

TERIYAKI SAUCE (pictured below left)

MAKES ABOUT 300ML (10½FL OZ/1¼ CUPS)

150ml (5fl oz/⅔ cup) soy sauce
150ml (5fl oz/⅔ cup) mirin
150ml (5fl oz/⅔ cup) sake
75g (2¾oz/⅓ cup) sugar

Place all of the ingredients in a medium pan and mix well to make sure that the sugar has completely dissolved. Bring it to the boil then simmer uncovered until the liquid has reduced by a quarter and is lightly syrupy. Let it cool down then transfer to a sterilised, airtight jar and keep in the fridge. Teriyaki sauce will keep in the fridge for four weeks.

The basic teriyaki sauce can be infused with myriad ingredients, but my favourites include garlic, chillies and ginger (see below); add any of these ingredients to the warm teriyaki sauce (off the heat).

For the garlic-flavoured teriyaki:
2 garlic cloves, peeled and lightly bruised

For the chilli-flavoured teriyaki:
1 large red chilli, cut in half lengthways

For the ginger-flavoured teriyaki:
2cm (¾in) piece of root ginger, peeled and lightly crushed

Ponzu is the most popular of Japanese sauces; it's used as a salad dressing, as a dipping sauce for hotpots, in fish dishes and as a light marinade. It is the Japanese equivalent of the French vinaigrette and every chef will have their own version. In its simplest form, it's a combination of soy sauce, mirin, lemon or lime juice, rice vinegar and dashi, but I also give a few other variations on the theme here that will accompany a range of different Nikkei dishes.

PONZU SAUCE

MAKES ABOUT 150ML (5FL OZ/⅔ CUP)

4 tbsp soy sauce
1 tbsp mirin
3½ tbsp lemon or lime juice (or a mixture of both)
1½ tbsp rice vinegar
¼ tsp instant dashi powder (see Cook's note, below right)

Add all the ingredients to an airtight container or jar, close tightly and shake well to dissolve the instant dashi powder. If the sauce is too sharp to taste, add ½ teaspoon of caster (superfine) sugar and shake it again to dissolve. Store in an airtight container or jar in the fridge. Ponzu sauce will keep for three weeks in the fridge.

SESAME PONZU SAUCE

MAKES ABOUT 300ML (10FL OZ/1¼ CUPS)

4 tbsp soy sauce
1 tbsp mirin
3½ tbsp lemon or lime juice (or a mix of both)
5 tsp rice vinegar
2 tbsp toasted sesame oil
2 tsp caster (superfine) sugar
½ small onion, very finely chopped
¼ tsp instant dashi powder (see Cook's note, right)

Add all the ingredients to an airtight container or jar, close tightly and shake well to dissolve the instant dashi powder and sugar. Store in an airtight container or jar in the fridge. Sesame ponzu sauce will keep for a week in the fridge.

TRUFFLE PONZU SAUCE

(pictured above)

MAKES ABOUT 110ML (3½FL OZ/½ CUP)

3 tbsp soy sauce
1 tbsp mirin
2 tbsp lemon or lime juice (or a mixture of both)
1 tbsp good-quality truffle oil
¼ tsp caster (superfine) sugar
¼ tsp instant dashi powder (see Cook's note, right)

Add all the ingredients to an airtight container or jar, close tightly and shake well to dissolve the instant dashi powder and sugar. Store in an airtight container or jar in the fridge. Use within a day or two as the truffle oil may lose its flavour soon after this. Shake well before using.

YUZU-PON SAUCE

MAKES ABOUT 150ML (5FL OZ/⅔ CUP)

4 tbsp soy sauce
1 tbsp mirin
2 tbsp yuzu juice (or a mix of tangerine, grapefruit and lime juices)
1½ tbsp rice vinegar
1 tsp caster (superfine) sugar
¼ tsp instant dashi powder (see Cook's note, below)

Add all the ingredients to an airtight container or jar, close tightly and shake well to dissolve the instant dashi powder and sugar. Store in an airtight container or jar in the fridge. Yuzu-pon sauce will keep for a week in the fridge.

SPICY PONZU SAUCE

MAKES ABOUT 150ML (5FL OZ/⅔ CUP)

4 tbsp soy sauce
1 tbsp mirin
3½ tbsp lemon or lime juice (or a mixture of both)
1½ tbsp rice vinegar
¼ tsp instant dashi powder (see Cook's note, below)
1 small red chilli, finely sliced (or 1 tsp chilli (dried red pepper) flakes)

Add all the ingredients to an airtight container or jar, close tightly and shake well to dissolve the instant dashi powder. Let the chilli infuse the ponzu sauce overnight in the fridge then drain it into another jar to remove the chilli. This sauce will keep for a week in the fridge.

Cook's note If you have the time and the ingredients, freshly made primary dashi (see page 230) is preferable to its instant form for a clearer and more refined flavour for any of the ponzu sauce recipes. Use the same volume of liquid dashi as soy sauce.

One of the major sauces of Peruvian cooking, Huancaína (pronounced, wan-kay-eena) sauce is usually served alongside sliced potatoes as in the popular Peruvian dish *Papas a la Huancaína*. It is made with *aji amarillo* chilli, evaporated milk and fresh cheese, so should be deliciously creamy with a kick of heat. I love serving it with potatoes or other vegetables, meat and fish and also as a pasta sauce.

HUANCAÍNA SAUCE

MAKES ABOUT 700ML (1¼ PINTS/3 CUPS)

2 tbsp olive oil
1 small onion, finely chopped
1 garlic clove, crushed
4 tbsp ready-made *aji amarillo* paste (available from Peruvian food shops)
100ml (3½fl oz/½ cup) sunflower oil
50g (1¾oz) fresh cow's cheese (or feta cheese)
400ml (13½fl oz/1¾ cups) evaporated milk
50g (1¾oz) cream crackers, crushed
2 tbsp lime juice
salt

In a frying pan (or skillet), heat the olive oil over a medium heat and fry the onion and garlic until translucent. Transfer to a food processor with the *aji amarillo* paste, sunflower oil, fresh cheese and evaporated milk and whizz until smooth.

Add the cream crackers and lime juice and whizz again. Check for seasoning and add more salt if required. The sauce should be smooth and creamy, a tad spicy but also tangy; if it's too thick, add a little more milk. This sauce will keep in the fridge for a week.

This aromatic, bright-green oil will add a refreshing herb flavour and a beautiful green colour to any dish it is used with, as in the Salmon sashimi the South American say (see page 64). It will keep for four weeks in the fridge.

CORIANDER OIL (pictured right)

MAKES ABOUT 300ML (10FL OZ/1¼ CUPS)

100g (3½oz/2½ cups) coriander (cilantro) stalks and leaves
300ml (10fl oz/1¼ cups) sunflower oil

Wash the coriander (cilantro), pat dry on tea-towels (dish towels) and then roughly chop.

Heat the chopped coriander (cilantro) and the sunflower oil in a small pan over a very gentle heat; warm the oil through until it's lukewarm and the coriander (cilantro) is wilted, for about 3 minutes. Take off the heat, place the pan in a bowl of iced water to cool it down quickly and so retain the vibrant green colour of the coriander (cilantro).

Once cool, blend the oil and coriander (cilantro) in a food processor until smooth. Transfer the coriander (cilantro) and oil mixture to a bowl, cover it and let it infuse in the fridge for 2 hours, or anything up to 48 hours.

Strain the mixture through a fine sieve (strainer) or a paper coffee filter into a sterilised jar and store in the fridge, where the oil will keep for up to four weeks.

Cook's note This oil can also be made with chervil, chives, basil, parsley or dill following the same instructions as for coriander (cilantro) oil, above.

A refreshing, creamy dressing that will add a real kick to any sushi or *tiraditos* or even salads. I love using wasabi lemon cream in the Salmon sushi, two ways (see page 55) and Tuna sashimi tostada (see page 81).

WASABI LEMON CREAM

(pictured below left)

MAKES 150ML (5FL OZ/⅔ CUP)

5 tbsp Japanese-style mayoneizu (see page 232)
5 tbsp soured cream
1 tbsp wasabi paste
a few drops of lemon juice
a pinch of salt

In a bowl, whisk all the ingredients together until well combined. Check the seasoning and add more salt, wasabi paste (if you like it a tad spicier) or lemon juice. The wasabi cream should taste spicy, but not overly so, with a refreshing acidity from the lemon. Once made, this cream lasts a week in the fridge.

Cook's note Whenever possible, use ready-made wasabi paste sold in small tubes as opposed to wasabi powder, which has to be made into a paste. The latter leaves a faint bitter aftertaste when mixed with other ingredients.

If you do not want to make your own Japanese-style mayoneizu, then you can buy ready-made Japanese mayonnaise; the most popular brands are Kewpie and Kenko. Japanese mayonnaise is tangier and more flavoursome than Western-style mayo.

This sauce is a fresh mayonnaise flavoured with rice vinegar and Chinese tobanjan, or chilli bean paste, and crispy chilli oil. You can use it as a topping for grilled (broiled) seafood sushi (as on page 82), or more broadly on any grilled (broiled) fish or seafood dish; its name is a nod to the Chinese ('Chifa') community of Peru.

CHIFA SAUCE
SPICY CHINESE-STYLE SAUCE

MAKES ABOUT 350ML (12FL OZ/1½ CUPS)

3 large egg yolks, very fresh
½ tsp salt
1½ tbsp rice vinegar
225ml (7½fl oz/1 cup) sunflower oil
1 tbsp preserved crispy chilli oil
1 tbsp tobanjan paste

Add the egg yolks, salt and rice vinegar to the bowl of a food processor and blitz to dissolve the salt.

While the processor is running, start adding the sunflower oil slowly and gradually to create an emulsion similar to mayonnaise. Next, add the preserved crispy chilli oil and the tobanjan paste and process a little more until everything is well combined.

Check the spiciness and, if necessary, add more tobanjan and preserved crispy chilli oil. The consistency should be of a runny mayonnaise; if it is too thick, just add a little water. Transfer to an airtight container and keep in the fridge, where it will last for up to four days.

A classic of Japanese cooking, this dressing or sauce can be used to flavour green vegetables or served as a dipping sauce for Japanese hotpots (hotchpotches) among other things.

SESAME DRESSING

GOMA-DARE

MAKES ABOUT 400ML (13½FL OZ/1¾ CUPS)

90g (3¼oz/⅔ cup) white sesame seeds
90ml (3¼fl oz/⅓ cup) soy sauce
30ml (1fl oz/2 tbsp) mirin
1 tbsp sugar
180ml (6¼fl oz/¾ cup) dashi (see page 230)

Dry-fry the white sesame seeds in a heavy frying pan (or skillet) over a medium heat until lightly golden; this should only take a few minutes. Shake the pan constantly and use a wooden spatula to stir the seeds as they brown. Be watchful as the sesame seeds can go from golden brown to burnt in just a few seconds; if they burn, you should discard them as they will make the goma-dare dressing bitter.

Transfer the toasted white sesame seeds to a pestle and mortar and grind the seeds until flaky. In Japan, a suribachi (a Japanese grinding bowl with an indented surface) is used for this. Then, add the soy sauce, mirin and sugar and mix well. Start adding the dashi a little at a time, diluting the mixture as you go and mixing well after each addition; you may not need all the dashi if you prefer a thicker dressing.

Store the dressing in an airtight container in the fridge for up to a week.

Cook's note You can substitute the toasted white sesame seeds with 6 tablespoons of light tahini (sesame seed) paste. The texture and flavour will be slightly different but it's a good standby option; you may need only a few tablespoons of dashi to dilute the goma-dare if you go for the tahini (sesame seed) option.

The Japanese characters for nanban roughly translate as 'Southern barbarians', and this expression, dating back to the 16th century, originally referred to Portuguese merchants and missionaries. The Portuguese were the first Westerners to enter Japan via Kyushu, the westernmost island of mainland Japan. With them, they brought South American chillies, their love for deep-frying foods and their habit of marinating them in vinegar and chillies – the 'escabeche' style. It was not long before the Japanese took a fancy to these new flavours, creating 'nanban' sauce, a fine example of what I suppose might be termed reverse-Nikkei cooking.

NANBAN SAUCE (pictured top right)

A SPICY, SWEET & SOUR SAUCE

MAKES ABOUT 800ML (1 PINT 7FL OZ/3½ CUPS)

500ml (18fl oz/2 cups) dashi (see page 230; or use ½ tbsp instant dashi powder and 500ml (18fl oz/2 cups) boiling water if time is tight)
2 spring onions (scallions), left whole
125ml (4fl oz/½ cup) soy sauce
125ml (4fl oz/½ cup) rice vinegar
70g (2½oz/⅓ cup) sugar
2 large red chillies, deseeded and finely sliced
chilli (dried red pepper) flakes or hot chilli sauce (optional)

Make the dashi following the recipe instructions on page 230 or opt for the instant version if pushed for time.

Char the spring onion (scallion) stalks over a gas ring or under a hot grill (broiler) until partially blackened.

Put the dashi, spring onions (scallions) and the rest of the ingredients (except the optional items) in a pan over a medium heat and mix until the sugar has completely dissolved. Bring to the boil, then take the pan off the heat and allow the mixture to cool down to room temperature. Next, check for seasoning; if you would like more heat, add a pinch of chilli (dried red pepper) flakes or a few drops of hot chilli sauce. Then, remove the charred spring onions (scallions) and transfer to a sterilised jar and refrigerate. This sauce will keep in the fridge for up to four days.

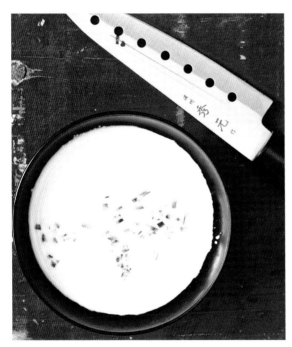

Leche de tigre, or tiger's milk, is a marinade used to 'cook' *ceviche*, one of the national dishes of Peru. There are thousands of versions of *leche de tigre*, but in its most basic incarnation it is made from lime juice, garlic, salt and chilli and other aromatics; sometimes scraps of white fish are thrown in for added flavour. Below I give a Nikkei twist to the recipe, using some Japanese ingredients and a touch of sugar for a less-bracing accompaniment to some of the Nikkei *tiraditos* and maki featured earlier on in the book (see pages 56, 60, 68 and 87).

NIKKEI *LECHE DE TIGRE*

(pictured below left)

MAKES ABOUT 125ML (4FL OZ)

1 fresh scallop, roughly diced (without its coral, about 35g (1⅓oz); other white fish can also be used instead)
½ tsp salt
1 tsp sugar
1 garlic clove, crushed
1 tsp minced root ginger
¼ tsp instant dashi powder
100ml (3½fl oz/½ cup) lime juice
½ red chilli, very finely diced
1–2 tbsp ready-made Japanese mayonnaise or Japanese-style mayoneizu (see page 232)

Put all the ingredients except the red chilli and Japanese mayonnaise into the bowl of a food processor and blend until you get a white, frothy and smooth sauce. Let it rest for 15 minutes.

Pass the mixture through a sieve (strainer), pressing down to squeeze every bit of juice from the mixture into a bowl.

Add the finely diced red chilli and the Japanese mayonnaise to the bowl and whisk until completely blended. Check for seasoning, then chill until needed. This marinade will keep in an airtight container for up to eight hours in the fridge.

Aji amarillo is a Peruvian native bright orange–yellow chilli, with plenty of heat and a fruity finish. Here, it is combined with soured cream and Japanese mayonnaise to create a aji amarillo cream to use as with the blow-torched salmon nigiri in my Nikkei 'surf & turf' sushi trio (see page 52).

AJI AMARILLO CREAM

MAKES ABOUT 150ML (5FL OZ/⅔ CUP)

50g (1¾oz/¼ cup) soured cream
50g (1¾oz/¼ cup) ready-made Japanese mayonnaise or Japanese-style mayoneizu (see page 232)
25g (1oz) ready-made aji amarillo paste (available from Peruvian food shops)
1 tbsp lemon juice
finely grated zest of ½ lemon
¼ tsp caster (superfine) sugar
a generous pinch of Maldon sea salt flakes

Mix all of the ingredients in a bowl until well combined. Transfer to a sterilised, airtight container and keep in the fridge for up to a week. Please note that the cream will become hotter over time.

Dried konbu seaweed can be rehydrated then caramelised in a mixture of soy sauce, sake and sugar. The resulting seaweed – known as konbu no tsukudani – can be used as a topping for white rice, as a filling for onigiri (triangular-shaped sushi) or simply added for flavour and colour to other dishes. I love cooking this with leftover konbu from making dashi (see page 230), then nothing is wasted. It will keep indefinitely in the fridge, so it's worth making a big batch – though, that can be dangerous as it is rather addictive!

CARAMELISED KONBU SEAWEED (pictured below left)

MAKES 50G (1¾OZ)

30g (1¼oz) leftover rehydrated konbu from making dashi (see page 230)
1 tbsp sake
1 tsp rice vinegar
1 tbsp soy sauce
15g (½oz/1¼ tbsp) sugar
1 tsp toasted white sesame seeds

Cut the leftover konbu into thin strips.

Put the konbu, sake and rice vinegar in a small pan. Pour just enough water to cover the konbu, bring to the boil and then simmer gently over a low heat until softened.

Next, add the soy sauce and sugar and continue simmering until the liquid has mostly evaporated. Remove from the heat and stir in the sesame seeds. Let the mixture cool down then transfer it to a sterilised airtight container or jar and refrigerated until needed.

Cook's note Rehydrated shiitake mushrooms (from the Shiitake dashi, see page 231) can be caramelised in exactly the same way. They're a wonderful addition to white rice or in ramen noodle soup.

This condiment is very easy to make, it takes just a little planning to prepare. This powder adds tonnes of natural umami flavours when dusted over *tiraditos*, as a coating for inside-out sushi or as a seasoning for small eats, such as *Pimientos de Padrón* Nikkei (see page 194).

RED MISO POWDER

MAKES ABOUT 50G (1¾OZ)

120g (4oz/½ cup) red miso (you could use brown miso for a milder flavour)

Preheat the oven to 70°C/158°F/gas mark ¼, and place a silicone mat or a sheet of non-stick baking parchment on a baking tray (baking sheet).

Using a palette knife or scraper, spread the miso as evenly and thinly as possible over the mat.

Place the baking tray (baking sheet) in the oven for about 3 hours. Check regularly after a couple of hours to prevent the miso from burning; it will become too dark and bitter if it burns.

Once the miso is completely dried out and crumbly, scrape it into a bowl and crush to a powder; I find that a mini-food processor comes in handy for this step.

Transfer the red miso powder to an airtight container or jar and store in a cool place. This powder lasts for four weeks.

These marinades are used for imparting a smoky flavour to Nikkei salmon and chicken skewers; I like to think of them as lighter versions of the delicious Peruvian classic *anticuchos de corazon*, which are made from ox heart and are sold freshly barbecued by street vendors all over the country. I use these marinades for the salmon *anticucho* in Nikkei chirashi-zushi (see page 72), and to marinate chicken in the Brazilian *churrasco* with Nikkei flavours (see page 157).

NIKKEI *ANTICUCHO* MARINADES

SALMON

MAKES ABOUT 150ML (5FL OZ/⅔ CUP) MARINADE FOR 500G (1LB 2OZ) SALMON

2 tbsp ready-made *aji panca* paste
2 tbsp ready-made *aji amarillo* paste
2 tbsp soy sauce
4 tbsp rice vinegar
2 garlic cloves, crushed
2cm (¾in) piece of root ginger, peeled and grated
1 tsp sugar
1 tsp salt

Make the marinade by mixing all the ingredients together in a bowl. Refrigerate until ready to use. This marinade will keep in the fridge for a week.

CHICKEN

MAKES ABOUT 200ML (7FL OZ/¾ CUP) MARINADE FOR 750G (1LB 11¾OZ) CHICKEN

4 tbsp ready-made *aji amarillo* paste
4 tbsp rice vinegar
2 tbsp soy sauce
2 tbsp extra virgin olive oil
2 garlic cloves, crushed
1 tsp cumin, ground
1 tsp salt
½ tsp freshly ground black pepper

Mix all the ingredients together in a bowl. Refrigerate until ready to use. This will keep in the fridge for a week.

The most popular ramen noodle accompaniment, these Japanese flavoured eggs are also delicious eaten on their own, or with other dishes, such as my Somen noodle & chicken salad (see page 95). They are best made a day in advance, and take your time and be gentle when handling the eggs, as they are very soft and fragile. Warning – these are very addictive!

JAPANESE FLAVOURED EGG AJITSUKE TAMAGO

SERVES 6

10 x 7-day-old eggs at room temperature (each weighing 60g (2oz))
3 litres (5¼ pints/2.6 quarts) water
1 tbsp coarse sea salt
2 tbsp rice vinegar

For the marinade:
150ml (5fl oz/⅔ cup) light soy sauce
150ml (5fl oz/⅔ cup) water
150ml (5fl oz/⅔ cup) mirin
6 tbsp caster (superfine) sugar
a pinch of instant dashi powder

Prepare a large iced-water bath in the sink or a big bowl. Have a thermometer and timer at the ready.

Using a needle, prick the bottom of each egg shell (at the wider end) to make a small hole; this allows air to escape from the eggs during cooking and stops them cracking.

Find a pan in which the 10 eggs can sit snugly in a single layer (you don't want something so large that they can rattle about and potentially crack). Fill the pan with the measured water and set over a medium heat to bring it to the boil (100°C (212°F) on a thermometer).

Add the sea salt and rice vinegar. When the water returns to the boil, gently lower the eggs one at a time into the water with a slotted spoon. Immediately turn down the heat so the water barely simmers (keep a constant temperature of 95°C (203°F)). From the moment all the eggs are in and the water temperature is 95°C (203°F), cook for 6 minutes exactly. Gently move the eggs about in the water every minute or so, so that they are evenly cooked on all sides.

Again using a slotted spoon, transfer the eggs immediately to the iced-water bath. Let them cool completely. When the eggs have cooled down, tap them very gently with the back of a teaspoon to crack the shells (don't be tempted to do this using the palm of your hand as the eggs will mostly likely crack in half). Carefully peel them under cold running water; the whites are extremely fragile so take great care while peeling and do not rush at this stage. Next, transfer

the eggs to a container in which they fit snugly in a single layer. If you don't have one, use a deeper container, but you will need to move the eggs around several times during the 2 hours the eggs will be marinating.

Whisk together the ingredients for the marinade until the sugar and dashi have dissolved. Pour this liquid over the eggs. Place two sheets of kitchen paper (paper towels) over the eggs and gently press down until the sheets are saturated with marinade; this process helps to keep the eggs submerged and an even tinting and flavouring.

Marinate the eggs at room temperature for 2 hours, then strain and gently blot dry; keep the marinade as it can be reused for making one more batch of ajitsuke tamago, then it should be discarded. Don't marinate the eggs for much longer than 2 hours or they will become too dark and strongly flavoured.

Serve, or store the eggs in an airtight container in the fridge for up to three days. To serve the eggs, take them out of the fridge a couple of hours before eating to bring them to room temperature. Or if you would like them hot, bring to room temperature and just before serving, immerse them in a bowl of hot water for 45 seconds.

Using a cheese knife (a blade with holes in so that the egg doesn't stick), cut the eggs carefully right through the middle lengthways, trying to keep the yolk from running out of the centre and onto the white. They're ready to serve.

This list covers the key ingredients used in this book, and is by no means a comprehensive inventory of Japanese, Asian and Latin American food products. You will not be required to purchase all of the ingredients listed, but to attempt most recipes you will need a handful of basic Japanese and South American ingredients, including soy sauce, mirin, dashi, rice vinegar, miso and short-grain rice. These ingredients make an appearance in many of my recipes and once you master their use, you are on track to enjoy some truly authentic Japanese and Nikkei dishes.

Besides Japanese food shops, you can often find these ingredients in Korean and Asian supermarkets or online. For a list of suggested Japanese, Asian and South American suppliers, see the Directory of suppliers on page 250.

JAPANESE & OTHER ASIAN INGREDIENTS

BONITO FLAKES – Known in Japanese as katsuoboshi, these feather-light shavings of air-dried bonito fish are mainly used as the key ingredient in dashi. These bonito flakes can also be added to other dishes as a flavouring or garnish.

CENTURY OLD EGGS – Despite their name, these eggs are preserved in a mixture of rice husks, clay and salt among other ingredients for about six months, not 100 years. The yolk goes creamy and takes on a dark green colour while the white hardens into an amber-coloured jelly. Available from Oriental supermarkets.

CHICKEN STOCK POWDER – Asian chicken stock powder contains soy sauce and other ingredients that give a different flavour to the Western varieties. It can be purchased from most Oriental supermarkets.

DAIKON – A giant white radish (*Raphanus sativus*), known also as mooli in Indian cooking, is an essential ingredient in Japanese and Nikkei cuisines. It can be grated and served as a garnish, cooked as a root vegetable or even pickled.

DAIKON CRESS – This cress has a spicy flavour and looks similar to baby cress but tastes very different. If you cannot find daikon cress, use baby cress instead.

DASHI – The Japanese stock made from water, bonito fish flakes and dried kelp (konbu). It is one of the pillars of Japanese and Nikkei cuisines and can be made fresh or from ready-made sachets, or from instant dashi powder, known as Hondashi. See dashi recipe on page 230.

EBI FURAI – These are stretched prawns (shrimp) coated in Japanese panko breadcrumbs. They are usually sold on a tray in the freezer compartment of Japanese food shops. They are a handy ingredient and go down a treat as a snack, garnish or as a filling to rolled sushi.

GINGER – In addition to the fresh variety, ginger also comes pickled in tiny red strips (known as beni shoga in Japanese). The red colour comes from red perilla, which is traditionally used in the pickling. The sliced pickled variety, sometimes lightly pink and sweet, is used as accompaniment for sushi and is eaten to clear the palate between different styles of sushi.

GOCHUJAN PASTE – This savoury Korean condiment is made from red chilli, glutinous rice, fermented soybeans and salt.

GYOZA WRAPPERS – Made from wheat flour, these very fine rectangular or circular wrappers are normally found in the freezer compartment of Asian food shops. They are used for making gyoza dumplings, also known as pot-sticker dumplings in the West.

KONBU (OR KOMBU) – A type of kelp seaweed. Konbu, a key ingredient for making dashi, is sold in Oriental supermarkets as dashi konbu. It is rich in natural monosodium glutamate. Never wash konbu as the flavour lies on the surface; at most, wipe it with a damp cloth.

KOUJI – A fungus used in various East Asian cuisines to ferment soybeans. It is also used to saccharify (that is,

Shiso

Aji limo

Aji rocoto

Aji amarillo

Matcha

Yuzu kosho

Aji panca

Yuzu juice

Kizami nori

Konbu

Black quinoà

Instant dashi
powder

Red miso

Brown miso

Bonito flakes

White miso

Dried shiitake
mushroom

新庄

五島灘の塩使用

塩麹

[しおこうじ]

200g

お料理いろいろ
おいしくなる。
お料理いろいろ
いろいろ
のに便利。
代わりに。

Shichimi
pepper

Instant
konbu dashi

Shio kouji

Somen noodles

Wasabi paste

Pickled ginger

convert starch to sugar) rice, other grains and potatoes in the making of alcoholic beverages such as sake, makgeolli and shochu. The 'national fungus' of Japan, it is important not only for brewing sake, but also for the fermentation of miso, soy sauce and a range of other Japanese foods.

MATCHA – This Japanese green tea powder is a very fine bright-green powder used for the Japanese tea ceremony as well as in myriad recipes ranging from cakes to ice cream. It is very bitter when tasted on its own, so sugar is nearly always added. Matcha has a high caffeine content.

MAYONEIZU – Also known as Japanese mayonnaise. This mayo is creamier and tangier than the Western varieties. It is also yellower in colour due to the higher proportion of egg yolk used. Check the recipe for home-made Japanese-style mayoneizu (see page 232) or buy it ready made; Kewpie and Kenko are the two most popular brands.

MENTAIKO – The marinated roe of pollock and cod is a common ingredient in Japanese cuisine. Of Korean origin, it was introduced to Japan after the Russo-Japanese War. A popular variety is spicy mentaiko (marinated in chillies), and is the number one ingredient of Kyushu Island.

MIRIN – This sweetened rice wine (sake) has an alcohol content of about 14%. It is used for cooking to add richness and depth to dishes, as well as to balance the saltiness of soy sauce. A 0.5% alcohol content variety known as Honteri Mirin is a more economical option.

MISO – This fermented soybean paste combined with either rice or barley and salt. It is mixed in dashi to make miso soup but also with other ingredients for marinades, sauces and dressings. There are many varieties – red, brown and white, smooth or grainy. As a general rule, the darker the miso, the saltier and more strongly flavoured it will be.

NORI – Most often seen as standard-sized, paper-thin sheets of toasted seaweed, nori is used as a wrapping for sushi rolls or onigiri rice balls (another style of sushi). Kizami nori are fine strips of nori used mainly as decoration. Aonori, translated rather misleadingly as blue nori, is in fact green and is sold in tiny flakes to be sprinkled over food.

RICE – See short-grain white rice.

RICE NOODLES – There are many different varieties, but the dried and thin vermicelli rice noodles as well as the Japanese hakusami noodles are featured in a few recipes in this book.

SANSHO PEPPER – The highly aromatic seed pods of the Japanese pepper (*Zanthoxylum piperitum*) are ground and used as seasoning in a variety of dishes. Sansho sprigs (kinome in Japanese) are used as an edible garnish.

SAKE – A Japanese dry wine made from polished rice with an alcohol content of about 15%. It is used for drinking (served either hot or cold) and cooking. There are many different grades of sake, but for cooking you can buy cooking-grade sake.

SAKE KASU – This is the lees left over from making sake and it is used as a pickling agent or as a cooking paste, as a wonderfully rich and creamy addition to miso soup, or as a marinade to add depth of flavour to food. See the recipe for a ton kasu jiro soup (see page 121).

SALMON ROE – Known in Japanese as ikura, these shiny red eggs are considered a luxury and taste delicious lightly seasoned with soy sauce and mirin, and as a topping over sushi or hot rice.

SESAME OIL/SEEDS – For the recipes in this book, always use toasted sesame seeds and oil, and whenever possible purchase a Japanese brand of sesame oil, such as Kadoya or Maruhon. Sesame seeds come in white or black colours.

SHICHIMI PEPPER – Also known as shichimi togarashi, this is Japan's Seven-spice chilli mix: red pepper flakes, roughly ground sansho, mandarin orange peel, dry ginger, black hemp seeds, tiny flakes of green nori and white sesame seeds. This is a key ingredient in many recipes in this book and goes particularly well sprinkled over buttered popcorn (see page 24).

SHIITAKE MUSHROOMS – The best known Japanese fungi, shiitake have a meaty texture and earthy flavour and can be purchased either fresh or dried. To rehydrate them, add the dried mushrooms to a bowl with warm water and a little sugar to help them plump up even more. Other popular Japanese mushrooms are oyster, enoki and shimeji.

SHIRATAKI NOODLES – These thin, translucent, gelatinous Japanese noodles made from the konjac yam (also known as devil's tongue yam). Shirataki means 'white waterfall', describing the appearance of these noodles. Largely composed of water and glucomannan (a water-soluble fibre), they are very low in carbohydrates and calories.

SHISO – A member of the mint family (also known as perilla in the West), shiso is a very aromatic herb with a unique flavour – a cross between mint and basil. It comes in purple or green; the former is used mainly to add colour and flavour to pickles and drinks, while the more delicate green-coloured shiso has many uses as a herb, in tempura and as a garnish in sashimi and sushi dishes. Shiso buds are also used as a condiment or garnish. Use only the leaves in dishes and discard the stems.

SHORT-GRAIN WHITE RICE – This is the rice used for all of the rice dishes in this book, including sushi and stir-fries. Its grains are smaller and rounder than other types of rice, such as basmati or jasmine. The rice part of sushi is called shari rice.

SICHUANESE GREEN MUSTARD PICKLE – Known as zasai in Japanese or zha cai in Chinese, this salt-fermented pickled vegetable is available in most Chinese supermarkets.

SOYBEAN POWDER – Known as kinako in Japanese, this toasted soybean powder is commonly used in Japanese sweets. It adds a toasty nuttiness to desserts.

SOY SAUCE – An essential ingredient in Japanese and Nikkei cuisines, soy sauce adds umami savouriness to many dishes. There are two main types of Japanese soy sauce – dark (koikuchi) or light (usukuchi). Unless specified, use the dark variety in all recipes in this book. Chinese or Korean soy sauces, while great for these cuisines, are not alternatives for Japanese or Nikkei dishes. The dark-coloured soy sauce is the all-purpose, standard soy sauce readily available in any Asian and Japanese food shops. The light-coloured variety, hailing from the Kansai region of Japan (around Kyoto), is lighter in colour but is saltier than the darker ones. Tamari is another type of soy sauce with little or no gluten, which is less salty and slightly thicker. In Peru, the native style of soy sauce is known as *sillao*.

SUSHI SEASONING – Known as sushisu in Japanese, this mixture of rice vinegar, sugar, salt and konbu can be bought ready made from Japanese food shops; a popular brand is Mizkan. For instructions on how to make your own sushi seasoning, see page 226.

TEMPURA FLOUR – Also called tempura batter mix, it contains a mixture of wheat and corn flours, dried egg and yeast. It is a practical alternative to making your own batter as it only needs the addition of water. Showa is a popular brand.

TOBIKO EGGS – These are the tiny roe of the flying fish; bright-orange salted eggs with a mild and sweet fish flavour. They also come in different colours, depending on the added flavours being used; popular ones are green wasabi and yellow yuzu.

TOFU – Soybean curd has a high protein content and is rich in calcium, iron and vitamins. It comes in many textures, shapes and sizes including soft (silken), firm or deep-fried.

TOBANJAN PASTE – This spicy, salty paste is made from fermented broad (fava) beans, soybeans, salt, rice and other spices. Originally from China, it is used in many Japanese and Nikkei dishes and sauces.

TSUKEMONO PICKLES – These Japanese preserved vegetables are served with rice as a side dish or as an accompaniment to or garnish for meals. A variety of different vegetables can be pickled, including cucumber and radish. They also come in different colours depending on the ingredients used in the pickling marinade, for example purple shiso will impart a dark red colour. They can be purchased ready made from Japanese food shops.

WASABI – Japanese horseradish (*Wasabia japonica*) is less harsh and more fragrant than the Western variety. Fresh wasabi is expensive as it grows wild in cool, shallow pools of water often high in the mountains. It can be purchased as a powder or paste. Whenever possible buy wasabi paste (as opposed to powder) and check the percentage content of real wasabi in the paste's ingredient list, it varies considerably from brand to brand. S&B is a popular brand of wasabi paste.

YUZU – This Japanese citrus fruit (*Citrus junos*) is highly aromatic with flavours of tangerine, limes and grapefruit, but is not very sweet. Both zest and juice are used in a variety of savoury dishes as well as desserts.

YUZU KOSHO – A paste made from yuzu citrus zest and juice, fiery chillies and salt. This cured paste comes in red and green colours, and a little goes a long way as it is highly flavoursome and aromatic. You can buy yuzu kosho from Japanese food shops or you could make your own – see my yuzu kosho recipe on page 232.

BRAZILIAN & PERUVIAN INGREDIENTS

AÇAÍ – A native of Brazil, the açaí is a small, round, black-purple berry about 2.5cm (1in) in circumference, similar in appearance to a grape, but smaller and with less pulp. Açaí is sold as frozen pulp, juice or an ingredient in various products from drinks, including grain alcohol and smoothies to foods, cosmetics and supplements. In Brazil, it is commonly eaten as *Açaí na tigela*. It has a rich and slightly tart but sweet flavour akin to a blackberry, with a hint of wine and with an aftertaste similar to dark chocolate.

AJI AMARILLO – The most commonly used hot pepper in Peru, *aji amarillo* or yellow chilli is a long finger-shaped chilli pepper with a bright shiny yellow–orange skin. It has an aromatic fruity flavour and is moderately hot. Deseeded and sliced, it can be added to dishes during cooking as well as used raw as a garnish. It can be bought as a paste that, added to dishes during cooking, will impart a hot fruity flavour and a light yellow colour to the food. The paste can be mixed with oil and used as a condiment or dipping sauce.

AJI PANCA – This variety of dried hot pepper with a dark reddish purple colour gives a deep, smoky flavour to dishes. It can be purchased as a paste available from South American food shops.

AJI ROCOTO – This medium-sized round pepper is fiercely hot. Thick fleshed with small black seeds, it can sometimes be yellow or green but it is most usually red. It's also available as a ready-made paste in Peruvian food shops.

CACHAÇA – Also known as *aguardente* or *pinga*, it is Brazil's national distilled spirit made from sugar cane juice. Outside Brazil, cachaça is used almost exclusively as an ingredient in tropical drinks, with the caipirinha being the most famous cocktail.

CASSAVA – Also known as manioc or yuka, this starchy vegetable is used extensively in Brazilian and Peruvian cooking. It has a thick, tough brown skin, which in the UK is usually waxed. It is cooked in a similar way to potatoes and is delicious deep-fried to make chips (fries), puréed or in pieces in various stews. It can also be purchased in a flour form for the popular Brazilian *farofa* dish (see page 156).

CHOCLO CORN – This variety of corn has large white kernels. *Choclo* is cooked and eaten as an accompaniment to meat and fish dishes but more traditionally to Peruvian *ceviche*.

CUPUAÇU – A tropical rainforest tree related to cacao. It is widely cultivated in the jungles of Colombia, Bolivia and Peru and in the north of Brazil. The white pulp of the *cupuaçu* (say it as 'coo-poo-ah-sue') is uniquely fragrant described as a mix of chocolate and pineapple.

DENDÊ OIL – Also known as palm oil, this edible vegetable oil is derived from the fruit of the oil palms. Palm oil is naturally reddish in colour because of a high beta-carotene content. Along with coconut oil, palm oil is one of the few highly saturated vegetable fats and is semi-solid at room temperature. Like most plant-based products, palm oil contain 'zero' cholesterol.

JALAPEÑO CHILLI – A medium-sized chilli pepper originating in Mexico. It is usually consumed green but also fully ripened when it turns crimson red. Jalapeño heat level varies from mild to hot depending on cultivation and preparation. The heat is concentrated in the membrane around the seeds.

GRAVIOLA – Also known as soursop, it is in the same genus as the *cherimoya* and the same family as the pawpaw (papaya). The flavour has been described as a combination of strawberry and pineapple, with sour citrus flavour notes contrasting with an underlying creamy flavour reminiscent of coconut or banana. Soursop is widely promoted as an alternative cancer treatment. There is, however, no medical evidence that it is effective.

LÚCUMA – This subtropical fruit hails from the Andean valleys of Chile, Ecuador and Peru. It's sometimes called 'eggfruit' in English, a reference to the fruit's dry flesh, which is similar in texture to a hard-boiled egg yolk. *Lúcuma* has a unique flavour of maple and sweet potato and is a highly nutritious fruit.

MANDIOQUINHA – Mandioquinha, also known as *batata baroa* in Brazil and *virraca* in Peru, is close to the potato family originally from the Andes. With a delicate flavour and natural sweetness, mandioquinha is extensively used in South American home cooking, and makes a great accompaniment to hearty meat dishes such as salt beef, its classic partner in Brazil.

PALM HEARTS or **PEACH PALM** – Known in Brazil as *palmito*, this vegetable is harvested from the inner core and growing bud of certain palm trees. Hearts of palm may be eaten on their own but are often seen in salads or as fillings for pies.

PICANHA – The most popular beef cut in Brazil; *picanha* comes from the cap lying above the top sirloin and rump (top round) areas; it is a triangular cut and has a beautiful layer of fat. It is not a muscle that moves much during the animal's life, and so it remains tender. In Brazil, *churrasco* (barbecue) and *picanha* are almost synonymous.

QUINOA – Pronounced 'keen-wa', there are two types of this wheat-free alternative to starchy grains: red and creamy white. Both types are slightly bitter when cooked and open up to release little white curls as they soften. Grown in Peru, Chile and Bolivia for thousands of years, quinoa formed the staple diet of the Incas and their descendants.

RAPADURA – Also known as *panela* in South America and jaggery elsewhere in the world, rapadura is unrefined whole cane sugar, typical of Central and of Latin America in general. It's a solid form of sucrose derived from the boiling and evaporation of sugarcane juice.

EUROPEAN INGREDIENTS

BACALHAU – The iconic ingredient of Portuguese cuisine, Portuguese salt-cod or *bacalhau* is also popular in Galicia (Spain) and in former Portuguese colonies, including Brazil, Cape Verde, Angola, Macau and Goa. It is sold whole, in loins or as trimmings. It needs to be rehydrated and desalinated for 24–48 hours before use. With a delicious firm texture and salt-umaminess, *bacalhau* is in hundreds of dishes from simple home-cooked meals to more elaborate, special occasion dishes.

ESPELETTE PEPPER – A variety of chilli pepper that's cultivated in the French Basque town of Espelette (right near the border of France and Spain). It gained AOC (*appellation d'origine contrôlée*) classification in 2000. Espelette pepper is one of the pillars of Basque cuisine – a mildly hot chilli powder, with a delicate, fruity flavour.

FOIE GRAS – The fattened liver of goose or duck; some of the best foie gras comes from the region of Landes in France. In recent years, the traditional feeding (gavage) of foie gras geese and ducks has received a lot of negative press, so please source this ingredient carefully, so that you're happy with its provenance. Buy the whole lobes of liver rather than the tinned pâté version whenever possible.

PIMIENTOS DE PADRÓN – This variety of peppers hails from the municipality of Padrón in the province of La Coruña in northwestern Spain. These are small peppers, about 5cm (2in) in length, with colours ranging from bright green to yellowish green. Their peculiarity lies in the fact that, while their taste is usually mild, a small minority – legend has it 1 in 10 – are mind-blowingly hot. In Japan, a similar pepper called shishito is very popular as a snack in Japanese pubs or izakaya.

There are a few pieces of equipment that are either essential or would come in handy when making the various dishes in this book.

Below are my list of go-to London suppliers for my supper clubs or events I'm putting on. There are also listed some suppliers abroad, many with websites too.

EQUIPMENT

PRESSURE COOKER – A relative inexpensive bit of kit that will save you time and energy. I find the latest range of electric pressure cookers that double up as rice cookers indispensable in my kitchen – slow cooking in a third of the time!

RICE COOKER – A vital piece of equipment in any Nikkei or Oriental household, a rice cooker will produce perfect rice every time with no guess work. Buy one with a clip-on lid that has a ventilation valve and ideally a timer. It will also keep rice warm after cooking and until it is ready to be served. I've been using my Tefal rice cooker for years with great results.

SUSHI MAT – Known as makisu in Japanese, this mat is made from bamboo and is used mainly for rolling sushi. However, it's also useful for shaping foods, such as tamagoyaki omelettes, and for squeezing excess water out of tofu. After use, sushi mats should be washed and completely dried to avoid the growth of bacteria.

SUSHI BARREL – Known as hangiri or handai in Japanese cooking, this round, flat-bottomed wooden tub or barrel is used in the final steps of preparing rice for sushi. This is essential in sushi making, but an unvarnished wooden bowl or large chopping (cutting) board could be used as a substitute.

TAMAGOYAKI PAN – This is an essential pan when attempting to make the Japanese multi-layered omelette known as tamagoyaki (see page 32).

WOODEN SPATULA – These large flat spoons (known as shamoji) are used for serving rice, and also to fold sushi rice while cooling and seasoning it. They are available in bamboo and plastic.

DIRECTORY OF SUPPLIERS

JAPANESE

ARIGATO
48–50 Brewer Street
London W1R 3HN
020 7287 1722

ATARI-YA
Finchley Branch
595 High Road,
London N12 0DY
020 8446 6669
www.atariya.co.uk

DOKI Japanese Tableware
207 High Road,
Middlesex HA3 5EE
020 8861 4277
www.dokiltd.co.uk

FUJI FOODS
167 Priory Road
London N8 8NB
020 8347 9177

JAPAN CENTRE
19 Shaftesbury Ave.
London W1D 7ED
020 3405 1246
www.japancentre.com

RICE WINE SHOP
82 Brewer Street
London, W1F 9UA

020 7439 3705
www.ricewineshop.com

TAZAKI FOODS LTD (Trade Only)
Unit 4, Delta Park Industrial
Estate, Millmarsh Lane,
Enfield EN3 7QJ
www.tazakifoods.com

ORIENTAL

KOREA FOODS
New Malden Branch
(largest branch)
Unit 5, Wyvern Industrial
Estate, Beverley Way,
New Malden,
Surrey KT3 4PH
020 8949 2238
www.koreafoods.co.uk

LONGDAN
25 Hackney Road
London E2 7NX
020 3222 0118
www.longdan.co.uk

SEEWOO
18–20 Lisle Street
London, WC2H 7BE
020 7439 8325
www.seewoo.com

SOUTH AMERICAN

BRAZILIAN CENTRE
223 Mare Street,
London E8 3QE
020 7682 3181
produtosbrasileiros.co.uk

SOL ANDINO
187 Old Kent Rd,
London SE1 5NA
020 7394 9203
www.solandinomarket.co.uk

SUBLIME FOODS
(for Brazilian frozen fruit
pulps – online only)
www.sublimefood.co.uk

VIVA PERU
Online shop only
www.vivaperu.co.uk

OTHER

LALANI & CO TEAS
(for green tea powder)
www.lalaniandco.com

**NEWINGTON GREEN FRUIT &
VEGETABLES**
109 Newington Green Road,
London N1 4QY

STEVE HATT FISHMONGERS
88–90 Essex Road,
London N1 8LU
020 7226 3963

TOM HIXSON ONLINE BUTCHERS
221 Central Markets,
London EC1A 9LH
www.tomhixson.co.uk

SUPPLIERS IN THE US

CATALINA FISH MARKET
5202 Lovelock Street
San Diego, CA 92110
(619) 297-9797
www.catalinaop.com

KATAGIRI
224 E. 59th Street,
New York, NY 10022
2127553566
www.katagiri.com

MITSUWA
100 E. Algonquin Road
Arlington Heights, IL 60005
(847) 956-6699
www.misuwa.com

UMAJIMAYA
600 5th Avenue South
Seattle, WA 98104
(206) 624 6248
www.uwajimaya.com

SUPPLIERS IN AUSTRALIA

ANEGAWA TRADING CO GROCERS
16A Deepwater Road,
Castle Cove 2069
(02) 9417 5452

FUJI MART
34A Elizabeth Street,
South Yarra 3141
(03) 9826 5839

TOKYO MART
Northbridge Plaza,
Shop 27/79, 113 Sailors
Bay Road,
Northbridge NSW 2063
(02) 9958 6860

BIBLIOGRAPHY

The author would like to acknowledge the following
sources used when writing of What is Nikkei cuisine?
(pages 6–17):

O Japonês no Brasil, Estudo de Mobilidade e Fixação
Hiroshi Saito PhD. 1961, Fundação Escola de
Sociologia e Política de São Paulo

*Uma Epopéia Moderna: 80 Anos da Imigração Japonesa
no Brasil*
Editora Hucitec. 1992, Sociedade Brasileira de
Cultura Japonesa, São Paulo; ISBN 85-271-0186-6

O Imigrante Japonês: História de sua vida no Brasil
Tomoo Handa, 1987
T.A. Queiroz Editor Ltda., Centro de Estudos Nipo-
Brasileiros
São Paulo; ISBN 85-85008-73-3

Guia da Cultura Japonesa no Brasil
Edited by Jhony Arai and Andreia Ferreira, 2004,
Editora Japan Brazil Communication;
ISBN 85-87679-18-X

Nikkei es Peru
Mitsuharu Tsumura and Josefina Barrón,
Telefonica 2013; ISBN: 978-612-45819-2-2

La Cocina Nikkei
Las Cocinas del Peru series by Gaston Acurio,
El Comercio 2006; ISBN: 9972-217-48-5

INDEX

ACKNOWLEDGEMENTS

There are a great number of people I am indebted to and without them, this book would not have been possible. First and foremost, my partner Gerald Coakley for his endless support and encouragement over the last two decades.

A huge thanks to Fritha Saunders for coming to my supper club, spotting the author in me and, along with Jacqui Small, believing in Nikkei cuisine. Massive thanks also to a group of outstanding professionals aka 'Team Nikkei' with whom I have been very lucky to work – editor Nikki Sims, photographers Lisa Linder and Fiona Kennedy, prop stylist Cynthia Inions, and the design and art director Manisha Patel.

Writing this book has involved a lot of research and fact finding, and I thank members of my family for their invaluable help – my photographer brother Ricardo Hara (www.ricardohara.com.br), and his wife Ana Paula Hara for the images on pages 12 and 13, and my cousin Caroline and my aunt Yoshiko Hara for sharing their family stories and photo albums. I would also like to thank my stepmother Lourdes Hara and my sister Natasha for their help tracking down a wealth of family archive material (pages 7–9).

I am greatly indebted to Ana Hasegawa of the Peruvian-Japanese Association in Lima, Peru, who gave me unlimited access to their precious archives of Japanese immigration images; some of which are included on pages 7 (top right), 8 (top left, middle right) and 9 (bottom left). I had a great deal of help and advice from Celia Abe Oi, of the Japanese Immigration Museum in São Paulo, Brazil, who shared many fascinating volumes on the early Nikkei migration and life in South America that were invaluable in researching this book.

Meeting Reiko Hashimoto in 2005 during my days in investment banking was a catalyst to my future career in Japanese and Nikkei cooking. I have always been greatly inspired by Reiko – she taught me so much about the food of my ancestors, its flavours and techniques, as well as the intricacies of human nature.

Many thanks to fellow Cordon Bleu chefs Patricia Cochoni and Natasha Mangla for their invaluable assistance during the shoots.

The publisher and I would like to thank the following chefs, most of whom I had the great pleasure of meeting while researching this book, for sharing their wonderful Nikkei recipes:

From São Paulo, Brazil – Adriano Kanashiro of Momotaro, Tsuyoshi Murakami of Kinoshita and Shin Koike of Sakagura A1.
From Lima, Peru – Toshiro Konishi of Toshiro's, Hajime Kasuga of Le Cordon Bleu and Mitsuharu Tsumura of Maido.
From Barcelona, Spain – Jorge Muñoz & Kioko Ii of Pakta.
From Miami, USA – Diego Oka of Mandarin Oriental's La Mar by Gastón Acurio; from New York, USA – Pedro Duarte of SUSHISAMBA.
From London, UK – Jordan Sclare and Michael Paul of Chotto Matte, London, UK.

Last but not least, I must also thank the many guests, staff and volunteers at my Japanese and Nikkei supper clubs and cookery classes who have been hugely supportive of my work since my departure from investment banking until the present day, many of whom are now close friends. I could not have done it without you!

Team Nikkei